I'M NOT HITLER!

What You're Not Allowed To Know About The Real "Right Wing"

Terry Leasure

Outskirts Press, Inc.
Denver, Colorado

The opinions expressed in this manuscript are solely the opinions of the author and do not represent the opinions or thoughts of the publisher. The author represents and warrants that s/he either owns or has the legal right to publish all material in this book.

I'm Not Hitler!
What You're Not Allowed To Know About The Real Right Wing Agenda.

Outskirts Press, Inc.
http://www.outskirtspress.com

ISBN: 978-1-4327-1393-5

Outskirts Press and the "OP" logo are trademarks belonging to Outskirts Press, Inc.

PRINTED IN THE UNITED STATES OF AMERICA

Contents

Chapter One   1
Confessions of a Former Liberal

Chapter Two   21
My Rude Awakening

Chapter Three   39
Let's Get it On!

Chapter Four   58
Give Us Your Tired, Your Poor,
Your Security Threats

Chapter Five   81
Welcome RACE Fans

Chapter Six   103
Stop! Or I'll Say "Stop" Again!

Chapter Seven   125
Crimes and Misdemeanors

Chapter Eight 145
From Tea Party to Twinkie Tax

Chapter Nine 169
Mother Nature is a Right Winger!

Chapter Ten 191
Fool's Court Press

Chapter Eleven 219
Hey, Norman Rockwell...Paint This!

Chapter Twelve 253
Parental Guidance Suggested

Chapter Thirteen 283
When it's left to the Left - My Katrina Rant

Chapter Fourteen 301
Judge Not, Lest Ye Be Liberal

Chapter Fifteen 325
The Point

"So, you've decided to write a book". I can almost smell the anticipation of failure in that statement. That's O.K., it's not the first time that I have crapped-out. There was middle-school wrestling, the trombone, Boy Scouts, karate, art school, the Army Reserves, and who knows what else. I gotta tell ya' though, I ain't looking forward to hearing my dad make that comment to me. So, I've decided to just not tell him.

I'm not totally sure why I'm doing this. I'm not a writer. I'm not a scholar. I'm not a politician or a celebrity. I never went to college and I slept most of the way through high school. I don't have lots of spare time to kill, and I have no reason to believe that anyone cares what I have to say.

I do have a few things in my corner, and one is my wife. I also have one of the most important things that anyone could ever dream to have - freedom. The most under-rated word in popular vocabulary is freedom. We all claim to want it. We all think we know what it is. We all think we have it, and we all take it for granted. I also have what I call "the Right to Fail."

How many of you have ever gotten mad about something, and proclaimed, "I should write a book!" Well, guess what, I'm doin' it!

Do I know what I'm doing? No, as a matter of fact I don't. I'm just tired of sitting on the sidelines, watching our country spiral out of control. From my *controversial* point of view, we are heading for a cliff at a high rate of speed. I am tired of feeling like part of the problem. I'm tired of feeling helpless. This country is the greatest conglomeration of ideas, beliefs, and values ever to hit the cosmos, but we are not taking full advantage of it.

We are one of the youngest countries on the block, and look what we've done in our short life. We built railroads, we invented air travel, and we put men on the moon. We even put a car on Mars. We've advanced medicine, communication, human rights, and just about every thing else that we get involved with. Hell, we even advance things that we *aren't* involved with, simply because other cultures want to be more like us. We are kind of like the little brother that some people have that always seems to succeed in what he does, he always has the hot chicks chasing him, and he's always first to cross the finish line. Meanwhile all the older kids sit around getting jealous hoping he'll knock-up the prom queen, or break his leg at the big game.

Even if you're a communist, a hippy, a stoner, or just a complete loser, you can't possibly get out of bed without realizing that if you are an American citizen, you have a definite advantage over most people in the rest of the world. Unfortunately, there are a whole lot of people here that just don't get that. There is another group of people that get it, but they don't take the time to think about what's going on around them. They believe the first sound bite or popular idea that comes across their TV screen. They don't want to hurt someone's feelings, they don't want to be *controversial*, or they're just afraid of being wrong, so they fall right in with the "flavor of the week" crowd, rather than stand on their own beliefs. There are a lot of *these* folks.

By writing this book, I think I'm just hoping to give people a little nudge toward independence. If nothing else, maybe just give them something to consider.

Chapter 1

Confessions of a Former Liberal

L et me introduce myself. My name is Terry. I am an average male, age thirty-two. I am a truck driver by trade. I live on the outskirts of a very small town in south central Pennsylvania.

I am married to a beautiful woman who I met four years ago. We are both members of the working class. She is employed by a very large credit card company, and I am employed by a very large grocery conglomerate. I enjoy driving for a living; it gives me the opportunity to see things that most people don't get to see from their cubical. I also get to meet a wide range of personalities, all of whom have a wide range of philosophies. I don't think this makes me any type of authority on any given subject, but it does give me an advantage.

My wife and I live in a nice little house in the country. I bought it two years ago after many years of working multiple jobs and making quite a few personal sacrifices. Our house is not very big and I'm constantly hammering, drilling, sanding, and painting. The funny thing is, even with all the splinters, smashed thumbs and back aches, I've never been happier.

I rented for many years. I always rented within my means so that

I would have enough money left over to have some fun with. Renting was easy; if the roof leaked, it wasn't my problem. If the water heater went bad, a new one was just a phone call away.

Nowadays, everything comes out of my pocket. You go through a serious attitude adjustment when you get your first mortgage bill. No longer can you just blow things off. If you are married, or have kids along with a mortgage, you can't even *think* of blowing things off! After all, it's not just all about you any more. You now have RESPONSIBILITIES!

Some people are terrified of being put in a position of responsibility; they have no ambition, they blame others when they screw up, or they try to justify their mistake by pointing out the fact that "everybody does it." I believe that we are all guilty of this on some level, but some people have made a career of it.

I had a fear of responsibility for many years. On any given evening, after work, I could be found on my couch, basically just running out the clock. I would just lie there and watch sitcoms or play video games for hours on end. In the back of my mind I was waiting for something to magically happen that would result in my becoming rich. I think I actually assumed that I would win the lottery, or some rich relative that I didn't know I had would leave me a few million dollars. The longer I thought this way, the more bitter I would get. Eventually, I began to believe that I deserved this imaginary windfall. I would see other guys my age with new cars or better jobs and get jealous. I automatically assumed that they had done something shady to get where they were. After all, I was a smart guy; I worked hard, and deserved the new truck!

I truly believed that the only way the other guy could have gotten that cushy job was if his uncle hired him, or he cheated on some test. I thought to myself, "If *I* couldn't get that job, then how could he?" The truth was that not only did I not have that cushy job; I never even applied for it! I never even tried to make an effort. I just kept on working the same crappy factory job, waiting for that magic money to show up. You see, I had no ambition. When you have no ambition, it means that you are not taking *responsibility* for your own life!

I'm Not Hitler!

I don't know how I got to that point in my life. Walking around fueled only by bitterness is no way to go through life. I don't think I was raised that way. My parents were not perfect, but they were head and shoulders above most that I've seen. I realize that it is not politically correct to make personal judgments about people, but lets be realistic. When you see a 13-year-old kid with a pierced tongue, you can safely assume that the cheese has slipped off mommy and daddy's cracker!

My parents were blue-collar types like myself. My dad was a mechanic by trade, and still is today. He owns his own business, which always allowed him to provide for his family. We were never rich, but we always had food in our guts and clothes on our back. We even had enough left over to have fun.

My mom had a few different jobs while my brother and I were growing up. She worked at a grocery store, she did hair for friends and neighbors, and she later worked at small store that did custom picture framing. She now owns the shop. Her main job, though, was being a mom. Being a mom seems to have lost its glamour over the years; we'll get into that later.

My parents are now divorced. They separated for a while when I was in middle school, then got back together for a time until my little brother left home. After that, it was "game on" for divorce. My brother and I both knew it was coming, and we were old enough to understand, so I don't think either of us feels like we were scarred for life. It wasn't an ugly divorce, so we all got through it all right.

I could very easily blame my parents for the bitter time in my life, but that would be a cop-out. It seems to be the popular way these days to handle things, but that doesn't make it right. Your parents might make you bitter, but unless you're a complete moron, you still know right from wrong! I wasted a big chunk of my life sitting around doing nothing, and that was MY fault!

Your attitude is something that is uniquely yours. You build it like a car. You cultivate it like a field. You start with a piece of junk. You make all the decisions. You can build a car that runs great, looks cool, and never leaves you on the side of the road, or you can fix it just enough to get you around. If you don't take time to work on your attitude, it will leave you on the shoulder of the road.

My attitude was just basic transportation. I knew the basics of right and wrong, I tried to treat people as nice as I could, and I had an adequate work ethic. But, there was a problem. I had a disease; I didn't know it until later in life. It was a deadly, crippling disease that was slowly eating me from the inside out. It was liberalism.

I don't know exactly how I contracted it. Did I catch it from someone? Was there a bad gene that I inherited from a distant relative? Maybe I should have washed my hands more often. All I know is, I was a carrier. Apparently, liberalism is highly contagious, and does not discriminate. It doesn't care if you are young or old, male or female, big or small. It doesn't even care what color you are, or where you come from.

When I was a kid, my parents took very good care of my brother and me. They got us all the shots that were available at the time. They bundled us up in the winter, and made sure we always ate the right foods and got plenty of exercise. Even with the yearly doctor's check-ups and chewable vitamins, I was doomed. Mom and Dad did their best to protect me from all the sickness that might try to invade my young fragile body, but there were no visible symptoms. Liberalism is a *silent* killer. Symptoms of liberalism don't show up until it is too late. By the time you see those first few signs, it already has you in its deadly grip.

Once people have developed full-blown liberalism, it is easier to tell who might be a carrier. Symptoms include: inability to stay focused, laziness, irritability, and learning disabilities. It decreases your awareness of what is going on around you, and can leave you completely dependant on the help of others. It was once thought that you could tell if a person had liberalism by the length of his hair, or his body odor. It was believed that you could spot liberalism in the way a person dressed, or even how they talked. These theories have long since been dismissed.

Today, after many years of study, we know that liberalism is not always identifiable on the outside of the body. Some carriers are very well dressed, and well spoken. Many look like everyday people, just like you or me. Someone you know may be a carrier. You could even have a close relative that is stricken with liberalism.

If this scares you, it should. Current statistics on liberalism are hard to calculate, but it is estimated that current carriers number in the millions.

Much progress has been made over the years in the war against liberalism. Many treatments were tried; in most cases they only compounded the problem. At one point liberalism was thought to be a *benefit*. Of course, this was wrong. After experiencing the horrible effects of liberalism, it was painfully obvious that this monster had to be stopped. Some suggested that you could ignore it and it would go away, never to return again, like chicken pox or the mumps. That was not the case. Today, popular theory dictates that you treat liberalism similarly to the way that some people once treated the common cold - by sweating it out. Giving liberalism extreme doses of what it demands seems to be the most common way to treat it now. So far, the results are not good. Liberalism is still the number one killer of young minds today, but there is hope.

After years of study, a group of people may have finally found the cure for liberalism. As it turns out, the cure was right under our noses from the very beginning. It is so simple and easy to administer that it's almost comical. This cure is available to everyone, and believe it or not, it doesn't even cost anything! After all these years of torment, after all the pain and suffering, we can rid ourselves of this cursed disease! The cure for the most diabolical scourge known to man is *education*.

That's right, education. It has been found that liberalism begins to decompose immediately when treated with even the smallest dose of education. We have also learned that when treated with a steady diet of *common sense*, liberalism cannot live. A healthy regiment of political discussion has also shown very promising results.

You might think that I have a lame sense of humor, but if you *think* about it, liberalism is very much like a bad disease. I should know, since I used to be a liberal.

This book is not simply all about liberal bashing. After all, liberalism bashes itself. I just got tired of hearing the opinions of experts on this, pundits for that, and all the other types of talking heads. Don't you ever wonder what a regular guy thinks? Haven't you ever driven down the road, looked at the car next to you, and wondered, "what does that guy think?" When the newspaper tells you that most Americans think a certain way, do you automatically believe it? If a politician says, "My constituents tell me..." do you assume it to be true? There are hundreds of people today writing opinions, shooting their mouths off, and trying to one-up each other. They all have one thing in common; they are not one of *us*. None of them are in the category of *common man* any more. That doesn't mean that they were born with a silver spoon in their mouth, it just means that when you become successful and/or famous, you move on with your life. You move to a better neighborhood, you eat at better restaurants and you hang with different people (notice I didn't say "better people", just different). You may still visit the old neighborhood, but you go to bed in your gated community. When was the last time you suppose that Rush Limbaugh or Al Franken fixed their own cars? Do you think that either of them put on their own brake pads to save a few bucks on installation? Would they even know how? How long has it been since they've had to bum a ride to work because they only own one car? Granted, "common man" is a subjective term. I'm just saying that when I drive down the road, I see a hell of a lot more Ford Escorts than Cadillac Escalades. It's probably safe to assume that at a certain level of success, you lose touch with the common man, whether you want to or not. Losing touch with the common man isn't really so bad; it's when you lose touch with common *sense* that all the problems start.

My point here is that we have more media access today than in any other time in history. We have TV, satellites, cell phones, books, newspapers, magazines, billboards, Internet, and 24-hour news channels. It's always the same people that we hear from, though. Why is that? Are these people really the only ones with a credible opinion? I think not. Do you really need a background in journalism to know right from wrong, or good from bad? With the exception of Jay Leno's "Jay Walking" segment, we rarely get to hear from an average Joe.Being an average Joe myself, I am personally offended by our lack of representation in the media. Even legitimate "man on the street" interviews are few and far between. Sure there are polls; we have more polls than the power company. Every day we are told what percentage of the population thinks *this*, or how many people surveyed think *that*. Is this the way to get inside the mind of everyday folks like you and me?

Just once, I would like to see Charlie Rose interviewing a forklift driver from Springfield, Virginia, or a hairdresser from Butte, Montana. Would Katie Couric's numbers really plummet if every now and then she had a pipe fitter from Kentucky on her show? I'm not assuming that every one who punches a clock or swings a hammer can hold the attention of any given audience. Let's face it, I'm willing to bet that a lot of us either don't *care* or don't *know* about what is going on beyond our back yards. I work with you people every day; you know I'm right about that. To have a guest on a talk show who holds no office, belongs to no organizations, and has no media history and is still able to have an intelligent conversation, would require a little more effort, but the results would be worth it. After all, who buys the paper, who watches the TV, and who listens to the radio? We do, the regular folks that you see every day. It stands to reason that we might want to hear from someone of our own ilk from time to time.

I have a few theories as to why nobody bothers with us. It may be because they are afraid of us. What would happen if the word got out that what the media says we think, and what we really *do* think, is completely different?

Let's examine this concept a little more closely. Let's say that you turn on the news, and you see a segment about "gooberism". I made up that term because it sounds funny. You see that there was a demonstration at a college in the Midwest promoting gooberism. The news guy tells you that this was a large demonstration, and most of the student body was in attendance. The camera focuses in on a young college student who is carrying a sign that reads, "Gooberism is not a crime!" She is crying and speaking very loudly. She tells us how gooberism is a private matter, and how much pain the "anti-gooberists" cause in the world. She proudly proclaims that she and her fellow goobers are just trying to bring awareness to the world.

By the tone of this news segment, and the fact that it even made the news, you would think that everybody is jumping up to embrace gooberism. The news folks forgot to tell you that this was a small college of about 350 students. They also forgot to tell you that the demonstration halted traffic, causing one woman to be late for work, and a policeman was taken to the hospital for a gash on his head. He got the injury when a demonstrator threw a battery at him. They spent very little time on the fact that gooberism is illegal. They also didn't dwell on the fact that gooberism is the leading cause of birth defects. The important thing is, the young lady with the sign got her message out.

If you were to form an opinion about gooberism from just this one news show, you might not endorse gooberism, but you would probably try to accept it. After all, all of your buddies saw the same show. You don't want to be on the wrong side of the fence. So rather than take the time to further investigate the downside of being a goober, you go along with whatever your coworkers say.

The next day you get a phone call. It's a national survey. They ask you if you would like to answer a question for a national poll. Feeling important, you say, "Yes, I would!" The woman on the other end of the phone then asks, "What issue concerns you the most?" Your options are gooberism, your health, and your children's health. Of course you would most likely choose your children's health. After a few days pass, you turn the news on again, and this time there is a debate between two famous political commentators. They are discussing whether or not gooberism will become a big issue in the next election. The pro-goober speaker then pulls out his big guns. You guessed it, a national poll (the one you took). He explains to the anti-goober guy that the American people are just not concerned about gooberism right now. Then the focus shifts to another topic.

Slowly thereafter, gooberism falls off the radar screen. Laws were not enforced; it became fashionable and popular. All the big names in Hollywood were doing it. It was in the movies, on TV, and soon gooberism was an accepted way to be a part of the "in crowd." It became a marketing gimmick. After that, goobers got younger and younger. Then, it was too late. Gooberism was killing our culture and putting our future at risk. Unfortunately, at this point everybody was doing it. Now that it was politically incorrect to speak out against it, and law enforcement was encouraged to tolerate it, gooberism became an epidemic! It was out of control. Society as a whole became dumber and dumber. This made us weaker and weaker. Soon, a rogue nation realized this, and took full advantage. First, they flooded our nation with their people. They came in unchecked. They came in illegally. After all, now that everyone has embraced gooberism, why would anyone hate us? And now that we're all goobers, we don't need to worry about communicable diseases, or criminal backgrounds.

One day, some jerk from this unnamed country comes to America. He is not stopped at the border. Nobody checks his bag, for fear of being reprimanded for *profiling*. Thanks to political correctness, his extensive record of terrorism is not investigated. He moves freely among the people. The new driver's license that was issued to him in California gives him access to banks, a job, medical treatment, and even the right to vote.

He uses his automatically issued freedom to get a job. He is the newest employee of The Acme Painting Company. He is a bridge painter. He goes to work everyday. He is a hard worker. He's a little quiet, but he doesn't cause trouble and he's always on time.

The job that he is currently working on is a large train bridge that spans the Mississippi River. After the first morning break, our guest climbs over to a main structural support. He starts to paint. A coworker notices that they are not ready to paint that beam yet, but to say something might hurt his feelings. Besides he doesn't speak English, so what's the point anyway? Off in the distance, he can hear a train coming down the tracks. This concerns no one, because the train comes by here everyday at the same time. The train gets closer, when one of the other workers hears our old buddy mumbling something. The worker can't make out what he's saying, but he keeps repeating himself...he's praying. As the train starts across the bridge, our ambassador of goodwill pulls something from his lunch box and attaches it to the beam. It's a bomb! Before anyone can think, the train crosses over the main beam section, and our friend detonates the bomb! He and the other painters are killed instantly. The train plunges 130 feet straight into the river. The three men on the train are also killed. This particular train was made up of 53 tank cars of highly poisonous chemicals on their way to a factory in the South. Many of the tanks ruptured on impact, spilling their contents into the Mississippi. The poison made it's way downstream, killing every living thing in the water. The crash created a mixture of water and chemicals that produced a toxic cloud in the air. The poison in the water soon got into the drinking water supply. As the cloud of poison gas went east, the surge of poisoned water went south. Thousands died.

There are two parties to blame for the outcome of this scenario. The first guilty party is the producer of the original news story. He took an issue that was not relevant, to say the least, and distracted everyone from the real issues of the day. He also covered this "red herring" in such a way as to subversively push a damaging agenda in the name of political correctness and feel-goodism.

The other party at fault is you! You were too interested in football, J-Lo, or what brand of underwear you have on to learn about the long-term effects of gooberism! You were too blinded by Britney Spears' boobs to realize that the poll you took was just a con. You were more concerned with Fifty Cent's new CD than you were about your senator's new bill to help strengthen our national security. You got played...sucker!

If you had taken the time to educate yourself, you wouldn't have bought everything they were selling. You would have known better. You would have known why to vote for a particular person, or not. That would have made it just a little bit harder for stupidity to take over. When you went to work, you had the option of bringing up a relevant point of an important topic; instead you opted to talk about some guy's batting average. I'm not knocking sports, but in these times, is who put the ball through the hoop at the top of our priority list? No matter which side of the gooberism fence you were on, you had the opportunity to inspire thought. Even if you didn't know anything about it, you might have come away from the conversation a little wiser after hearing someone's point of view. Instead, you taught nothing, and you learned nothing. You did find out how many yards Payton ran for, though. I'm sure that is worth something to someone.

Surely, this could have an effect on our daily lives in the future. Never mind the fact that there is some really shady stuff going down that could ruin you or your children's future, keep paying attention to the important things like WWF, NFL, NBA, NASCAR, and baseball. After all, politics is boring, all politicians are the same, and nothing will ever change, because what you think doesn't matter. When was the last time Dionne Sanders called *you* for advice? How much has professional sports really changed *your* life over the years? I may be too idealistic, but I do believe that your vote still counts. This is why I think that the mainstream media fears the common man. If he is on the ball and educated, then they are not in control. If shiny objects distract you, they can get anything by you. Is this a giant conspiracy? Did our leaders plan this? Is there a secret "star chamber"-type group that is planning this elaborate scheme to keep the people down from behind closed doors?

No, I doubt it. Our government is neither smart enough, nor organized enough, to pull that off. I do believe that they saw the advantage of an uneducated society, and have been exploiting it for a long time now. Early on, I think they realized that our attention spans are very limited. Unless something is right up in our face, we don't make a big fuss. We might gripe about something when we first hear about it, but once we get back on the couch and turn the game on, we'll be just fine.

I was just as guilty as anybody else. My shiny object wasn't sports; it was prime-time sitcoms. I was in deep. I was very particular about my viewing habits. I had the prime-time lineup memorized. I knew what time and what channel all the popular shows were on. I didn't watch the news, I didn't read the paper; I didn't see the need. I got all my news and opinions from shows like *Murphy Brown* or *Northern Exposure*. Don't get me wrong, these were both very well written and entertaining programs, but the liberal agenda that they promoted was never-ending. I had friends at work that would try to point this out to me, but I didn't want to believe that they could be right. I couldn't believe that they had seen something that I missed.

After all, they were Bible-thumpers. After my years of "research", I had learned that religious fanatics controlled the right-wing conspiracy. So I knew they would try to make me believe that I didn't know what I was talking about. I was on to them. I was smarter than them; they were just gun toting, money-hungry racists, like the retired astronaut on *Northern Exposure.*

These were the guys that I worked with every day. We did the same jobs, ate the same lunches and made the same wage, but I truly thought I was superior to them. They were not as cool as I was. They didn't understand pop culture. How could you be intelligent if you didn't listen to Pearl Jam? How could you possibly know what was going on if you didn't watch "Friends"? How could you know about the real world, when you spent all of your time with your wife and kids?

The shiny things had me. I took myself for granted. I was being led by Hollywood, I and assumed they had all the answers. I never gave common sense a chance. Looking back now, I realize that I was ignorant. That ignorance caused my greatest shame; I voted for William Jefferson Clinton. At this point in my life I live with the shame of knowing how much has happened in recent years, and knowing that in some small way, I am to blame.

How many others did I convince to follow suit? How many times did I make fun of Dan Quayle for his misspelling of potato? How many times did I applaud Clinton's plan for free college tuition? Who else did I misinform?

They say that hindsight is 20/20, but that doesn't make you feel better when you can see how stupid you were.

This brings up another theory as to why the media treats the common man like a plague carrier. They seem to think that we are all cut from the same cloth. Apparently they believe that we are all morons. Yes, it's true, I wouldn't trust a lot of us to sit the right way on a toilet seat, but that doesn't mean that we are all worthless. Much of the knowledge that we *all* gather in life comes from other people. My father, not a talk show host, taught me how to drive. My mother, not some rock star, taught me to treat other people with respect. A friend of mine, not some washed-up actor, taught me most of what I know about the trucking industry. My point is, even though we gain most of our knowledge from other *commoners* similar to ourselves, the media seems to think that commoners have nothing to offer.

Why is it that when there is a controversial situation in the world, I am spoon-fed the political perspective of Susan Sarandon? Do I need to know what Tim Robbins thinks of the war in Iraq? Am I to believe Martin Sheen is more informed than the guy who installed my cable? Just what is the average educational background of the average actor? Just because some guy's name is more recognizable than yours, does that mean that you're an idiot?

I apply my criticism across the board. I recently heard an interview with one of my favorite actors, Gary Sinise. He and I seem to have similar opinions, and he strikes me as being a very decent person, but why is his opinion any more noteworthy than anyone else's? I'm sure that this interview was an attempt by the network to appear fair and balanced, but why do I care what a liberal *or* conservative actor thinks? I must say though, it is funny how a conservative actor's point of view is rarely given screen time. I'm sure it's just my imagination, not a liberal bias.Being a truck driver gives me the opportunity to meet lots of people. Trust me, some of these people are more informed on the issues than anybody living in a gilded cage. I would also say that most people I talk to are far more interesting. The most important thing that is not considered about "Joe Paycheck" is the fact that no matter how much he does or doesn't know about something, his response is almost always genuine. The truck mechanic that fixed my radio doesn't have a publicist feeding him politically correct responses. He doesn't need to worry about his ratings. He will never need to put on a front for the network executives. He doesn't have to "keep it clean" during prime time hours. You get the real deal when you talk to *real* people.

You would also be surprised how much the average guy *does* know about the real world. After all, he does live in it. Some of us can read. Some of us can write. There are even common people who can think. I have heard a rumor that there are common folk who have been to college. My stepfather went to college. He has more than one successful business venture, but you'll never see him on the Oprah show, because he's never been in a sitcom.

You see, if word was to get out that people are really not very liberal, the power structure would shift dramatically. In the minds of those in power, this cannot be allowed to happen. When I refer to people of power, I don't necessarily mean presidents or generals. The real people that are in the driver's seat are controlling what you see on TV, what you listen to, and what you read. It's a rare occasion that any politician can affect the way you think, but actors and musicians do it all the time. I remember when the movie *The Fast and The Furious* was released. At every theater in the country, after the movie let out, every car in the parking lot left in a fury of burning rubber and grinding gears. We didn't drive like that on the way to the show, but after watching that movie, even a card-carrying pillar of the community such as myself found it hard to not drop the clutch and catch second!

It's the same thing with music. If you limit yourself to one style of music, you will almost always start to pick up some of the attributes of your favorite artists. If you listen to nothing but country music, you might pick up a slight southern drawl. If you listen to hip-hop, eventually you might forget how to pronounce the words "the" and "ask". If you listen to gothic rock, you might start wearing more black clothing.

My point is that few things in this world alter our subconscious more effectively than the things that entertain us. Music, movies, and books have been guiding public opinion since the dawn of man; from Shakespeare to Clint Eastwood, and all the way back to the first cave paintings, we have been influenced by the stories of others. Who doesn't feel just a little cockier after seeing *Enter the Dragon*? Who hasn't questioned the morality of war after seeing *Platoon*? Didn't you hate rich people when you first saw the movie *Wall Street*?

Look at the young people today. At some point, it became fashionable to drive a spike through your tongue. This was prominent in the punk rock community in the early eighties, but that was just a small segment of the urban landscape. Later, punk rock became more popular, and now every other time I go to a fast food joint, some little freak asks me in slurred and barely decipherable language, "Do you want fries with that?" All I can think of in this situation is, "Can this kid be trusted to prepare my family's food?" How can I take a person seriously when they have purposely punched a hole in their lip? Could a person with a tattoo on their neck be of much help to me?

I don't think any president, congressman, or senator will ever have enough persuasive talent to convince someone to mutilate themselves, but what about a popular hard rock band? People will most likely never line up in droves to start speaking like Colin Powell, but what about Snoop Doggy Dog? Do you gizzle my drizzle?

The real power is in the power of persuasion, not in the power of legislation. Washington can't touch Hollywood, even on a good day! If Hollywood ever lost its ability to control the masses, the entire balance of power would change. If people were no longer led around by the nose in the quest to be cool, then maybe they would think for themselves. We can't have that! This is why we hear from Sean Penn from California, and not John Smith from Iowa.

As I said earlier, I don't believe that this is massive conspiracy. I do believe that the people are still the driving force of this nation. I still believe that we have the power to steer this country in any direction we choose. The problem is that we forgot how to drive. Right now, this country is just bouncing off whatever obstacle is in its path. We are letting the wrong people take the wheel. We have freedom of speech, and freedom of the press, but we actually pay people to use it for us, and they are only too happy to oblige. We have become comfortable in our own ignorance. If our kids can be convinced that to be cool you have to punch holes in your face, then who is really at the wheel? When does the common man get to decide what's cool? When does the common man get to influence the kids at the fast food joint?

I don't want to give you the wrong impression. I don't blame the media for the stupid things that kids do today. I offer this analogy. Think of mass media as a buffet. Let's say that children are, well...hungry children. If you send the kids to the buffet unescorted, they will eat whatever they want. They will gorge themselves on pudding, pie, donuts, cake, and every other sugary concoction under the sneeze guard. Eventually they will become fat. Soon after, they become less active, then lazy. Later on, they learn that they have a vitamin deficiency, which makes them vulnerable to disease. They become sick all the time. More time goes by, and the kids are diagnosed with diabetes. The diabetes causes one to lose his foot, another to go blind. This scenario ends with the kids having a very short, painful life.

Now imagine these very same kids, going to the very same buffet, with a responsible adult at their side. Mom watches as they reach for the pudding. With a scolding glance she says, "No! Not until you eat your vegetables." She then proceeds to fill the children's plates with reasonable amounts of corn, peas, chicken and potatoes. They clean their plates, and are provided with a proper portion of pudding. This same discipline is provided at every meal until the children grow to be adults. This scenario ends with kids growing up to be healthy adults of average size, and without disease.

Mass media is no different than that buffet. If you don't pay attention to what is going into your kid's mind, don't get all bent out of shape when they blow themselves up trying to get on TV. Don't blame the gun manufacturer when your fourteen year old pulls a Columbine! You were the one that put a TV in his room. You were the one that didn't take the time to explain the value of human life to him. You were the one that assumed he knew the difference between right and wrong, or fantasy and reality. You were too wrapped-up in who's going to the Super Bowl to notice that your own son was slowly going insane. It was you who sent him to the buffet unescorted!

Have you ever wondered why TV shows are called *programs*? Is it just me, or is that just a little too coincidental? You know what they say, "garbage in, garbage out"!

So what do I think should be done about the garbage being pushed on our helpless young children? I thought you would never ask. For the sake of our children's well being, and our own personal safety, we must act now. To protect our children from the pervasive sex and violence in the media today, we must resort to the extreme act of...*parenting*. I know, it seems excessive, but desperate times call for desperate measures. If you thought I was going to suggest that we take legal action against the media, you were way off. Who am I to tell someone that they aren't allowed to create a TV show, just because I don't like the content? Who am I to tell an author that they can't write about something, because *I* think it's indecent? How arrogant would I have to be, to tell a singer that he needs to modify his lyrics, because a child may hear them?

At one point in my life, I remember believing that it was the government's responsibility to protect people from the bad things in the media. I remember the day that the K.K.K. came to town. They weren't actually coming to *my* town, but they were scheduling an event, two towns over. Assuming that I knew all there was to know about racism, I was instantly outraged. I thought to myself, "The Klan should be rounded up and arrested! They have no right to preach that kind of hatred!" I actually believed that some government agency should step in and stop them from coming to our area. I never gave the First Amendment a thought. I was so comfortable in my superior ideals that I completely ignored the rights of others. I didn't consider the notion that if the government had the power to suppress one man's ideas, then they could suppress mine too. Yes, the K.K.K. is the epitome of ignorance. Yes, they are a pimple on the ass of humanity. They make morons look scholarly, but they have the right to say whatever they want to in America.

That was a big pill for me to swallow for a long time. I had trouble getting my mind around the concept that our Constitution was designed to allow "the people" to decide what they wanted to be exposed to. It is not the job of the F.B.I. to shield us from concepts and ideas. It *is* their job to shield us from nut-jobs with box cutters. I had forgotten about the fact that most of the music I listened to was considered controversial by some people. Should they be able to have my tape collection confiscated? I never took the time to look at the big picture.

The K.K.K. is practically defunct and nobody takes them seriously anymore. It wasn't because the C.I.A. shut them down. It was because "the people" made a choice! They heard what the Klan had to say; they didn't agree with their ideals, so they rejected them.

That is exactly how the system is supposed to work. The common man has the ability to make his own decisions, and is encouraged to do so.

I had been focusing on the message, and not on the freedom to send the message. I was distracted by my own high opinion of myself. I didn't understand this until later in life, when someone told me that we have "the right to be stupid." I wish now that I could remember who told me that. That one simple statement stuck with me; to this day I think it is one of the wisest phrases I've ever heard.

It never dawned on me that the Constitution is not there to protect the speech that

we agree with. The Constitution is there to protect the speech that we *disagree* with. After all, isn't that one of the reasons that we left England in the first place? The British didn't like what we were saying, so they tried to keep us down. We didn't have a constitution that guaranteed our right to free speech, so we had to leave. Then, when we got to our new pad, we still had to fight for the right to speak our mind. Those Brits really liked us: look how pissed they got after we left.

Eventually, the K.K.K. did come to town; I decided to take the high road. I stayed home. The more I thought about my plan to sneak onto the rooftops and spray their parade with skunk urine, the less realistic it sounded. I don't have access to enough skunks.

I heard from a friend of mine that only a few people showed up. Most of them only went to point and laugh at the idiot parade as it passed by. In the years since, I haven't heard of the KKK returning. Score one for freedom!

When the people speak, it truly is a great thing. The power that the common man possesses is staggering. An educated man has the power to move mountains. I'm not just talking about the kind of education that you receive in a school. I also mean the education that you get when you pay attention to what is going on around you. The kind of education that allows you to see beyond what you are shown. Looking at the big picture is the most important thing that a free person can do. Unfortunately, it seems to be a lost art. Even as a group, the common man does not have the right, or the power, to stifle another man's idea. However, we all have the right to *reject* his idea. If a guy on the street tries to sell you a cheap product, it is his right to do so. It is your right to say, "No, thanks!" An *educated* person knows what kind of junk the guy is peddling, so he won't buy it. An uneducated person will buy one for himself and one for his kids at home.

An educated population can reject a dangerous idea. We have done it for hundreds of years. An uneducated population will buy into any crazy philosophy that comes down the pike. This is what I fear is happening now. We seem to be getting dumber by the day. This is exactly what has happened to most of the failed civilizations in the past. They took their eye off the ball, misplaced their priorities, and faded into the pages of history books. If you think that it could never happen to us, guess again. We are losing our grip on our own freedoms. There are people pushing concepts and ideals on us that if not rejected, will sink us! Instead of rejecting these ideas, we are lapping them up. Our lack of interest in real education is clouding our view of the big picture. We are becoming slaves of the people in power. The common man is being downgraded. We are being reprogrammed as a society, slowly and gradually. Common sense is fading into obscurity, slowly being replaced by ignorance. Our natural will to be free is being co-opted by absolute dependency. The self-defeating shell game of liberalism is gaining ground. If the common man doesn't wake up soon, we are all doomed!

For example, you could have read the last paragraph and considered it to be nothing more than a rambling list of talking points from someone with a "doomsday complex." But if you take the time to think about each line, you will see that they are actually pretty accurate; a little heavy, maybe, but accurate.

Hopefully, by the end of this book you will come away with a better understanding of why there is a growing group of people who feel that there actually *is* reason to be concerned about the future of our country. My goal here is not to scare you into building a bunker in your back yard and surrounding your house with razor wire. I simply want to scare you just enough to spark your interest in things beyond your front stoop. And if I can't scare you, maybe you will be *curious* enough to find out if there is any validity to the things I am saying. Either way, if this book prompts you to find out more about what's going on in the world, then I will consider it a success. If it prompts you to *do* something about what's going on in the world, then it will have exceeded my wildest dreams.

Chapter 2
My Rude Awakening

A wise man once said, "Ignorance is bliss." I never really understood the true depth of this statement until I started to outgrow my liberal beliefs. Looking back, I remember how happy I was. I think about how superior I felt in the company of others. I was filled with confidence. No one could convince me that I was wrong about anything.

Today, confidence is a foreign word to me. Lately, I am starting to wonder if I would be better off returning to my original way of thinking. Back then, I didn't feel the need to excel in anything. I didn't worry about much. Now, it seems like everyday there is something else to be concerned about. Things that many people seem to take for granted really mean something to me now.

You see, at some point in my life, I woke up. I started to pay more attention to the things that really count in life. This is even truer right now, because just last week I learned that I am going to be a father. This is something that my wife and I have been working toward for some time now. It will be interesting for me to see how far this book project gets by the time our child is born. Today is Sept. 27, 2003; I'll keep you posted as you read on.

Now, back to my confidence issues. I am by nature a "glass half full" kind of guy. I always have been. My parents tried to steer me in that direction. My dad would always try to tell me that most problems in life have a way of working themselves out. My mom would try to get me to look at other people's situations and compare them to mine. Naturally, after years of this, I try to maintain a positive attitude. I feel that I have a good sense of humor, and I try to make people laugh whenever possible. Even with these character traits, I seem to be losing my faith in people. Now that my blinders have come off, I'm not sure I like what I see.

I can't pinpoint exactly when I started to become more conservative, but a few instances stand out in my mind. I think it may have started with a phone call I received late one night. I was in my apartment, enjoying my two favorite things at the time - pizza and TV. It was about midnight when the phone rang; it was my mom. She told me that my brother had been in a car accident. This is a horrible thing to hear at any hour. She told me that he was O.K., but he was in the hospital for observation. I was very relieved. She told me that his car was totaled, and that his friend John was with him at the time. He also was going to be fine. I automatically assumed that it was my brother's fault. After all, he was still just a kid. Then my mom informed me that it was a hit-and-run, and they hadn't caught the guy yet. It was at this point that I got pissed. I couldn't believe that someone would do that. My dad got on the phone and told me how bad the car was. He told me that they were both lucky to be alive. At first I thought maybe he was just exaggerating, until he told me about the crash scene. My brother David was traveling on a main road that leads out of town. We had been on this road at least twice a day since as far back as we could remember. It's a wide, smooth road with very few dangerous spots. David was beginning to crest a hill, when a car hit him from behind. According to the police, they looked at this guy's skid marks and estimated his speed to be about 90 to 100 miles per hour. He hit David's car squarely in the rear, pushing him into a graveyard on the *left* side of the road. This road is very busy, even at that hour. I was extremely thankful that no one was coming in the other direction, and that the phone pole that David missed was not two feet to the right.

After hearing my dad's description of the crash, and realizing how close I had some to losing my brother, I went into "detective mode." The police said that they were looking for a blue and grey Mustang GT with a pink stripe. I assumed that it couldn't have gotten far with a smashed front end. The radiator had to be shot, and I knew I had seen that car around town a few times. I just never knew who owned it.

I got dressed, and went hunting. Beginning at the crash site, I went further down the road. I was hoping to figure out which way the guy had turned off. I stopped at the first turn-off, assuming that he would have gotten off the main road as soon as possible. I was right. With the help of my trusty flashlight, I saw pieces of my brother's taillights on the ground. They had fallen off when the Mustang made the turn. This worked at a few more intersections, and then I was able to follow the antifreeze trail. I could tell by the quantity of antifreeze that he was moving slower at this point. I knew he would try to get the car out of sight somewhere nearby. I lost the trail; he had run out of antifreeze, but I kept going. I drove around the general area for at least an hour. I found one blue and grey Mustang, but I could tell it was not damaged in the front, so I gave up and started home. On the way I kept an eye out, just in case. I passed a house that had two vehicles in the driveway, a pickup, and what looked like a Mustang. The pickup was parked in front of the Mustang, so I could not get a clear view of it without trespassing. There was a light on in the house, so I didn't want to risk getting my head blown off. Who says owning a gun doesn't deter crime?

I went home and called the police. After hearing about what I had found, they said they would check it out. A few hours later, my dad called me to tell me that they had picked the guy up at that very house. Of course, he was drunk. Not only was he drunk, but he also had a history of drunk driving.

The next day, I went to see my brother's car. The entire trunk was pushed flat against the back seat. David and John *were* lucky to be alive!

That was also the day that I started to think about things more clearly. Actually, I started to think about more things in general. I started to ask questions. How was this moron allowed to drive, with his record? Why could I find this idiot when the police couldn't? Did the guy possess any common sense, and if not, why?

This may have been where I started to lose my hope for humanity. Most importantly, I believe that this was when I began to see that there is a connection between what happens to everyday people, and what our elected officials do.

You see, the ass that hit my brother had a valid driver's license, despite his record of abuse behind the wheel. This happened because we have a very weak judicial system. At some point, a judge dropped the ball on this guy. Another contributing factor was the lack of parenting on the part of this jerk's parents. He was an adult at the time when he hit my brother, but what values fell by the wayside when he was growing up? I don't know anything about this guy's childhood, but it is obvious to me that his parents dropped the ball too. Didn't anyone teach him that if you get drunk, you can't get behind the wheel of a car? Did they forget to mention to him that you have to take responsibility for your actions? It must have slipped their minds to tell him that hit-and-run is a felony. Since he has yet to apologize, I guess they forgot to explain common courtesy to him also. To this day, he is still driving, and still frequenting the local tavern. I have to assume that he will strike again...literally.

Around the same period in my life, something else happened that made me wonder if I really had it all figured out. It was 1993; I was watching my old friend the TV. There was a news break. Someone had detonated a bomb at the World Trade Center in New York. I was glued to the TV screen. I was trying to figure out what kind of person would do something like this. I have always had a knack for engineering and mechanics, so I pictured in my mind what might happen if this bomb had weakened the right support structure. The image that came to mind was horrible. I remember seeing the footage of the people streaming out of the towers. I thought back to the class trip we took to New York City. Man, those towers were the biggest things I had ever seen. Being terrified of heights, I could never even think of going into them. I couldn't get my mind around the concept of purposely trying to knock them down. There couldn't be someone out there *that* evil. I didn't know how many people were normally in the towers at any given time, but I knew it was in the thousands. I had never heard of anything like this happening in America. Who was the nut job responsible for this?

In the coming days and weeks, I kept hearing the name Osama Bin Laden. He sounded like some wacko with mental problems. As time went on, I heard less and less about the bombing. One day, I heard that they had arrested some old blind guy that was allegedly the brains behind this attack. Not much else was mentioned about Bin Laden. I just assumed that we either took him out covertly, or that he wasn't that big of a deal after all. I knew that either way, our President had things under control. I didn't notice that Bill Clinton never even went to visit the World Trade Center after the bombing. It was never mentioned on the news that I *did* watch. I heard that the President threw a few missiles over bin Laden's way, so I assumed that we got him and it was over. Bill was a hero. Eventually, the attack was no longer newsworthy, and we seemed to have lost interest.

I still had questions. I wanted to know more about this Bin Laden guy, and his operation. Did we know much about him? Did the government have an eye on him? Did they get him or not? What was his problem? I had heard about terrorism before, but it was always someone else's problem. Occasionally, an American would become an innocent bystander and get killed in some foreign country, but it never happened *here* before. Was this the start of a new trend? Were we ready?

I was beginning to take a small interest in world events. I wanted to know about things that I had never paid attention to before. This was only a spark of casual interest, but it was a start. Like most people at the time, I eventually lost interest, and fell back into my comfortable life.

I was on the couch again in 1995 and heard about the bombing in Oklahoma. Hundreds died. It was a horrible thing to have happened, but I didn't pay as much attention to the aftermath. They found the culprits and sentenced them to death. It was a done deal. The press said that Timothy McVeigh and his accomplice, Terry Nichols, were "right wing fanatics" that wanted to destroy the government. I thought this seemed a little far-fetched, but at this time in my life, I was still willing to trust the mainstream press. I also took the path of the mainstream during the standoff in Waco, Texas. I wasn't yet ready to believe that the press could be misrepresenting the truth. I couldn't stop wondering, though, about a few things. Was this the best idea that the A.T.F. could come up with to bring David Coresh to justice? Yes, he may have been a religious weirdo with some firearms violations, but did that justify this massive siege? I didn't understand why they didn't just pick him up earlier, away from the compound. Again, I just figured that the government knew what they were doing. I thought back to the Ruby Ridge situation and remembered having the same questions then too.

Later in life, I would find out that my questions were justified. The important thing was that I was asking questions.

Around this time I had started a new job working for a large grocery store chain as a truck driver. In our area, this was the job to have if you were going to be a truck driver. The benefits were good, and the pay was great. I tried very hard to get in at this place. After many trips to meet with the personnel dept., and turning in quite a few applications, I told the man in charge of hiring, "Your either going to hire me, or you're going to put a restraining order on me." I was hired the next week and I am still working there today.

One cool thing about working for a big company is you get to work with a lot of people. Exposure to a lot of people means exposure to a lot of opinions. This, I consider a good thing. There were a lot of people my own age at my last job; at the new one I would be working mostly with people much older than me. Many of my new coworkers were former over-the-road, long haul truckers, with millions of miles worth of life experience, and thousands of stories.I worked a lot of hours, and I worked late at night. This turned out to be a blessing in disguise. My love affair with the television set was about to end. I was no longer a slave to primetime TV. I was working a job that would keep me confined in a truck for hours at a time. FM radio got old real quick. I kept hearing the same box of records over and over, on all of the stations. Even my tapes were getting old; I needed something different to keep my brain occupied during the long trips to make my deliveries. One night, I decided to hit the AM button, just for something to do. This was the smartest move I had made in a long time. Things were about to change; I didn't even see it coming.

I found a channel that came in pretty clear, so I gave it a chance. A guy started talking about crime. He was rejoicing in the fact that a man had been shot and killed while attempting to rape a young woman in front of her child. She pulled out her gun and shot him. He then began to tell the listeners where they could find this story, so that they would know it was true. He gave names, places, times, and sources. I couldn't believe what I was hearing. I was blown away. His tone was one of joy and satisfaction. He talked for more than two hours. His topics ranged from gay rights to the Middle East conflict. He was only giving his own opinion, but he was following it with facts. I heard more useful information in those two hours than I had ever seen on TV. He was obnoxious, but he wielded facts like a broad sword! There was no generality, there was no ambiguity. He offered analogies that ran exactly parallel to the topic. He didn't mince words, and political correctness was not even considered. I had never heard anything like this before. The idea of someone shouting their opinion from the rooftops, but explaining in rational terms why they felt that way, really hit me like a Mack truck. This man's name was Neil Boortz. He opened up a whole new world to me; talk radio...I was hooked.

The next day, I went to work, got in my truck and headed down the road. I turned on the radio, and immediately hit the AM button. I scanned the dial. I doubted that I would be able to find Mr. Boortz again, but I was curious to hear what else was on the less popular bandwidth. Again, I was surprised. As I drove down the road, I heard the voice of what I thought was a crotchety old man. He was talking about women in the military, and he was clearly against it. At first I thought he was just an old geezer who was out of touch with "mainstream society." As a liberal, my attitude was, "Hey, women have the right to do whatever they want, and they are equal to men on every level." The old guy on the radio had a different take on the subject. He brought up the point of male/ female relationships, and their consequences on the battlefield. He also examined the possibility of an enemy force exploiting females in times of war. He followed this up with the burden that a military force would carry if a soldier were pregnant.

Like Mr. Boortz, the old broadcaster presented his theories, and backed them up with facts. He mentioned names and had no problem with telling the audience where to find out more about the subject. He brought up the opposing opinion, and quickly pointed out the error in their thinking. He, too, drew perfect parallels and presented matching analogies. By the time he finished his diatribe on women in combat, I had to take a second look at my opinion on the subject. After all, mine was the *opposing* opinion. Just then I noticed something; I was thinking, and the more I thought about it, the more I realized that my politically correct ideal wouldn't hold water.

A few weeks later, my best friend from high school came to visit. He is a soldier in the U.S. Marines. His name is Scott, and he is a great person to know. He's the kind of guy that I believe most people want their sons to be like when they grow up. He's got a great sense of humor, he's very smart, and would do anything for you. He is one of the few people in this world that I trust.

While he was visiting, I asked him about women in the military. I remembered meeting some of his female coworkers when I had gone to visit him. One in particular stood out in my mind. She seemed to have her head on strait. She also struck me as being very independent and headstrong. I thought she had a great attitude, and until I heard the old guy on the radio, I assumed that there was nothing wrong with her being a Marine. After hearing this guy's radio show, I thought about Scott's coworker. It didn't hit me at the time I met her, but it was hitting me now. This girl couldn't have been more than four feet nine inches tall, and I'm willing to bet that she didn't weigh one hundred pounds. I started to picture what an enemy soldier would do to her in battle, and it gave me chills.

I wasn't sure how Scott felt about the whole subject; we never talked much about world events or social issues before. We always talked about guy stuff - chicks, cars, and work, not much else. When I asked him what he thought about it, I was surprised at his answer. He agreed with the old guy on the radio. He even brought up an issue that the old guy missed. He started telling me about rumors of *prostitution* in the ranks. I had never even thought of *that*. He told me how he had heard rumors of women in the military who make a tidy profit selling themselves to other soldiers. He also said that for the most part, women are accepted and respected, but some soldiers were not looking forward to walking onto a battlefield with them.

After my conversation with Scott, I noticed something about myself; not only was I learning about something, I was researching too. The old guy on the radio who inspired me to check something out for myself was G. Gordon Liddy.

Today, I have a new opinion about women in the military, but you will have to wait until later find out about it.

After my experience with Mr. Boortz and Mr. Liddy I started listening to talk radio almost exclusively. I didn't limit myself, though, to shows about politics and social issues. Occasionally, I would listen to comedy talk shows like "Don and Mike," or variety shows like "A Prairie Home Companion."

A new pool of information was slowly seeping into my brain. The only problem was, even with exposure to new ideas, I was still a liberal at heart. I was at a point where I would get mad at the radio, because I got tired of conservative hosts blowing holes in my philosophies. I would call them names and pound on the dashboard, but no matter how hard I tried I couldn't catch them in a lie. I couldn't even catch them making a significant mistake. Of all the names I called them, liar wasn't one of them. I wondered to myself, how the radio hosts could be saying these things about such important people? They're giving names, dates, and sources. How do they do this everyday without getting sued for slander? With all the nasty things that they are all saying about President Clinton and his people, why are they all not in court? The answer was right in front of me, but I was too proud to look at it. They weren't being sued because they were telling the truth!

I tried not to notice that conservative radio hosts weren't afraid to read quotes or play audiotape of the people they were confronting. I had rarely seen this in the mainstream media. Years of "hit and run" commentary was all I knew. Making a statement that sounded legitimate, but contained no actual facts or information, was what I assumed real news was. I was taking their word for it, while only hearing the parts that *they* thought were important, or supported *their* agenda.

Talk radio was different. No matter how hard I tried to deny it, they *did* give the names. They *did* tell the times. They *did* give the sources of information. They *did* have their facts straight. They *did* tell you how to research the facts for yourself. They *did* take the calls from liberals. They *did* roll the audio tapedquotes. Their arguments *did* consist of more than general comments or making fun of someone's looks.

I still tried to hold my liberal ground. The questions I had about social issues, politics, and our culture were beginning to multiply. The philosophies that I had cultivated in my youth were clashing with the new information that I was receiving. I was conflicted. Pride was running the show. Trying to make my square peg ideologies fit the round holes of reality was becoming more and more difficult. Apparently, there is something to that old cliché, "the truth hurts." It would take something serious to bring everything into focus for me.

On the morning of September 11, 2001, I was sound asleep when my girlfriend woke me up. She said something about a plane crash. I wasn't planning to wake up for at least another hour or two, so I only processed about half of what she was saying. I asked her what she was talking about. She told me that an airplane had hit a building in New York. In my half-conscious state of mind, I rationalized it this way: it was bound to happen. I assumed that a plane had gone off course in a fog bank, and hit a building. I knew I would see the news footage when I got up, so I mumbled my theory to my better half, and fell back asleep.

A few minutes later, she came back into the bedroom and demanded that I come out to the living room and see what was going on. By the tone in her voice, I knew something wasn't quite right. I sat down in front of the TV, and as someone who is not a professional writer, I must admit, it's hard to put into words what I saw, and what I thought about it, but this is what I've come up with.

I sat down in front of the TV, and tried to compute the images that my eyes were relaying to my brain. I remember thinking, "That looks like the World Trade Center, but it's on fire. That can't be real." I double checked the channel indicator, and started changing stations. My girlfriend said she had already done that and it was on every channel. I asked her what had happened. She said that she was watching her morning show, when they broke in with a bulletin about an airplane that had hit the World Trade Center. She said "that's when I tried to get you up the first time. Then a few minutes later, while they had the cameras on, another airplane hit the other tower."

I asked her if she was sure that there were two separate airplanes. Before she could answer me, they ran footage of the second airplane hitting the other tower. At this point, I rubbed my eyes, and looked around. I wasn't totally sure that I was awake. I have always had extremely realistic dreams, so I wanted to be sure I was really seeing this. I was.

Darlene (my girlfriend and now wife) asked me how this could happen. I didn't exactly know what to say, but I was sure it wasn't an accident. Even though I had just woken up, I could see that the sky was crystal clear. I knew that the odds of two planes running out of fuel at the same time and hitting the same set of buildings were probably impossible to calculate. I told her that I had a feeling that someone had done this on purpose. She asked me why someone would do that. The only thing I could think of was "religious wackos." Then, I thought back to the *first* attack on the Trade Center; those guys were members of a crazy Muslim outfit. I thought we had taken care of those guys a few years back. Apparently not.

The question she asked me next still replays in my head from time to time. She asked me what was going to happen to the people in the buildings. As I mentioned earlier, I have a knack for mechanics and basic engineering. On this day I considered it to be a curse. I didn't want to upset her, but I didn't want to sugar coat it either. We were both adults. On the TV screen, I pointed to the sections of the buildings underneath where the fire was visible. I said, "Everyone under this point should be OK for the most part, as long as they can get out of the buildings before the fire spreads to the lower floors." Then she asked, "What about the people above those points?" It took me a second, but I said, "They're gone."

She suggested that we pray for them. I'm not a very religious man, but I didn't know what else to do. Darlene is a great person, and she knows that I am very private about my religious beliefs; she respected that and went back to bathroom to get ready for work. I did as she suggested.

My brother works for my dad, and they don't have a TV at the garage they own; they rarely listen to the radio either (my dad doesn't want to offend his Mennonite customers). I knew they would want to hear about this, so I called the garage. I told my dad everything I was seeing and hearing on TV. He said that he would run up to his house and check it out; he only lived two blocks away at the time.

After hanging up with Dad, Darlene came out of the bathroom; it was time for her to go to work. I didn't feel too comfortable about Darlene going to work, but I didn't want to scare her. Still, I wanted her to be careful and stay alert. I explained to her that things were going to change in America from this day on. I told her to go straight to work, and to come straight home. I told her not to stop for anything or anyone. I reminded her that she worked for a large financial institution, and I told her to pay attention to her surroundings at work, and to follow whatever security procedures that they were using. She started to cry.

I didn't know what to do; I knew that I would be going to work in a few hours, and I didn't want her to get in trouble for not going to work. I had to assume that the Trade Center was the end of the attack. I couldn't imagine that anything else could happen after something this major. I assumed that she would be OK at work. After trying to calm her down, I suggested that she go to work. I kissed her goodbye, and she left.

As I heard her get into her car, I called my mom. I knew that she would be at work, and most likely listening to her Christian music CD collection, so I thought that she might not know what was going on. I was right. I told her to turn on her radio, and tune in a news channel. I tried to describe to her what I was seeing on TV. "Both towers of The World Trade Center are on fire," I told her. I explained to her how it had happened. I was describing the massive amounts of smoke and debris coming from the upper sections of the buildings. As I was talking, they were showing footage from a helicopter, and that's when the first tower fell. All I remember saying as this happened was "no, no, no, Mom, one of the towers just fell down!" I never even considered this as a possibility. Somehow, I pictured them slowly burning to the ground. I figured that there would be a long battle with the fire, but it would eventually burn itself out. After all, once the jet fuel burned off, the firemen could get closer to the fire. I never thought the tower would fall.

After the tower fell, I was still trying to give a play-by-play to my mom. I described the giant cloud of dust that was covering the city. The more I talked, the harder it got to find words.

Finally, I told Mom that I was going to hang up and watch the news. A few minutes later, a different picture came on the screen. It was the Pentagon. It was on fire! I called my dad again. I said, "They just took out the Pentagon, I think we're being attacked!" As always, he sounded skeptical, but he humored me. He told me that this was bound to happen, and to keep my eyes open at work tonight. The conversation was very short. Talking to my dad takes patience and skill. This subject was so serious and unusual to both of us that discussing it was not an option. I said goodbye.

I called my mom back, and told her that the Pentagon had been attacked too. She told me that she had heard on the news that a plane went down somewhere near Pittsburgh, and that one might be headed for Camp David. Now I was starting to get scared. What do you do when your country comes under surprise attack? They forgot to mention this in grade school, or maybe I was out that day. My mom was in no position to offer any advice either. She did offer Darlene and me a space at her and my stepfather's mountain retreat, in the event that this was going to be a full-scale war. At first, I thought she was overreacting, and then I looked at the TV screen again. My mom is prone to overreacting; we usually just make fun of her. That day I wasn't laughing. I actually considered her offer. I thought back to the previous year when she and my stepfather Denny were so concerned about the "Y2K bug" that they fortified Denny's hunting cabin with months of supplies and ammunition, just in case anarchy ensued. We ripped on her for a long time after that; now it was looking like a viable option.

Having no idea when this was going to stop, who was going to get hit next, or what other methods of attack were going to be implemented, I did the only thing that a Pennsylvania good ole' boy could think of. I got out my .45 semi-automatic, and started cleaning it. I didn't know what else to do. I wasn't worried so much about meeting up with a terrorist, I was more concerned with how *we* would react. Would there be panic in the streets? Would there be looting? Would I be able to get to Darlene again if this all got out of hand? Looking back now, reaching for my gun as a first impulse may have been a little presumptuous, but think about it. Unless you were around on Dec. 7, 1941, this situation hadn't occurred here before. What did you do on that day? Did you just blow it off as something that didn't concern you? Did you hide in the closet? Maybe you pretended that you were watching a movie, and smoked another bowl. Did you consider your family, and how to defend them if necessary? Whatever you did, you did *not* know for a fact that you were safe; I don't care how detached from reality you were.

On that day, the most productive and practical idea I could come up with was to clean my gun. For you city folk, understanding someone's desire to carry a firearm may seem a little foreign, but in the country it's not much more unusual than carrying a Palm Pilot. We'll get into that later.

As I was sitting on the couch, cleaning my gun and watching the news, I watched the second tower fall. I just couldn't believe that this was happening. I started feeling something inside my chest; it was anger. Someone was attacking my country, the only home that I have ever known. A spark of liberalism shot through my mind; I tried to imagine how other countries felt as they saw a US tank coming over the hill in *their* homeland. I almost considered the idea that maybe we had been *asking* for this. That concept faded into oblivion as soon as I looked at the screen again. We didn't deserve this. Those people jumping from the top of the building just to get one last gasp of fresh air never asked for this. They just went to work that day. I remembered that America is the good guy. We don't invade countries for no reason. If you see a US tank coming at you, it means that we are trying to free somebody. It means that we are trying to help. I tried to think of a country that we had invaded and claimed as our own in the last couple of hundred years, and I couldn't think of one. Pilgrims invading the New World don't count, because we were fleeing an oppressive country, and we would have shared with the Indians, but they weren't the sharing type.

As I watched our country come under attack, I knew that things would never be the

same. I knew that our enemies would be exposed and our allies would help us. I knew that our attitudes would have to change.

I had big ideas about how our nation would join together and rise up to fight the evil bastards that had done this to us. I assumed that there would be lines around the block at the recruiting offices. I just knew that everyone would be on the same page from now on. I thought back to all the times I had said, "War is never the answer." After September 11, it was clear that pacifism was not an option. How could anyone disagree with that now?

Looking back, I know that I was being too idealistic. I don't think I was being naïve; I truly believed that was how it should have happened. Of course I was wrong, but one thing was sure, September 11, 2001, was the day I woke up. From there on I was a different person. Those terrorists killed more than thousands of people that day; they killed the liberalism in me.

The day went on. I went to work, just like every other day, except this day, everyone was different. Usually, I got to work early to socialize with the other drivers before we headed out on our runs. We joked around, and talked about the latest company gossip or current events. On this day, everyone was very subdued. There was no joking around. We all had the same look on our faces. To this day, it's hard to describe that look. I imagine it's the same look you might have if your doctor just told you that you had cancer. A look of disbelief, helplessness, shame and anger, all rolled into one. We talked about what had happened that morning, and how it was going to affect traffic in Washington DC, as well as the effects it would have on our job in general. We kept the conversation simple. We didn't plan it that way; I think we just didn't know what to say, or how to say it. We all just wanted to be home with our families, but we had jobs to do.

My run was to be a "back-haul." A back-haul is when you are dispatched to a warehouse or factory to bring a certain product back to your distribution center. As I was walking out the door with my paperwork, another driver was coming in from his run to DC. His face was lit up like a Christmas tree. He was talking as fast as he could, and you could tell he was shook up. He had been on the road all day and was only able to hear about the attacks on the radio. He told us how he had been sitting on the DC beltway when a group of jet fighters buzzed his truck. He said the sound of the jets coming up on him, without warning, scared him to death. He said that he could see the smoke from the Pentagon from the highway. The more he talked, the more animated he became. I went on out the door to get my assigned truck.

For me, the safest place in the world is behind the wheel of an 18-wheeler. That is where I am the most comfortable, but that day, I just wanted to be home with Darlene. I was worried about her, and hoping that she was doing OK at work. I didn't feel safe at all. I still had no reason to believe that the attacks were over. I still hadn't found out about the rumor of the plane going down at Camp David. I only live 30 miles from there. DC isn't that far away either. If I had been allowed to carry my gun in the truck, I may have felt a little better. My destination was no real comfort to me, either. I was to pick up a load of detergents in Camp Hill, PA, which is right next to Harrisburg. There is an international airport there, not to mention Three Mile Island Nuclear Power Plant. Would a nuclear power plant be considered a target? I tried not to think about it too much. As I made my run that day, my ears were glued to the radio. Again, AM stations were proving to be the most informative. You could definitely tell that the press was shook up. The reports were many; no fluff pieces, no commercials. Some of the FM stations were still playing their boxes of records. I found out later that most of them didn't even activate the Emergency Broadcast System. I guess they felt that an attack on our country didn't justify cutting into a Motley Crue tune for a newsbreak.

I got to my destination ahead of schedule. I had to wait for a while until a forklift operator was available. I went to the driver's break room to get a soda. In the break room was a television with a crowd of truck drivers around it. Again, the images of destruction were in vivid color. It was unusual to see big, surly truck drivers with such a sobering look about them. I got a soda out of the machine and watched for a while. It seemed as though the attacks were over, but no one on the news would risk saying that yet. By this time, more footage was coming into the newsrooms and making its way onto the TV screen. None of it was pretty.

Eventually, a forklift operator was available, I was loaded, and then I returned to the distribution center; I was glad to be going home. Darlene was there when I got home; we were both relieved to see each other. That night we held each other a little tighter than usual.

I decided to call this chapter "My Rude Awakening" because it took something that big, that horrible, to snap me out of my "cruise control" mind set. I had to experience something catastrophic to learn that there are a lot of bad things going on out there that can't be wished away, or put on the back burner. I needed to see thousands of people die to learn about appreciating our freedom. It would take the destruction of some of man's greatest architectural achievements for me to realize that our way of life is good, and worth fighting for. I needed to see people risk their lives to save total strangers in order to learn how much of my own life I had wasted

Ever since that day, I have different priorities. I pay more attention to the way I treat other people. I pay attention to what is going on in the world around me. I have taken the time to learn what our leaders are doing to keep us safe. More importantly, I am learning what they are *not* doing to keep us safe.

I have realized that there is something to those family values that I used to ridicule. Most importantly, I now have something that I was lacking before September 11th, and that is ambition. I want to be a better person. I want to learn more about everything. I want to have a family. I want to raise a child who will grow up to be part of the solution, not part of the problem.

I have more motivation, and I don't spend nearly as much time on the couch as I used to. When I *do* watch TV, I watch real news shows. I pay attention to all sides of an issue and apply common sense to it *before* I form an opinion. I no longer pay attention to popular opinions. You are either right or wrong. Something either makes sense, or it doesn't. I don't let political correctness cloud my judgment anymore. I now know that doing the right thing may get you some dirty looks from time to time. I have learned that most of what I have been led to believe about conservative values is way off base. I learned that I am no longer a victim. I consider the "ripple effect" of decisions that our so-called leaders make. I have a new sense of independence. I also have a better idea of what *independence* is.

In the coming chapters we are going to get into a whole mess of subjects. I am going to contrast and compare the liberal and conservative way of dealing with these subjects. I will also try to apply some good old-fashioned common sense while I'm at it.

Remember, I'm just a simple truck driver from southern Pennsylvania; you don't have to believe or agree with anything I say. I just want to help you get out of cruise control.

Chapter 3
Let's Get It On!

It is a very weird time in the world right now. I just watched as Arnold Schwarzenegger swept a recall election for Governor of California. We are currently fighting a war on terrorism in Iraq and Afghanistan, Johnny Cash has died, and Rush Limbaugh has just checked himself into rehab for addiction to prescription painkillers.

Lately, real life has become much more entertaining than anything coming out of Hollywood. "The Terminator" is now the Governor of the largest economy in the United States! You couldn't write a more ridiculous script than that, but this is real life! Don't get me wrong, as screwed up as California is nowadays, there is nowhere to go but up. When it comes to the West Coast, I think that most of us just hope for the best, but expect the worst. Those guys are nuts over there. I will never understand how a state with such a pioneering history came to be the Mecca of liberalism. How did they go from John Wayne to Sean Penn? Leading men in Hollywood used to be proud of their country. They jumped at a chance to promote American ideals and the spirit of patriotism. In World War Two, actors like Audie Murphy, Jimmy Stewart, and "The Duke" lined up to make movies that emboldened our nation, and reminded us of what we have here. Now, you can't turn on the TV without seeing some overpaid water-head putting down every action we might take to protect our country.

I remember when I was in high school all the latest trends would come to our school about six months to a year after they first hit in California. Chuck Taylor sneakers, rap music, skate boarding, and just about every other pop culture phenomenon, starts in California, then spreads across the rest of the country. Apparently, liberalism is no exception.

I don't know exactly how it started, but it's choking us all. Some people think that California's liberal stranglehold is the result of the peace movement of the sixties. One theory assumes that the college students who protested the Vietnam War grew up to become the college professors of today. Now, with a captive audience of naive young minds, they can put whatever spin they want to on our nation's history. Being ex-hippies of the flower power generation, they have no concept of true evil, and seem to have a real problem with law and order. We'll get more into that later.

I don't know if Arnold will be able to do much to help California, but I sure hope he can. He has been very vague about his plans to fix his state, and most of the people that he is picking to fill his team seem to be from the left side if the aisle. Just the fact that most of the people in the California legislature probably won't take him seriously could be a problem. In any case, I wish him the best of luck.

When I decided to write this book, I basically just jumped into it. I had thoughts about many issues and wanted to chronicle them in a way that would make sense to anyone who might actually read this. I am giving you fair warning, I don't do political correctness, and I don't care if I offend anyone. That being said, I'm not *trying* to offend anyone either. I speak in plain terms, I don't beat around the bush, and I hate sugar coating the things that need to be left bitter.

From this point on, I am going to randomly pick topics that I feel are important, and try to give you one common man's perspective on them. All of my comments are open to debate, and there is no law that says you have to agree with any of them. I do request that you give these concepts some thought before you dismiss them. Like me, just considering and thinking about a topic could actually put you onto the road to a new education.

Finding segues into particular subjects has never been my specialty, so I would like to jump right into a subject that is on everyone's mind these days - the war in Iraq.

After September 11, 2001, I have been paying close attention to what is going on in our nation, and in the world. I don't like what I see. The problem is, most of what I see comes from my old friend the television. According to my TV, we are bogged down in a quagmire and losing the war on terrorism. My TV tells me that the war in Iraq has nothing to do with terrorism. If I was smart, I would take my TV out into the driveway, and run over it a few times with my truck. Maybe then it wouldn't act so negative all the time. A little attitude adjustment never hurt anybody. I am so tired of having to read between the lines to figure out what the real story is. I don't always have time to research every news story that I see. If I took everything that I see on TV for face value, I'd hide under the bed.

If you believe what the media is currently spoon-feeding you, the war in Iraq looks like a big mistake. If you apply your memory skills, deductive reasoning, and just a pinch of common sense, you start to get a much clearer picture. It wouldn't hurt to do a little research on your own either. As I said in the first chapter, the media hates it when people do this; they rely on you to just accept the trash that they are giving you. You have no excuse for letting them do this to you. Here are a few reasons why; libraries, newspapers, books, radio, mail, magazines, the Internet, and most importantly, your own brain.

When the subject of Iraq comes up, I hear the word "quagmire" a lot. I also hear references to Vietnam. Did I miss a memo? Was I supposed to forget the events leading up to the war in Iraq? Was I supposed to erase the past twelve years of my life? Did someone forget to tell me to ignore the people I know who *actually were* in Vietnam, and who *were* in Iraq? Maybe I was never properly instructed on how *not* to talk to the friends and relatives who are in Iraq now, or know someone who is. Apparently, I shouldn't be making comparisons to other wars in the past either, such as World War I or II. According to the news, I should forget everything. I think not.

You see, unfortunately, I do remember the events leading up to the war in Iraq. I remember the time that Saddam Hussein gassed his own people. He killed thousands of men, women and children. Not soldiers on a battlefield, just regular folks. He used poisonous gas, which has been banned by every civilized nation on the planet. I remember when he invaded one of his neighboring countries, Kuwait. His army rolled in there, killing anything that got in the way. America had to step in and kick him back out of there. You might remember a little thing called Desert Storm. In the process of adjusting Saddam's attitude, he lit all the oil wells on fire; I guess he was not much of an *environmentalist*. We rolled over him so easily that it was almost embarrassing.

We had the option to take him out of power, but that was not the mission. Our mission at that time was to push him out of Kuwait, and we did that. We let him go because we made the mistake of assuming that the United Nations had a real purpose in existing. Saddam signed an agreement with the U.N., allowing him to stay in power as long as he would allow inspectors into his country to check out his weapons stash. He also had to agree to a "no fly zone".

I remember the weapons that the U.N. found; Scud missiles, poisonous gas, nerve agents, biological agents, and all kinds of goodies that are banned everywhere else. I specifically remember the giant gun that he was building into the side of a mountain. It had a range of a few hundred miles, and it just happened to be pointed at Israel. He was planning to build an even bigger one with a 500-foot barrel. It would have been capable of shooting a nuclear device into orbit. I remember seeing the confiscated barrel components on the news.

These things were all documented by the United Nations, and found to be violations of the treaties that Saddam himself agreed to. Enter Resolution 1441. Hussein agreed to show the world that he had destroyed or dismantled all of the weapons that the U.N. knew he had. He put on a good show for a while, but he could never seem to remember where he left all of those nasty toys. He gave the world the run-around for years. He even kicked the U.N. inspectors out of Iraq. The U.N. said that there would be serious consequences if he didn't comply with them. I don't blame Hussein for not trembling with fear over the prospect of the U.N. flexing *their* muscles. They couldn't resolve a parking ticket.

Am I supposed to forget that all this happened? I haven't even mentioned Saddam's history of torture and human rights violations yet. When he first took power back in 1979, one of his first acts as a dictator was to assassinate twenty-some members of his own cabinet. So much for job security.

I didn't forget about the fact that if an Iraqi citizen left his country without permission from the Iraqi government, his family would be raped and tortured in public.

Look, I could go on for hours on end about the atrocities that Saddam Hussein and his sons committed, but you have heard it all before. The bottom line is, he was the personification of evil. You either believe that or you don't. Listing all of Saddam's greatest hits will probably not change your mind. For some reason, there are people out there who seem to tune out the ever-expanding list of evil things that this guy did. I don't know if they just don't believe it, or they just don't want to admit that bad people don't respond to "please" and "thank you". These folks seem to believe that since we have not yet found weapons of mass destruction, that must mean they didn't exist in the first place. Never mind the fact that just a few weeks prior to the writing of this chapter, U.S. forces found a bunch of Iraqi jet fighters buried in the desert sands. They didn't look like they were destroyed to me. It makes me wonder what else might be buried in the sand. I guess we shouldn't pay any attention to the fact that it has only been a few months since we rolled into Iraq. I'm sure that Saddam hasn't been trying to hide anything for the past *ten* years. We should have expected to see all of his weaponry displayed in plain view, in the parking lot of the Baghdad Mall. Is it possible, that if someone knew that they were going to be invaded in the not too distant future, they might try to *hide* the things that they are not supposed to have in the first place? Is it beyond the realm of possibility, that this person may have even smuggled them into a neighboring country? Some people are not giving common sense a fighting chance. If you are one of these people, I offer you the following analogy.

Let's say that you are a policeman. You have just been dispatched to a robbery in progress. When you get there, you recognize the suspect. You have busted him before. You know that he has a violent past and that he has had gun violations before. You know that he has used guns to murder people before, too. You also know that he has never turned in the guns that he has been caught with before, *and* that he has been trying to get more guns as well. On this night, he is wearing an overcoat, and something is being pointed at the grocery store clerk from the perp's coat pocket. Knowing what you do about this guy, do you assume that it is just his finger in the coat pocket, or a gun? Do you walk up to him and politely ask to see the contents of his coat, or do you pull out your service revolver and treat him as an armed and dangerous criminal? Maybe you should just keep on driving, and let the "neighborhood watch" take care of him. What do you think you would want to happen if you were the grocery store clerk?

If you had decided to treat him as an armed and dangerous criminal, would you have been wrong, even though it turned out to only be his finger pointing from his coat? Of course not. You were acting in the best interest of the grocery store clerk. The option of assuming that you could play cat and mouse with this guy, without any possibility of the clerk getting hurt, just wouldn't be the way to go. Hindsight is 20/20, but no one can predict the future. When it comes to protecting the clerk, or your nation, you only have history to guide you - and maybe a little common sense.

The liberal idea would be to continue with more diplomacy and inspections. This looks good on paper, but only if you are dealing with a civilized human being. The people on the left side of the fence still don't get that. They seem to believe that Saddam is someone who can be negotiated with or that he can be trusted to see the error of his ways. I wish that was a possibility, and I'm not even saying that it isn't. I'm just saying that history doesn't bear that out.

I'm Not Hitler!

Sure, Saddam could wake up tomorrow and realize how evil he is, turn himself in and beg forgiveness from the millions of people whose lives he destroyed, but if you were in Vegas, would you put your kid's college fund on a bet like that?

I don't care if he still has weapons of mass destruction or not. We know that he did, and he has never explained in any detail what happened to them. We could be sifting through that sand for decades before we find them. We may need to go into his neighboring countries to find them. This does not mean that it was a mistake to go to Iraq. It just means that Saddam is sneaky. Who didn't know that already? I still believe that we will find his toys, even if it takes a while. Iraq is a pretty big chunk of real estate. The things we are looking for aren't much bigger than a Volkswagen, in some cases the size if a Pepsi bottle. If I told you that you had three months to find a Pepsi bottle in a foreign country the size of California, do you think you could find it? Don't forget, I had at least ten years to hide it.

I don't care if this was a "War for Oil" either. We *need* oil. Even the most die-hard, tree-hugging, vegetarian, pierced-lipped, pot-smoking pacifist uses oil is some way. If you are one of these folks, what did you use to light up your bong with today? My guess is you used a lighter- a plastic lighter. And what is plastic made from? OIL. What is the fuel in the lighter made from? OIL. You may have used the same lighter to burn your dreadlocks. Does your microbus run on OIL, or happy thoughts? Do you drive on pavement? Do you use electricity? Do you cook your food? What was the paint that you used to vandalize that fur coat made from? OIL.

What would happen if we had allowed Saddam Hussein to monopolize the oil supplies in the Middle East? Would you be willing to pay five dollars a gallon for gas? What good is your weed if you can't afford to go get it? When you get the munchies, how much will it cost to have a pizza delivered then?

Do you really believe that he could have been trusted not to use his oil supply to blackmail or extort the rest of the world?

I like oil; I not only *like* oil, I love it. I don't like crappy oil either. I want the good stuff. When I step on the gas I want to get my money's worth. I don't want to get run over by a truck because the cheap gas in my tank made my engine cut out. I don't want to need a valve job every other year either.

Letting Saddam remain in charge of the fuel spigot would definitely be a bad idea, because no matter how evil or politically incorrect you think oil is, we all use it, and we all need it. Until they invent an engine that runs on good intentions, oil is our nation's lifeblood.

I don't care if all of George Bush's best friends make a profit from this war. So what if they do? Who is spending the most money on this war? America. Who should have the first chance to make a few bucks in the process? America. George Bush was a millionaire before he became President. He was already a rich oilman. Am I to believe that he risked the lives of thousands of people, our national security, billions of taxpayer's dollars, and possibly a world war, just so he could buy another gold plated back scratcher? I have to believe that if George W. Bush was that greedy or *that* evil, it would be a little more noticeable. *That* kind of evil is hard to cover up. Saddam has been trying to look like a nice guy for years, how successful has *he* been?

On the surface, it may look like a conflict of interest for a Texas oilman to be invading an oil producing country. Here is where you get to put on your thinking caps. If we only wanted the oil, then why didn't we just take it the first time after Desert Storm? Why aren't we just taking it now? Have we ever done that in the past? Can you remember a country that we just invaded and then stole their resources for ourselves? What other choice did the President have? Would it have been better if Bush kicked the problem on down the line, giving Saddam time to get his toys put together? I guess he wouldn't have looked like a nasty old oil baron then, and *that's* what is most important today.

The same can be said for Vice President Dick Cheney. I know that he has business ties to Halliburton. I also am fully aware that this is the same company that is going to make a lot of money from reconstruction in Iraq. Again, on the surface this looks like a conflict of interest. But did you know that Halliburton is one of only *three* companies in the entire world that is big enough to handle the massive job of reconstructing Iraq's entire country? Having that job put up for contract bids would have made no sense, because Halliburton was really the only game in town. There is a company in France that could do it, but let's not kid ourselves; France has no business making one penny off of this war. *They* were the ones who helped create that nut-job Saddam. Their dealings with him are well documented. He had an oil deal with the French that was going to cost them billions if he were to fall from power. The French knew that Bush wasn't going to play around with Saddam like Clinton did, so they did everything in their power to stop the war. I don't recall hearing about any *French* soldiers helping in the effort to free the Iraqis. I don't remember any reports about any *French* soldiers giving *their* lives or sacrificing *their* time and money for the cause of freedom. They deserve nothing.

Back to Bush and Cheney. America is the most powerful nation in the history of the world. We are the most technologically advanced society ever to walk on the big blue marble. This did not happen overnight, and it didn't happen without using the resources that are available to us. Our nation's energy policy is the most important key to our survival. If we ever lose our focus on energy production, use, or exploration, we will fail as a country. We will end up being slaves to whatever nation surpasses us in the energy game. Keeping that in mind, who better to run a country dependent on energy than someone who has been in the energy business? A person who is familiar with the ins and outs of large-scale oil production is more likely to have some insight on the energy needs of his country than most other people.

I offer this analogy. Let's say you want to hire someone to manage your bakery. Would you hire the kid who went to college and studied journalism, or would you hire the kid whose father owned a successful chain of donut shops? If you hire the donut shop kid, would you get mad at him if you found out that in his spare time he was lobbying for a police station to be built across the street from your bakery? It may be a conflict of interest, but who is the victim, and who is the benefactor?

You see, if you are an American citizen, you are going to benefit from a free Iraq, whether it *is* all about oil or not. Iraq is going to benefit no matter who really started the war, or why. Even if it were true that Bush and Cheney started the war in Iraq for personal gain, what's the downside? We freed an entire population from a murdering bastard. We helped to stabilize the price of oil for the entire world. We are bringing democracy to a people who could never have dreamed of it before. We closed the rape rooms. We are setting up a new government, *of* and *by* the people of Iraq. We are essentially creating a new friend in the Middle East. That alone is going to benefit everyone. If Bush and Cheney were smart enough and ambitious enough to plan and execute this whole scheme, and make a few bucks from it in the process, I say BRAVO!

Yes, this war has cost lives on both sides (more on Saddam's side than ours) but freedom is *not* free. Saddam Hussein killed hundreds of thousands of people. We are finding mass graves of his victims every week. These were mostly just regular folks like you and me, who said something that he didn't like. Or he *thought* they had said something he didn't like. He was the Grande Puh-ba of human rights abuses. Even the British weren't treating us *that* bad when we fought and sacrificed for *our* own freedom back in the Revolutionary War. War is a nasty business; people die. They don't always die quickly, or in a blaze of glory as in the movies. Unfortunately, as long as there are bad guys, there will always be a need for good guys to give their lives to free the victims of tyrannical misfits. The men and women who are risking their lives to free complete strangers in Iraq are the best that mankind can offer. They volunteered; they were not drafted, or forced by an oppressive regime to join a dictator's military force. They took an oath to defend the cause of freedom. They left behind all the comforts of home, including their friends and family. As of the writing of this chapter, we have lost nearly 200 American lives in the effort to free Iraq, heroes all. If Saddam would have been left to continue at his previous rate, within a few years, *millions* more could have died. Assuming that no human life is more valuable than any other human life, I can live with these odds.

For me to say that I can live with these odds may seem to be incredibly insensitive, but it's not. A person who sacrifices on any level so that someone else can live free is a hero. It would be great if it were always possible to negotiate our way to global freedom. The sad fact of life is, this will never be realistic, at least not in *our* lifetime. There are people in this world who are just evil. There is no other way to put it. They don't respond to treaties, negotiations, political or financial pressure, and least of all, capitulation. Sometimes, as painful as it is, you need to use force. There are people in the world who don't understand any other language than violence. In many cases throughout history, violence has been the method people used to come to power in the first place. Were Saddam Hussein, Pol Pot, Idi Amin, or Al Capone *voted* into power by free democratic elections by the people? I highly doubt it. I used Al Capone as an example because *his* methods were very similar to the methods that have been used by dictators since the dawn of man. These methods can be best described in one word...bullying. I would bet that most people, at one time or another, have been bullied by someone. I am no exception.

When I was in school, I rode the bus every day. It was a long bus ride because we lived in the country. It was made even longer by one boy who also rode my bus. His name was Steve, and he was a bully. Every day he would try to intimidate me in one way or another. He would flick my ears from the seat behind me. When the bus driver wasn't looking, he would jump in the seat with me and punch me in the thigh or arm. It was very embarrassing. This kind of torture would continue throughout the day, because we were in the same class too. I would try to talk to him and ask him nicely not to pick on me; this usually resulted in more beatings.

One day, I had enough. I didn't want to get in trouble, so I did what the teachers had told us to do if we ever felt like we were being bullied. I told my teacher about what Steve was doing. I assumed that this would be the end of Steve's daily torture. I was wrong. The next day, he jumped into my seat again. This time he wasn't going to pick on me for fun; he was pissed! He punched me harder than ever. The rest of the day, whenever he would see me, he would push, punch, kick, or trip me. Each time, he would dare me to tell on him again.

I went home that day tired, and consumed with shame. I was out of ideas. I was afraid of what my parents would say, but I needed help.My father is a very uncomplicated man. To him, most things are either black or white. There is not much room for gray areas in his philosophies of life. I went to him with my problem. For some reason, I assumed that he would go talk to Steve's father. Again, I was wrong. His first question was, "what do you want me to do about it?" I suggested that he call Steve's dad on the phone. He said "no." I asked him what I should do. He grabbed my right arm and held it up in front of me. He said, "Make a fist," so I did. As most kids at that age would have, I made my fist with my thumb tucked inside my fingers. He said, "not like that," and proceeded to show me how to make a proper fist. "Now what do I do?" I asked. He told me that the next time Steve came up to me, if he even looked like he was going to touch me, I was supposed to punch him in the face with all of my strength. He told me not to hesitate, and to aim for his nose. I told him that I would get in trouble at school if I did that. He told me that I would get in trouble at *home* if I didn't. I didn't know what to think of this, but he was my father and I trusted him. After all, getting in trouble at school usually meant writing something on the chalkboard, or standing in the corner. Getting in trouble at home usually meant losing my bicycle for a week; I hated *that* more than anything.

The next day I got on the bus just as I had a hundred times in the past. I sat down as usual. When we stopped at Steve's house, I could feel the butterflies in my gut. I was hoping that he would forget about me. I was hoping that maybe he wouldn't be coming to school at all. At this point, I was hoping for the bus to catch on fire, or the sky to fall, anything! No such luck. Steve came out of the front door of his house and headed toward the bus. He came through the door and up the steps. He passed my seat and sat down behind me. I did my best to summon the power of invisibility, but that didn't work either. I felt a sharp pain behind my ear; he flicked me. My next move was not planned, it just sort of happened. I stood up. To this day, I don't know how I stood up, and I don't think I even had a plan for after I was on my feet. Steve seemed surprised to see me standing in front of him, but he wasn't scared. He stood up too and got right in front of my face. He said, "What are you going to do, cry?" Again, I had no plan, and I was pretty convinced that I was going to be going home with a bunch of empty spaces where teeth once were. Before I could think, my right arm was in the air, and a small hand-shaped object was headed toward Steve's face at an alarming rate of speed. My newly discovered fist hit his mouth and nose with a squish-like noise. He flew backwards and landed a few seats back. I was standing there, waiting for him to get up and start pummeling me. The retaliation never came. He looked at me, and with blood running from his lip and nose he whimpered to me that he was going to tell his father. He then went to the back of the bus and hid behind the seat in front of him.

To this day, I can't recall what punishment I received in school that day. I'm sure it wasn't something that scarred me for life. I *do* remember what happened the next day on the bus ride to school.

I was anticipating a surprise attack of some kind. I was sure that Steve would not be able to let this go. After all, had I embarrassed him in front of everyone on the bus, as well as everyone who saw his fat lip. I was sure that he would try to get me back. When Steve got on the bus that morning, I tried my best to ignore him. I was caught completely off guard by what happened next. Steve sat down in the seat next to me; I was bracing for a punch to the face. He said something to me, but I couldn't make out the words over the noise of the bus gearing up. "What?" I asked. "I said I'm sorry that I was messing with you", he said in a sheepish kind of way. He then informed me that he was just kidding around, and didn't mean to make me mad. I had no idea what to say, or how to react. The only thing I could think to say was, "no big deal."

Even at the ripe the old age of a fifth grader, I knew that he wasn't just "kidding around," but I decided not to push the issue. From that day forward, Steve never bothered me again; in fact he became somewhat of a buddy, until he moved away a few years later.

The lesson that I learned from this situation was sometimes you *do* need to resort to violence. There *are* people in the world who do not respond to anything else. You can be as polite, respectful, or diplomatic as you want to be, but in some cases you might need to punch them in the face in order to protect yourself. Right now, Saddam Hussein is getting his fat lip, courtesy of the United States armed forces.

I don't believe that violence is *always* the way to solve problems. We are better than that, but what if your mother was being mugged? Would you ask the mugger nicely to stop and apologize, or would you fight to save your mom? Even the most devout pacifist will fight for *something*, his mom, his wife, his children...a tree.

I truly feel that this country is worth fighting for. It is worth protecting. We cannot afford to take chances with our future. What other country offers as much opportunity and freedom as America? Relying on dictators and despots to change their ways, and not seek to destroy our allies or us, is just plain stupid. Relying on a giant useless bureaucracy like the United Nations to save the day is just insane.

I am trying very hard not to turn this into just another "bash Clinton" book, but it isn't easy. Bill Clinton had just as much opportunity to take care of the Saddam situation as George Bush had. He opted to throw a few missiles over there and call it a day. He was well aware of the fact that Hussein was not honoring his agreements. He was well aware of the fact Hussein was a major human rights abuser. He was aware that Hussein was interested in acquiring and/or developing weapons of mass destruction. He was even aware that Saddam had used these types of weapons in the past, on his own people. At the end of Clinton's presidency, no matter how you slice it, or who you blame, Saddam Hussein was still in power.

I don't really care why Bill dropped the ball. I don't care if it was a "pass the buck" thing. I don't care if it was a "Let the U.N. handle it" thing. I don't care if was a "fear" thing. I don't even care if it was an "I don't want to risk my political career" thing. All I know is, he left this big mess for the next guy to handle. I can only thank God that the next guy was not Al Gore. I wouldn't have blamed Saddam if he would have invaded downtown Washington DC. Gore would probably still be trying to play nice with him, as he perfected more ways to kill us, or at least control us.I still believe in diplomacy, but there does come a time when you need to step back and recognize when it has failed. Diplomacy is *a* tool for peace, not *the* tool for peace. Sometimes you need to *carry* a big stick, and sometimes you need to *use* a big stick.

Something else that seems to be a popular topic lately is the media's reporting of what is really going on in Iraq. The average American does not have the time, money, or ambition, to go to Iraq and see for themselves what is really going on over there. We have no other choice but to trust the news coverage offered up by the mainstream press. At least, that's how it used to be. Today, we have been blessed with the miracle of the Internet and instant satellite communication. If you want to know what the weather in Tikrit is like today, all you need to do is look at the TV, and you can see it live and in high definition. If that doesn't satisfy you, just turn on your computer, and you can get the entire history of weather patterns in Iraq, as well as real-time satellite images.

The information age has hit us like a Mack truck. If you don't know what is going on in the world, you're just not trying. We have the ability to talk with people, and see them at the same time anywhere in the world...live. The only problem is, apparently somebody forgot to tell the mass media outlets.

They seem to have forgotten that they are not the only game in town anymore. If I want to know how my friend is doing while he is stationed in Iraq, all I have to do is email him. In return, he can send me digital photographs right into my living room, instantly. I don't have to wait for a letter and a month-old snap shot. He can give me instant feedback as to how well the war effort is going, and I don't have to worry about liberal bias, or any other bias for that matter. I know he'll give me the real scoop, because he isn't competing with anyone for ratings. I don't need to worry about his personal agenda tainting his reports.

When you turn on the news right now, you would think that the liberation of Iraq was a waste of time and money. The reporting of this war has been shameful lately. The sad part is that the press did so well covering the actual invasion of Iraq. They used what is now commonly referred to as "embedded reporters." I was amazed at this concept: putting reporters in with the soldiers on the ground, and using real-time technology to relay video coverage of the war, as it is happening. I stayed up until the early morning hours to watch this. Every night I would be glued to the screen. It was hard for the networks to put a spin on their reports, because so much footage was coming in at such a high rate of speed.

My question is, where are the embeds now? Here we are, only a few months after the end of the invasion, and the information well seems to have run dry. The only news that comes out of Iraq now is the daily body count. The media has forgotten how to report *good* news. If you are the type of person who trusts the "alphabet channels" you probably have no idea of the good that is happening as a result of our intervention in Iraq. You might even be ashamed of our involvement.

Thanks to the media's policy of "all bad news, all the time," it is going to be harder to win the peace and fight the war on terror. When you convince the masses that things are going sour, they will react in a way that reflects that. So now, rather than everybody working together to help a newly freed country get back on it's feet, we are wasting time pointing fingers at people for a *failure* that never happened.

The networks seem to have trouble reporting things like the schools and hospitals that have been opened. They forget to mention the introduction of Internet services, and other new technologies, to a people who were never allowed to have them before. They skip over the fact that a new Iraqi police force has been trained, and is currently working to keep the peace. The finding of weapons caches and mass graves doesn't seem to get much airtime. The fact that right now, cars in California are already being powered by fuel that is being pumped by Iraqi oil workers has fallen by the wayside. People can travel, speak, protest, sing, dance, and live better lives now, without having to worry about a dictator's son slowly dropping them into an industrial chipping machine for his own amusement. This *also* doesn't seem to warrant a prime time expose.

One thing is for sure; you will get your hourly close-up of an angry Iraqi citizen whose vegetable stand got backed over by an evil American tank. You will also get the hourly update on the cost to the taxpayers of "Bush's war." They have to call it that; anything else wouldn't be sensational enough. If "Bush's war" becomes too repetitive, then "Bush's unilateral occupation" will do just fine. As long as we put the blame on the Republican, and not the murdering bastard dictator. They still use the word "unilateral", even though there are countries from all over the globe helping in the effort. I guess "unilateral" means without France, Germany, and Russia.

I almost forgot to mention the obligatory, wide-panning shot of the Air Force transport planes bringing home the flag-draped coffins of soldiers killed in Iraq. What liberally biased news report would be complete without a good ole' fashioned "coffin shot," to get the blood of the population boiling? Nothing says "thank you for sacrificing your only son for the cause of freedom" like a media circus. So much for a private, dignified, homecoming for a fallen hero. Let's just focus on the negative, and ignore any evidence of positive.

Another favorite of the left-leaning media is regular coverage of anti-war protests. Whenever there is an anti-war rally anywhere in the United States, there is bound to be a flock of cameras covering it. Is this really news? Is coverage of these events really important?

Today, as I was making my deliveries, I was listening to radio coverage of a big protest in Washington DC. Rather than do a news segment, the radio network opted to do a direct feed of every word being said at the rally. I couldn't believe the words I was hearing. You would have thought that President Bush was Hitler, Hussein, and Dr. Evil all rolled into one. They were all repeating the same propaganda. None of what they were saying made any sense to me. Their accusations didn't seem to match my memory of the past few years' events. They didn't seem to be applying much logic to their arguments, let alone common sense.

One protestor after another complained about how we have ignored the U.N. That made no sense to me, because I remember how hard we tried to get them on board. I remember Colin Powell's speeches in front of the U.N. Over and over: Bush's war! unilateral occupation!, blah, blah, blah. It was funny how I didn't hear from too many Iraqis though.

I'm not saying that the press has no right to print or broadcast whatever they want to, but they *should* consider the consequences of their actions. They *should* use better judgment. If the media had used these same tactics in Word War II, we would probably be eating a lot more sauerkraut today.

This is what I don't understand about the press and their constant drift to the left side of the road. What if everyone accepted liberalism? Let's say, for the sake of argument, that we handed the keys over to the U.N. and let them take our country for a spin. Does the mainstream media really believe that they would still have the same amount of power and freedom that they do today? The U.N. is the same outfit that thinks that Yasser Arafat is one of the *good* guys. They put *Libya* in charge of overseeing *human rights*, for God's sake! The U.N. would make us sitting ducks. I can assume that with America under U.N. control, all bets would be off. The biggest jerk on the block would take a poke at us right away. This would most likely be China. They have the brains and the brawn to do it. How far do you think the press would get under communist rule?

From my point of view, the media seems to be shooting themselves in the foot under the guise of objectivity. I think they need to start rooting for the home team, while we still *have* a home team.

The fact is - war is hell. Nobody wants war, nobody likes war, but if war happens, you should want to help your side win. At the very least, you shouldn't want to do something that will make your side lose. If your side loses, so do *you*. The ironic thing is, we are on the right side of this war, and we are the good guys. We don't need to lie about anything we are doing. We don't even need to *distort* anything. There is no reason for anyone in the press to worry about losing his or her objectivity. If the only way you can be objective is to only report the bad news, then maybe you should look into a new line of work. If the press undermines our resolve, and costs us the war on terror, they are just as likely to be blown up by a terrorist as anyone else. Considering their higher-profile social status, they may even be *more* likely to get up close and personal with a car bomb. Liberalism is so self-defeating.

I'm Not Hitler!

You may have noticed that I have not said anything about the link between Saddam Hussein, and Osama Bin Laden. I haven't mentioned it because it doesn't matter. We know that they are both terrorists. I don't care if they are complete strangers, or if they are conjoined twins. They are both murderers who hate America. The only difference I can see is, Hussein usually sticks with killing his *own* people, and Bin Laden kills *us*. I don't think that should matter though. I offer this analogy. If your neighbor's wife is being raped, do you let it happen? After all, the guy isn't raping *your* wife; he's not doing it on *your* property. Is your neighbor's wife less important than yours? Just how sure are you that the rapist won't come to *your* house next week, or tomorrow?Just in case you didn't hear, though, there *have* been reports of contact between Hussein's people and Bin Laden's people. They have also found terrorist training camps in Iraq, complete with a commercial jet airliner fuselage. I'm sure they were just using that for fire drills.

Does it really matter which homicidal maniac killed what innocent person? Do we *need* to see them in bed together to realize that they *both* needed to be dealt with? Where do you draw the line between evil enough to be left alone, or evil enough to be taken out? What is the acceptable number of murder victims? How much torture is too much? How many rape rooms are too many?

What is the limit on public beheadings?

You would think that the ACLU, Amnesty International, the United Nations, and all the other human rights organizations would be cheering us on. But let something as benign as the word "God" getting into the Pledge of Allegiance happen, and watch them work. I smell hypocrisy.

I still chuckle every time I hear someone refer to America as a nation of "cowboys." I think Willie Nelson said it best when he wrote, "My heroes have always been cowboys."

Chapter 4
Give Us Your Tired, Your Poor, Your Security Threats

O K, here is a simple subject that has been made so unnecessarily complicated that it makes me think that our leaders have thrown their brains out the window and onto the pavement. Immigration is the backbone of our country. Every last person in the United States can look back in their family tree and discover that they came from somewhere else. One exception, of course, is the handful of "pure blood" Native Americans.

Our heritage is based on the idea of immigrating to a new land in the hopes of making a new and better life for our families and ourselves. I have never traced my family tree, but I know I am descended from German immigrants on my dad's side, and Native Americans on my mom's. For me to be anti-immigration would make me a hypocrite. I know that there are a small number of people who would like to see all immigration stopped, permanently. These people are called "jerks." Most of the people I have encountered in my life are decent folks who understand that, for the most part, we are all products of immigration.

Can you imagine what the food court at the mall would look like if we had not allowed immigrants to come here? We wouldn't have tacos, pizza, egg rolls, croissants, or bagels. All we would have to eat is chicken. How much fun would that be? You probably realize by now that I am a big fan of food.

America truly is a melting pot. This alone has made us the most successful nation that the world has ever known. Think about it. We have gathered ideas and culture from all over the globe into one big family called America. If there is one group that has a problem, then there is probably another group that has a solution. The list of achievements that has come out of our country would choke a horse, maybe an elephant.

This did not happen by locking the door to people from other countries. If you don't take a look at another guy's ideas, you only have your own to work with. Unless you know everything, you may miss a chance to make an improvement. This principle applies to countries, too. Countries that shut out other people are usually a few steps behind the rest of us. Look at Russia, China, Iraq, Cuba, Iran and any other country that has ever closed its doors. They *have* technology, but they rarely *invent* it. If a man is not free, his ambition is squashed. If he has no ambition, he will be less likely to invent the light bulb or the telephone. As a result, these countries offer little to humanity. Russia has recently figured this out, and is finally trying to do something about it. Many others will need to learn the hard way.

America knew this from day one. This is why we have always been the most welcoming nation on the planet. We have never been perfect, but when it comes to freedom, we are the only game in town. Yes, there are other countries that come pretty close, but why settle for less when you can have the real McGilla.

We have been sending out this message since we first hit Plymouth Rock. We still do today. Think of America as a big house. We have a giant "welcome" mat at the front door. We are the nicest people on the block, and we always let the neighbors in to visit. A lot of the time, we let neighbors move in with us. We don't mind this because we took the time to get to know them, and we have the room. Unfortunately, for some people this concept is not good enough. This is where some people start to come unglued. Whenever somebody complains about ILLEGAL immigration, they are automatically labeled a Nazi, or a jerk. People seem to be having more and more difficulty understanding the difference between LEGAL immigration, and ILLEGAL immigration. To these people there is no difference. Again, I am referring to liberals. The difference between LEGAL and ILLEGAL immigration is wide enough to drive a fleet of 18-wheelers through.

For those of you who may not see the difference, I am glad to explain. LEGAL immigration is when you come to America in search of a better life. You respect all laws concerning the act of becoming a U.S. citizen. You go through all the proper immigration procedures. This means that you are checked by doctors for any diseases you may have. This is done so that you don't infect anyone already living here. People come here from all over the world and many different climates. A communicable disease does *not* care what country you are from, or what country you are going to. If you have tuberculosis, we may not want you in our house.

As a LEGAL immigrant, you are then checked for a criminal history by the proper authorities. If you are wanted for murder in Istanbul, we may not want you in our house. If you are a member of a known terrorist group, we may not want you in our house. If you are a rapist from England, we may not want you in our house.

A LEGAL immigrant will then make an effort to learn our language and customs. After all, he truly does want to be an American, and wants to be able to communicate and identify with his new countrymen as much as he can. This will also help him succeed here, as well as make new friends.

After he has completed these steps, a LEGAL immigrant will be asked to take a Pledge of Allegiance to his new homeland. He will also be asked to renounce his former country. If he does not vow to protect and defend his new home, then he may have other reasons for being here, so we may not want him in our house.

After a LEGAL immigrant completes these few steps, he is then welcomed here with open arms. He is then free to go in whatever direction he wishes, and is an American citizen who is entitled to all America has to offer. Hopefully, he will take full advantage of this and become the next Arnold Shwarzenegger. Basically, we have looked out the peephole and opened the door to our house, and he is now one of the people in our house. Welcome.

This is a very general description of what LEGAL immigration should be, and once was. These are the same steps that immigrants have been using for a long time to come to our country. It has never been a perfect system, but it has been a pretty good one. It has also been a *common sense* method of bringing people into our house.

Now let's take a look at ILLEGAL immigration. Take notice to the first two letters in "ILLEGAL". They are easy to overlook, but they change the meaning of the word dramatically. This may be the problem. Everyone on the left side of the road must be overlooking the "I" and the "L".

When you come to this country ILLEGALLY, you are breaking into our house. You are also breaking the law. You are not being checked for communicable diseases. If you have tuberculosis, you will be spreading it all over our house, and no one will know it until it is too late. You have made the people in our house sick.

An ILLEGAL immigrant is not checked for a criminal history. You have already broken into our house, which speaks volumes about your morals and ethics. You just might happen to be a murderer, rapist, or terrorist. No one will know until it is too late. You may have killed or raped the people in our house.

As an ILLEGAL immigrant, you have less motivation to learn our language and customs, because you are not working toward becoming a legitimate American citizen. Not only have you broken into our house, but also we can't even talk to you now that you are here. You have separated yourself from the people in our house.

ILLEGAL immigrants do not pledge their allegiance to our nation. They take no vows to defend it. At this point, you have broken into our house, and may not even try to help out if the gangs of thugs down the street try to burn it down. You might even be the type of guy who would tell them the best way to start the fire. Again, by the time anyone figures this out, it is too late. You may have helped someone else kill the people in our house.

Now that you are here ILLEGALLY, you are using many of the

resources offered by our country. If you are a criminal, you are enjoying our prisons as well as our law enforcement and judicial system. You are using our hospitals, ambulances, schools, roads, and any number of public facilities. The only problem is that you are only paying a fraction of the taxes compared to the people who are here legitimately. You are mooching off of the people in our house.

As you can see, there is more to the discussion of ILLEGAL immigration than you might see on the alphabet channels. Liberals would have you believe that it is just a matter of compassion. They seem to think that if you are against ILLEGAL immigration, then you must be against ALL immigration. The liberal approach to immigration seems to be "Hey, let's let everybody in, no matter who he is, or what his motives are." We seem to have forgotten that some of the September 11th attackers were here ILLEGALLY. Not much is mentioned of the fact that one of the Washington DC snipers was here ILLEGALLY. Rarely are crime statistics brought up in debates about ILLEGAL immigration. Apparently it is assumed by everyone that if you are here ILLEGALLY, you are a law- abiding person. Liberals seem to have caught on to this oxy-moronic concept. Nowadays, they refer to ILLEGAL immigrants as "undocumented citizens". Does this change anything? What is worse, someone "peeing" in your Cheerios, or someone "urinating" in them? To me, both are equally likely to make me vomit. A dog is a dog, even if you call it a "canine citizen". No matter what name you put on it, ILLEGAL is ILLEGAL. Calling it anything else does not change that.

We seem to be losing the meaning of words like "illegal" for the sake of political correctness. I wonder what this will mean years down the road. Liberals seem to be preoccupied with worrying about alienating ILLEGAL immigrants. This makes no sense to me, because I thought that they were *supposed* to feel alienated. That is why they are called ILLEGAL ALIENS. They *should* feel alienated, because they *are* different. They are different from anyone who has ever immigrated to America LEGALLY. The last thing we should be concerned about is insulting them. Were they worried about our feelings when they broke into our country? If someone breaks into my house, the last thing I am going to be thinking is, "I hope he feels accepted." I will be thinking about whether I should use the .45 or the .357.

Let's not get carried away; I am not suggesting that ILLEGAL ALIENS should be shot on sight. I like to use extreme analogies in order to get my points across. This has always worked for me. Sometimes, you need to make a bold statement in order for people to get what you are talking about.

I do believe that when you break the law, there needs to be some consequence. My analogy was designed to demonstrate that. The same analogy demonstrates that human beings do not naturally consider political correctness when faced with a dangerous situation. They consider self-preservation, and how best to protect themselves and their loved ones. So before you label me a blood thirsty, gun happy redneck, you need to consider the fact that political correctness and *common sense* are worlds apart.

This same principle applies to our nation. If we lived in a world where there were no criminals, and no diseases, we could get away with a more liberal policy of immigration. Until that day comes, we have no choice but to ask, "Who's there?" when someone shows up at our front door.

Unfortunately, the issue of ILLEGAL immigration has been put on the back burner for a long time. We have been paying little attention to the realities of ILLEGAL immigration. At the same time, a movement to try to decriminalize ILLEGAL immigration has gained a lot of momentum. For years now, we seem to have been losing focus on why we had immigration laws in the first place. Apparently, it is now assumed that if you are an ILLEGAL immigrant, you couldn't possibly be a criminal. Never mind the fact that you disregarded our immigration laws. It is also assumed that an ILLEGAL immigrant couldn't possibly have a disease that he could give to someone else. Never mind the fact that people in other countries get sick too. I missed the memo that stated that unemployment was no longer a factor in America. Apparently, we have so many jobs here, that we can afford to give them away to anyone who wants one, whether they are here LEGALLY or not.

Never mind the fact that the liberal media is constantly shouting about the high unemployment rate. It seems that we can all rejoice, now that we are all making enough money to cover the expense of ILLEGAL immigration, without sacrificing our own wants or needs. Never mind the fact that just the cost of emergency medical care to ILLEGAL immigrants costs America millions in insurance premiums.

There are actually people in our own government who not only don't want to fix the ILLEGAL immigration problem; they want to make it worse. There are bills being passed around that would require states to issue driver's licenses to ILLEGAL immigrants. There are other bills that would give welfare and college tuition to ILLEGALS. There is a push to officially end the practice of deporting people who are found to be here ILLEGALLY.

These same people push bilingualism, and segregation. Yes, segregation. It's time to put some of that gray matter between your ears to use. I know, thinking is hard, but you've still got to do it. You may have expected me to rail against bilingualism, but I probably took you by surprise when I made accusations of *segregation* among our left leaning friends. Allow me to explain.

Webster's dictionary defines "bilingual" as relating to, or expressed in two languages. There is nothing wrong with learning other languages. In fact, it is generally a good idea. You broaden your education, as well as your ability to communicate with people around the world. I have always envied people who took the time to learn another language. I had enough trouble getting the hang of English. As you may have already figured out, I am still working on it today.

The problem with bilingualism is that it is being forced on the wrong people. More and more, I am seeing everyday things presented in Spanish, as well as English. I hear advertisements on the radio in Spanish. I see sale flyers at the grocery store printed in Spanish. Even the men's room signs have Spanish subtitles. I run across bilingualism all the time. Bilingual radio stations, TV channels, and phone messages have become a normal part of everyday life. There is only one problem; THERE ARE MORE THAN TWO LANGUAGES ON PLANET EARTH!

I always wonder how someone from Romania feels when he looks at the subtitles on the gas pump, and doesn't see *his* native language represented. I wonder the same thing when a Chinese gentleman does not see his home language written on the hand dryer in the men's room. Is someone trying to send these people a message? Are they not worthy of equal representation on everyday items? The last time I checked, America was a melting pot of people from all over the globe. Our population is made up of people from *many* countries, and *many* cultures. It may shock some of you, but these same people do not *all* speak English.

For some reason though, it seems to be assumed that they all speak Spanish. Being the realist that I am, I can only imagine how confusing everyday objects would be if they had every language represented on them. The men's room sign would cover the entire door, maybe even the whole wall. Television would be impossible to watch. Radio would make no sense at all. I doubt that an average truck driver like myself would be able to find time in his busy day to learn how to speak every language from every culture either. I would probably kill myself half way through French. Even the Pope can't speak *every* language, and he's the Pope!

On the surface, this seems to be a pretty good deal for people who emigrate here from a Spanish-speaking country. Consider this. Imagine yourself as an immigrant from Ecuador, and you only speak Spanish. For the sake of argument, let's say that you are here LEGALLY. You entered America with a temporary visa, and hope to become a citizen someday. It is likely that you are staying with family members. In their home, only Spanish is spoken. While you are here, you pick up a job washing dishes at a local restaurant. At this restaurant, all of the labels and signs have Spanish subtitles. While you work, your boss lets you listen to the radio. You find a Spanish speaking station, and listen to it every day. When you go home at night, you watch your favorite soccer team on the all-Spanish channel, and then go to bed. When you wake up, you read the Spanish newspaper, and start another "all Spanish" day. You find your new life in America to be much easier than you expected. You *are* working, and you *are* a productive member of your community.

I'm Not Hitler!

You continue on like this for months.

Eventually, on your day off, you decide to explore the city a little bit. You go to a part of town that you haven't been to yet. As you get further away from your neighborhood, you notice something. There seem to be fewer and fewer Latinos. You don't dwell on it, and keep going. You decide to go into a clothing store to look at shirts. You look around, but you are not sure where the fitting room is. You decide to go up to the counter and ask for help. The lady behind the cash register tries to understand you, but she only speaks English. Slightly embarrassed, you walk away and leave the store. You walk down the block to a jewelry store where you see a necklace in the window. You think of how happy your mother would be if you could buy it, and send it to her in Ecuador. You walk in, and ask the salesman if you can see the necklace. He looks at you helplessly and says, "I'm sorry, I don't know what you are saying." This man does not know how to speak Spanish either, although he does speak fluent Russian, as well as English. You speak neither. Again, you walk away, without the gift for your mother. At this point, you start to get a little frustrated. You go into a bar to have a beer, and try to forget your frustrating adventure. You point to the beer tap, and hold up one finger. The bartender understands. You put your money on the bar and he slides you your change. You notice that a group of guys about your age are watching a soccer game on the big screen TV in the corner. You recognize one of the teams that are playing. It just happens to be a team from Ecuador. It is the same team that your cousin plays for. You have been to many of his games, and know many of the other players.

You look at the guys who are watching the game, and notice that they seem to be decent hard working folks, just like you. You decide to go over and introduce yourself in hopes of meeting new friends. You just want to talk soccer with someone your own age. You think that they might find your personal connection to the game interesting. After approaching one of the guys, you ask him what the score is. He too gives you a puzzled look. He then looks around at his buddies, and asks if any of them know what you are saying. They all shake their heads. Having dealt with enough disappointment, you walk out of the bar and go back to the neighborhood where you can have a conversation with people. You don't have the shirt, or the necklace you wanted, and you didn't make any new friends.

It dawns on you that once you leave the community where everyone speaks Spanish, life gets a little more difficult. Within just a few blocks the communication gap widens, until the simplest things become difficult. So you decide to stay in your community.

You have been living here for months, but since you live in a Spanish-speaking community, you have never needed to learn English...so you didn't. Most of the people in your neighborhood only speak Spanish, so they have little reason to learn English either. After all, everything they ever need is in Spanish. If they need a policeman, a Spanish-speaking officer is dispatched. If they have questions about their credit card, a Spanish-speaking customer service rep, will help them out. You name the service, it's probably offered in Spanish.

Even though you would like to see more of America, and meet more people, you don't bother trying to leave your community anymore, because the communication gap is too frustrating. Besides, everything you need is right here in your neighborhood. You opt to stay among your Spanish-speaking neighbors, and never get to have conversations or friendships with anyone else. You missed out on job opportunities, friends, and even a date. You didn't get to find out, but the girl at the clothing shop thought you were cute. She was single, but you didn't know that because you couldn't talk to her. Thanks to not learning the language of the country you are living in, you are now separated from the rest of the population. You are SEGREGATED.

Now that you are already here, and you have friends and family here as well, the pressure to further your immigration status is starting to fall by the wayside. You know that these days, it is politically incorrect for the authorities to deport you when your visa runs out. You also know that there are people in the American government who see you as a potential voter. You know that these same people are working behind the scenes to let you become a citizen by default. So why would you bother going through the bureaucracy of the LEGAL immigration process?

Sure, every now and then you will be in a situation where it might be easier to speak English, but that is not a big deal. After all, America has gone out of its way to accommodate Spanish-speaking people. These rare situations do not justify the time and expense of learning English, so why bother? As long as you don't stray off the "reservation," your life here is not too shabby. Your visa eventually expires, but you don't lose much sleep over it. After all, what do you have to worry about? You opt to become an ILLEGAL alien. Since you know that you are not a terrorist or a drug dealer, you don't see why anyone could complain. You do have a job, and you still work hard. You even pay *some* taxes. What's the problem?

Another argument that you use to justify your stay here is the idea that you are doing a job that no one in America would want to do. So you consider yourself a hero for saving American citizens from the downside of hard labor. You are also quite comfortable with the idea that you are saving American employers millions of dollars in labor costs. You weigh the pros and cons of ILLEGAL immigration, and decide that you should be looked at as a pillar of the community.

This of course, is a general depiction of the current situation that many of our nation's newest guests are in. They are in the unenviable position of wanting so badly to leave a less desirable habitat that they break the law to get here, but don't want to go through the steps to actually become an American. I think that this says a lot about a person's true intentions. I try to see the good in people, but this paradox of conflicting intentions really makes me wonder.

Even though the fictitious example just used is a common situation in real life, it is not the *real* problem with ILLEGAL immigration. If our only concern was Latino immigrants who just want a better life coming here ILLEGALLY, then people like myself would probably not get angry enough to write a chapter about it in a book. The real problem with ILLEGAL immigration lies beneath the surface. It is not visible to the untrained eye. In some cases it is not visible to the naked eye either.

Yes, there is a good case for not breaking our immigration laws.

Yes, there is a good case against ILLEGAL immigrants taking jobs from our economy. Yes, there is a good case against a self-imposed communication gap between Americans and ILLEGALS who refuse to learn English. Yes, there is a case to be made for the fact that someone who comes here ILLEGALLY and is allowed to stay without penalty is slapping the face of every immigrant who ever took the time and had the dignity to respect our immigration process. There is even a pretty good case to be made for the fact that people employing ILLEGAL immigrants have an unfair advantage over an employer who respects the law.

Even as controversial, debatable, or important as these points are, none of them are as important to me as SECURITY. More to the point, NATIONAL SECURITY. You see, when you slip under the fence, no one is checking your passport (if you even have one). This would be OK if everyone had labels on their foreheads that would tell us if they were a terrorist or a health risk. If we could have the ability to look at someone's face and instantly be able to see that they are a rapist or a drug dealer, then ILLEGAL immigration wouldn't matter to me as much. After all, I was born here. Why would I care if ILLEGAL immigration were an insult to LEGAL immigrants everywhere? I have a job. So why would I care if a job that an American could be doing is being held by an ILLEGAL ALIEN? I'm not usually a very social person, so why would I care if I can't have a conversation with an ILLEGAL immigrant? I don't plan to own a business anytime soon, so I'm not going to stay up at night wondering how to compete with another guy who is not afraid to break the law.

But I *am* planning to live as long as I can. I *do* enjoy life. I *do* want to see my child born and grow up. I *do* want to get old. I do *not* want to see people die, get sick, be robbed, raped, or molested. I do *not* want to see bad things happen to innocent people. Call me crazy, but that's just how I am.

As an advocate of self-preservation, I have no choice but to get angry about ILLEGAL immigration. How are we supposed to know if a person who comes here from another country is a friend, or foe? Are we just supposed to roll the dice and assume that person is not a member of a terrorist group? Are we really asking too much to see his passport, or check his criminal record? Does this really mean that America is an oppressive nation? Are we really the bad guy here?

Maybe you know someone who is here ILLEGALLY. What is his or her medical history? Do they have all of their shots? Did they receive them in their native country? Are the vaccines in that country up to date? What about the records? Do you somehow know, for a fact, that they did not come here carrying a virus? If so, *how* do you know this? I would like to apply the same method to ILLEGAL immigrants that may come in contact with *my* family. Will this same method tell me if an ILLEGAL immigrant has a history of mental illness?

Would you be willing to bet your life, or the lives of your children, on the odds that this person has no history of violence? Are you sure that this person is not here because he is running from the law in his home country? Again, please tell me how you can be sure; I would like to feel safe too.

You see, ILLEGAL ALIENS do not get checked for *anything*. When they come into our country, they don't bring much luggage, but they can bring a heap of baggage. If they have tuberculosis, it comes with them. Viruses don't fall off upon reaching the United States. A murderous past does not disappear when you cross the border. If you were a child molester in Yugoslavia, it is a pretty safe bet that you will be a child molester in America. Are we really out of line for wanting to know this about you? Are we anti-Yugoslavian for wanting you to stay out of our country?

I am not assuming that health screening and criminal background checks are a 100% success when determining if a person is fit to become an American citizen. What I don't understand is, how can you argue with the logic of trying? How can we be blamed for looking out for the safety and well being of our own country?

In most books, discussions, or TV documentaries that I have seen on the topic of ILLEGAL immigration, people always like to throw around statistics. People on both sides of the argument spend a lot of time and energy tossing numbers around like some pathetic tennis match. I never pay attention to these numbers. Most of the time, the numbers even seem to back up my theories, but numbers rarely make you think. I could very easily list numbers that bolster my opinion and help my position, but you might dismiss them, assuming that they are made up anyway. Besides, numbers are so boring. Instead, I have been asking questions. Questions force you to take a look at the issue for yourself.

If I tell you that X number of ILLEGAL immigrants leave their homeland because they are wanted for violent crimes, you will waste precious time and brain cells trying to figure out if that number seems right to you. If I ask the question "Is it possible that some of the people who immigrate to America ILLEGALLY have a criminal history?" you stop focusing on a number, and start to see the root of the issue.

ILLEGAL immigration is one of many issues that really don't require statistics. This is a *common sense* issue. I believe that common sense does not need to be backed up by numbers. It only needs to be presented in the right way. Most people are so used to hearing statistics that they can't seem to make a decision without hearing a number.

Do you really need to hear exactly how many people break into our country ILLEGALLY every year to know that it is a bad thing? Do you really need to hear a number to realize that a certain percentage of ILLEGAL immigrants are here to harm us? What percentage would it take to convince you that people need to be checked out before they are allowed to come here? This begs the question; how many ILLEGAL aliens does it take to strike terror into the hearts of an entire country? If September 11th were any indication, I would say it takes about nineteen. If you want real numbers, it only takes one ILLEGAL alien to build and detonate a truck bomb. It only takes one ILLEGAL alien to infect an entire nation with the Ebola virus. It only takes one ILLEGAL alien, running from the law in his home country, to rape or murder someone in your family. One is the loneliest number that you'll ever know. It is also the most important number, when discussing ILLEGAL immigration.

Let's assume that we *did* have proper border control, and we *did* have all the technology and resources to screen out people who are a risk to our country. Would we be able to catch every person who wanted to come here and hurt us? Of course not. This does not mean that we should just throw up our hands and do nothing. We still have an obligation to try.

We have an obligation to every man, woman and child who are in this country LEGALLY. It doesn't matter if your family came here on the Mayflower, or you came here last month on a jet airliner. If you live in America as a LEGAL citizen, you are entitled to a basic degree of protection. Our government's obligation is to protect our entire nation from things that may put us all in danger.

These things include criminals, diseases, and ideas. No, that was not a typographical error; I said "ideas." Here is another concept that may require a little intellectual effort on your part. In most cases, ideas are a good thing. In most cases, ideas should be protected to the farthest reaches of our ability. The problem is, not all ideas are *good* ideas. If you were a person from Istanbul who has a new idea for the production of steel, America would be wise to welcome you with open arms. What if you are a person from Syria, who has a new way to recruit potential suicide bombers? How wise would we be to allow you access to our country? What if you are a communist from the former Soviet Union, who has a new idea for indoctrinating young college students into socialism? Would it be a smart move for us to roll out the red carpet for you?

Again, these are things that we as a nation have a right to know about you, BEFORE you get here. At first, you may think that people have the right to believe or think whatever they want, so this also must mean that they have a right to bring these thoughts and beliefs with them to America. If you think this way, you are only half right.

Yes, a human being has the right to believe whatever they want, no matter how crazy or insane it might be. At the same time, other people have the right to protect themselves from the results of these thoughts. This applies to nations as well.

We are a sovereign nation, as well as a free nation. This is worth protecting, for the sake of us all (even liberals). Ideas like communism, socialism, terrorism, and globalism are enemies of freedom. When these concepts are introduced to the population, they put us all at risk (even liberals).

If you are a communist, should you be allowed to emigrate here, where you could end up being a teacher in a high school in Vermont? I am *not* suggesting that you do not have a right to be a communist. I *am* suggesting that you do not have a right to spread communism to America. This means that you should not be allowed to enter.

After all, if you *are* a communist, what possible reason could you have for becoming an American citizen, unless you wanted to undermine our freedoms? We are capitalists; our way of life goes against everything that you believe in. I can understand you wanting to visit. Maybe you have family here, but a "Communist American" is an oxymoron.

Just like crimes and diseases, bad ideas do not announce themselves when they enter the country. Immigrants who want to bring down freedom or democracy do not wear signs that read, "Hi, my name is Igor, I teach children about communism". If they did, it wouldn't be necessary to check them out before they emigrated here. Unfortunately, reality forces us to use *common sense*. The problem is, we are losing our grip on *common sense*. The concept of controlling ideas is nothing new; liberals have been advocating this for years. You would think that they would be right behind conservatives in the fight against communism, socialism, and terrorism. In the real world though, this does not seem to be the case. In the glory days of liberalism (back when it had a legitimate purpose), people spoke out against racism and fascism. At the time, racism had already been holding on with a pretty tight grip here in America. Racism was a classic example of a bad idea. Most of the population knew that it was wrong, but there were a lot of holdouts.

Back then, the so-called "liberal establishment" was on the front lines, fighting against a bad idea. They held marches, protests, sit-ins, and practiced civil disobedience in an effort to stop a bad idea. If you tried to stand up and say that racists had a right to be here, you were immediately called a nut. The concept of someone having the right to be a bigot was a complete mystery to liberals back then.

I think that it is safe to assume that if there had been evidence to show that there were groups of racists trying to enter the United States ILLEGALLY, liberals would have been at the forefront of the anti ILLEGAL immigration movement. Of course, this is just a theory; most of our racists have always been home grown.

Today, communism, like racism, is a bad idea. It is a different bad idea, but it is a bad idea nonetheless. Who wants to stop the bad idea this time? Not liberals. They seem to be too busy trying to make sure that *this* bad idea has full access to our population. The irony is, liberals would suffer just as much, if not more, if we were ever to lose our freedoms. They don't seem to be thinking long term.

Please bear with me as I paint with a broad brush for a moment. I know a lot of people who proudly claim to be liberals. Most of these same people claim to be lovers of music and poetry. These same people jump at the chance to protest. They protest everything from the war in Iraq to fur coats. Now I don't claim to be an expert on communist ideology, but the last time I checked, protesting was not very popular among the leaders of communist countries. I have a feeling that there are a few people in Siberia who would back me up on that. If they wouldn't, I'm sure I could find some Tiananmen Square residents who would. Ask Paul McCartney how many years it took him to be allowed to sing *Back in the USSR* in Russia. Ask Hillary Clinton what the Chinese government did to her latest book when it was exported to their country. Can you say "censorship"?

It makes no sense to me how a group of people who are as vocal, out spoken, and just plain loud as liberals are, can be for any policy that would put their ability to be vocal, outspoken, and loud in jeopardy. This is what liberals are doing when they say that we should loosen, or even eliminate border control. This is what they are doing when they try to legitimize the actions of people who come here ILLEGALLY. This is what they are doing when they refuse to see the dangers of ILLEGAL immigration.

I wish that I could say that the only ones to blame here are liberals. The truth is, there is plenty of blame to go around. There are so called "conservatives" who can't see the forest for the trees when it comes to ILLEGAL immigration. It seems that these guys want to risk it all, just for the favor of big business. Maybe they are just trying to look more politically correct, or compassionate. Maybe some of them are guilty of hiring ILLEGALS to work for them. I don't actually know why anyone, especially a conservative, would want to give ILLEGAL immigrants a free pass, but some of them are.

Does someone who broke into our country deserve a driver's license? I don't think so. Do they deserve free health care? I doubt it. Do ILLEGAL immigrants deserve money for college? No. For some reason, there are people in our government trying to make these things happen. Who gets to pay for it? You do. Is that fair to the guy from Turkey, who busted his butt trying to emigrate here LEGALLY? No. Is that fair to taxpayers like you and me, who have no say over where our tax money goes? No.

Apparently, we have been electing leaders who have no testicular fortitude. They are so afraid of being labeled that they refuse to make tough decisions. They would rather sacrifice the well being of the people than be called a name. It seems to me that these people can't make a decision unless they run it past a focus group first. Right and wrong are only vague concepts that are no longer applicable.

Today, if politicians were to start a debate about immigration policy, they would be trying so hard to please everybody that they would miss the point entirely. Some of them would get the point, but deflect it in order to not offend anyone. Where are the people of character that I assumed I could vote for? Where is the guy who is not afraid to stand up and talk about the bad things that go hand and hand with ILLEGAL immigration?

The irony here is that ILLEGAL immigrants take no vows to obey the laws of our nation. They are also not required to learn about our system of government. This means that if given a driver's license, the right to vote follows suit. So what does this mean to an aspiring politician? How will he get the vote of someone who does not even know how our voting system works? The answer is, money. Money is the universal language. So now that a "so-called conservative" politician has alienated his voter base, he will be forced to rely on the votes of ILLEGAL aliens. I hope he can afford it, because I know that I would never vote for someone who would put us at risk by decriminalizing ILLEGAL immigration. Basically, in the effort to not offend a group of criminals, this same politician just told his entire voter base to take a flying leap by pushing these concepts. This is not what conservatives want, so they will not vote for him. So now, not only has he lost his base, but also he has to compete with the left wing for the votes of criminals. Unless he can outspend the liberal candidate, he will lose. If he had just stayed with the tried and true concepts of right and wrong, and common sense, he would not have to come up with so much money. He could have just debated his way to office.

Back in chapter one, I told you that education is the worst enemy of liberalism. Our immigration policy is a good example of this. As long as you don't give much thought to the downside of ILLEGAL immigration, you might not think it is a big deal. The more you learn about it, though, the more you will realize that it is a very big deal.

I have only scratched the surface of why we all need to be concerned about ILLEGAL immigration. I didn't spend much time on the economic effects on our nation. I didn't spend much time on the cultural effects either. These are also important problems that need to be looked into, but I'm not writing specifically about immigration policy. I am trying to write a book that shows everyday people like you and me why liberalism is not what it appears to be. I am trying to make some basic points about how liberalism affects everyone in so many ways. ILLEGAL immigration is just one of many issues that get made complicated by liberalism.

Before we move on to another subject, consider this. We don't let people on a commercial airplane until a basic check of their intentions is conducted. We look at them, we ask them questions, we run them through special scanners, and we even strip-search them if someone thinks it's necessary. This is done in the attempt to make the flight safer for everyone on the plane and on the ground.

If we applied the same logic to air travel that we do to immigration, September 11th would happen every week. Can you imagine in today's world, letting anyone who wants to get on a plane without checking his or her bag? Why would we take the same risks with our entire country?

Last but not least, I would like to talk to all of you who may have immigrated here from another country, LEGALLY of course. Think of the United States as a roller coaster. Not just any roller coaster, but the biggest, fastest, and best roller coaster around. Everyone wants to get on and take a ride. You are no exception.

You pay for a ticket, and get in line. It is a very long line, and it is the hottest day of the summer. There are kids yelling and screaming, old people complaining, and you just ran out of soda. You stay in line though, because you really want to ride this coaster. Finally, you get near the end of the line. This is the point where the roller coaster staff begins to announce safety tips over the intercom. You are taught how to use the safety harness, and are told all of the precautions that you should take.

After standing in this God-forsaken line for almost two hours in the blazing sun, it is finally your turn to get on the roller coaster. Just then, a group of young punks jump over the security fence, and butt in front of you. They get on the roller coaster and have no idea how to work the safety harness. You look around expecting to see a group of security guards. You also assume that they will shut down the coaster until the punks are forced to go back to the end of the line and buy a ticket.

Instead, the roller coaster conductor welcomes the punks, and tells them to have a good time. They are even told to bring their friends next time. They are also given complimentary soda pops and hot dogs. You watch as the coaster takes off. On turn two, five of these jerks are thrown out of coaster cars. They have various injuries, and are taken to the theme park infirmary.

One of the punks jumps off at the top of hill seven. You can't tell what he is doing up there, but he seems to be tampering with the tracks. You look at your ticket, and read the fine print. It seems that there is a $3 surcharge for "the nourishment of young punks" which is used to pay for the hot dogs and sodas that they ate. There is also a $3 charge for "young punk medical care" which pays for the injuries that these freeloaders got when they fell out of the roller coaster cars. There is one last charge for "track maintenance." This charge goes toward fixing the track when someone tampers with it.

After reassessing the situation, you wonder why you stood in line all that time. What was the point? Angrily, you approach the ticket taker. You ask her why those guys were allowed to get on the roller coaster when everyone else had to pay for a ticket and stand in line. Her response was, "We don't want to offend them, and that is our policy." You tell her that this policy offends *you*. She looks at you with a blank expression, and says, "Thank you, come again" as if she never even heard you. *Your* feelings have no bearing on the issue, but the feelings of the jerks that butted in line were the first and only consideration.

Eventually, the park fell into disrepair. Fewer and fewer people came to ride the coasters. Profits fell, and crime became too much for the security guards to handle. There were often riots among the gangs that had taken over the park, and the people who paid the ticket, and stood in line. After a while, the park closed. From then on, no one rode the coaster.If you are a person who has opted to respect the immigration laws of our nation, and immigrated here LEGALLY, then you can identify with the man in line at the roller coaster.

If you have never considered the effects of ILLEGAL Immigration, or even the concept of it, then I hope that the roller coaster analogy has cleared a few things up for you.

I cannot stress enough, that no decent American wants to end immigration, myself included. But anyone with the vaguest concept of logic should be able to understand why there needs to be a more efficient and secure method of bringing people from other lands into our country. The stakes are way too high to let anyone and everyone come here without first checking them out. Notice that at no point have I suggested that we close our doors to other people. I just want these people to knock first, and then identify themselves.

The next time you walk up to the front of your house or apartment, ask yourself these questions. Why do I have a door? Why do I have a lock on that door? Why do I ask, "Who's there?" before I open the door from inside? Would I let anyone who wanted to just come into my house? Do I trust everyone who knocks on the door? Do I know for a fact that someone knocking on my door is a good person? Am I being insensitive to others, or am I just being careful? Am I willing to risk the safety of my family, to not hurt someone's feelings?

Chapter 5
Welcome RACE Fans!

OK, now it's time for everyone's favorite subject, racism. Just in case you think it is important for some reason, I'm a white guy. Or, if you want to sound educated, you could say that I am a Caucasian. You could go a step farther and say that I am a Caucasian-American. The irony of that is, I have never been to Caucasia. I can't even find it on the map (that's a joke). Since I am of German and Native American descent, you might as well say that I am a German, Native American, and Caucasian American. Let's not forget, I am a truck driver. This makes me a German, Native American, Caucasian, truck driving American. But you can call me Terry.

There is more irony in my personal description. I told you that I am a white guy. Like most people, you probably accept that as a personal description. The problem is, I am not white. Granted, I have been out of school for a good while now, but I do remember some of what I learned. I believe I was in kindergarten when they first taught us about colors. I remember when the teacher wanted to teach us about the color red, she held up a stop sign and a toy fire truck. To teach us about green, she showed us a leaf, and a dollar bill. Then it came time to teach us about the color white. She held up a blank piece of paper, and pointed out the window at the snow-covered playground.

At the time, I thought back to when my parents said that we were white. I didn't understand why snow and blank paper looked so different from the color of my skin. I held a blank piece of paper up to my arm, but they didn't match at all. The same thing happened when I put my hand in the snow at recess. Either my teacher was wrong, or my parents were. I was more of a tan color, or maybe the color of bare wood. I looked in my big box of crayons, trying to find a color that matched my skin. The closest color that I could find was called peach.

Being a young kid, I didn't spend much time on the subject. I had more important issues to deal with; cartoons, my bratty little brother, and cooties.

Then one day, we got a new kid in class. He had really dark skin. I suppose that I had seen people with skin that dark before, but I guess I had never paid much attention to them. I kept hearing people say that the new kid was black. This didn't make much sense to me. When the teacher taught us about the color black, she held up a piece of black licorice, and pointed to the chalkboard. This kid did have dark skin, but he didn't match the color of black licorice or the chalkboard. I thought he looked more like the color of a Hershey bar. When I found the crayon that was closest to the color of his skin, it was marked "brown". The *black* crayon was way off.

To this day, I have yet to meet a person whose skin matches a black crayon, or a white crayon. The closest I have ever come to meeting a white person is an albino guy that

unloads my truck sometimes. As pale as he is, he is still not white. He is actually more of a pink color. I have also met a lot of people with *dark* skin, but none of them matched the black crayon. I have met a lot of people who seem to match the brown crayon though. The darkest skinned person that I can ever recall meeting happens to be another truck driver that I work with. He is more the color of a Hershey's Special Dark chocolate bar. I am very familiar with this blend of chocolate, because I am one of the few people I know that like it. In fact, I love it. As dark as it is though, it's still not quite black.

Webster's defines race in four different ways; 1. *A division of the human population distinguished by physical characteristics transmitted by genes.* This definition does not do much to help me sort out the concept of "racial division." According to definition No. 1, you could belong to a race of tall people, redheaded people, big-nosed people, or arrogant people (people often say that your attitude is genetic; my mom always says that I am just like my father).

That's all well and good, but what if you are a *short* black man, and your neighbor is a *tall* black man? Are you from a different race according to your stature, or the same race according to your pigmentation? Which "physical characteristic transmitted by genes" should we consider when classifying someone as a particular race? Does it really matter?

Diabetes is usually considered hereditary, so if you are a white diabetic, are you the same race as a black diabetic? Is there a race of freckled people? I have seen "black" people with freckles. If your father has big ears, you might inherit them also. Does this mean that you belong to a race of big-eared people?

What if you are a tall, brown-skinned diabetic, with freckles and big ears? What race would you be then? After all, these divisions are all part of the human population, and they are all hereditary.

Definition No. 2 states as follows; *a body of people united by a common history or nationality.* According to this definition, Pennsylvanians could be considered a race of people. The same could be said for employees of a company. If you work at McDonald's, you share a common history with everyone else who works at McDonald's. You all work for the same company, so you have all been hired and trained to work under the same company policies. By definition, you are a part of the race of McDonald's employees. You are a "McDonaldian."

What if you are constipated? You share a common history with anyone who has ever been constipated. What if you are constipated while you are working at McDonald's? I guess that means that you are bi-racial. You are a McDonaldian/Constipatian mix. For you to please those who are against race mixing, you will need to quit your job, or take Ex-Lax.

Definition No. 2 also implies that if you are united with other people by a common nationality, you are a member of a certain race. Does this mean that French and

Canadian people are not from the same race? Are Mexicans a different race than Brazilians? If you live in Australia, are you a different race than someone from New Zealand? After all, France, Canada, Mexico, Brazil, Australia, and New Zealand are all nations. In fact, Webster's uses "The Spanish *race*" as an example. By definition, if you are an American, you are part of the "American race." I like this concept.

For my money, definition No. 3 seems to sum things up pretty well. It simply says - *Humanity as a whole.* There are no specifics implied. There are no examples given. This is because they are not necessary. If you are a human being, you are all of the above. You *are* a division of the human population. You *are* distinguished by physical characteristics transmitted by genes (two arms, two legs, ten fingers, ten toes, opposable thumbs, and lack of a fur coat). You *are* part of a body of people united by a common history or nationality. Whether you believe in evolution or creation, it is safe to assume that you believe that humans were *all* created by the same method, which by default means that you are a human being, no matter what nation you are from. Besides, even though it is an unrealistic pipe dream (thank God!), it is *theoretically* possible for the world to become one nation. This would not change any physical characteristics of humans; only cultures and borders would change. I believe that the Webster people were smart enough to realize that cultures and borders change all the time. So in order to account for any possibility, even globalism, they covered all of the bases by not specifying any particular nation.

This brings us to the definition, "Humanity as a whole." Unless you are a fish that knows how to read, and have nothing better to do than read this book, this means you. You are a human. You are a member of the human race. I have no idea what color you are, or what country you are from, but I am reasonably sure that you are a human.

I'm Not Hitler!

Webster's final definition of race reads as follows: *a subspecies or breed, as of domestic animals.* This is the last definition of race, as it applies to this discussion. Still no mention of skin color. In fact, if you look up "color" in the dictionary, the definition as it applies to this discussion is as follows; skin tone, complexion.

I have never met a person that had *no* skin tone or complexion. I *have* seen a movie about one though; it was called "The Invisible Man." Have you ever seen an invisible man?

By definition, aren't we all "colored people?" Doesn't that mean that The National Association for the Advancement of Colored People would be glad to help *me* get to college too?

If you ask the Webster folks what "racism" means, they will say: 1. The belief that some races are inherently superior to others; 2. Discrimination based on race. Again, no mention of skin color.

Well, they say that confession is good for the soul, so I need to come clean about something. It has taken a long time for me to admit this, but I am ready to tell the truth about myself. I am a racist. I am not proud of this fact, but it is true nonetheless. I have always believed that humans are superior to the animal kingdom. I hope you can still respect me despite my personal shortcoming.

I have been a racist all of my life, and though I am not a member of any racist organizations, I have owned a cat. I also believe that cows should never be allowed to vote, or use the same water fountain as I do. I do not believe that a horse should ride the bus at all, even if it is only allowed to ride in the back. It will be a cold day in hell when I ever share a lunch counter with an elephant. You can also bet your last dollar that I would never let a chipmunk date my daughter.

Now that you know my secret, I can tell you that I make no apologies for my racist beliefs. I will always believe that humans are the superior race, and that animals have no business breeding with humans. I just don't think it's right. Animals should stay on their side of the fence, and humans should stay on ours. I don't want my kid to go to school with a goat either. The government doesn't have the right to make us let hippopotamuses into our schools. They're not like us; they don't belong here! The government is full of panda lovers! Otters go home! Human power!

I'm sorry; I got carried away there for a minute. We human supremacists get fired up now and then. We're not bad people, we just believe in keeping the human race pure. If we start mixing animals and humans, we will end up becoming a "mutt race." We can't let that happen. I just don't like animals; they are always jumping around, making funny noises. They don't talk like the rest of us. They all have fur, and snouts, and they smell bad. Some of them have shells, and even scales. They are lazy too. Have you ever seen a sloth work hard? A bear will sleep all winter long if you let him get away with it.

OK, I have a warped sense of humor; sue me. My point is that most people don't even know what racism is, much less what it is about. So, what I am going to do is try to give you something to think about on the topic of "racism."

First of all, I think that if you agree with the good folks at Webster's, then you really can't call the personal differences between people of different skin tone "racism," even though that seems to be what we have been doing for a long time. I believe the term "colorism" is more appropriate.

As long as I can remember, anyone who I have ever met who could be considered a "racist" focused on the *pigmentation* of the person that they have a problem with. This concept has always been a two way street. I have met *light* skinned people, who don't like *dark* skinned people. I have also met *dark* skinned people who don't like *light* skinned people.

Even at age thirty-two, this has never made any sense to me. These "colorists" never seem to have a valid reason for disliking someone, except for the color of somebody's skin. By this logic, at Christmas time you would throw away your gifts before you open them, just because you might not like the color of the wrapping.

For you NASCAR fans, does a red car run faster than a blue car? Is the paint job the key to winning the race, or are the driver and the pit crew?

Color is a matter of taste. I like blue myself. But not on everything. I think blue looks good on a Corvette, but not a house. The funny thing about color is; it is only as important as the eyes of the person who sees it.

If you were blind, how important would color be to you? Could you explain the concept of color to someone who has been blind since birth? Would that person care if your skin were the color of bare wood, or a Hershey bar? Would they know the difference between the two colors?

In keeping with my earlier explanation of "racism," a blind man would probably not know or care about the skin color of a doctor that is about to perform brain surgery on him, but he would probably be able to tell if a kangaroo was about to cut him open. He would probably also care what the doctor's credentials are.

As a *light* skinned man who has 20/20 vision, I can tell you that I don't care what color my doctor is, as long as he is the best person for the job. Yes, I did say person. I see no reason why only men can be good doctors. This is not a matter of political correctness, just common sense.

This brings us back to liberalism. One of the most controversial liberal ideas that I can think of is "affirmative action." The fact that it is considered controversial scares me. It makes me think that there are a lot of people out there that are not using "the old bean."

To me, there is no controversy. It's just a bad idea. Yes, I said it. Before you throw the book out the window and call me a racist (colorist), allow me to explain myself.

First, you need to know what affirmative action is, was, and is supposed to be. Back in the days of segregation and *real* racism (colorism), equal rights were not as common or popular as they are today. If you were a "black" man in those days, you were not allowed to do many of the things that some people take for granted today.

Imagine getting on a bus today and having the driver tell you that you have to go to the back of the bus just because of the color of your skin. Imagine not being able to vote, or go to a public school. What if you were not allowed to sit at a lunch counter in a restaurant, or not allowed into the restaurant to begin with, just on the basis of skin color? Can you picture having to use a separate water fountain?

Going even further back, can you comprehend owning another person? Can you comprehend being owned? Having no rights at all, and being kept as a possession? How would you feel if you were traded for a mule and a bushel of corn?

These were *real* civil rights abuses. Though it was misnamed "racism," no matter what you call it, it was wrong. At different times in our history, these concepts were the normal way of life. Was it a good thing? No. Was it something that we should celebrate? No. Was it something that we should forget? No.

Thankfully, "racism" is all but a memory. Discrimination does still exist on some levels of American culture, and I suspect that this will be the case for a long time. But *true* discrimination on the basis of skin color has been outlawed for some time.

Thanks to the efforts of people like President John F. Kennedy and Dr. Martin Luther King, people of different skin tone are considered equal in the eyes of the law. This is what our forefathers intended when they wrote the Bill of Rights. For all intents and purposes, "racism" is dead.

Now before you start thinking that I am living in a dream world, I know that there is still a great divide between people simply due to their melanin level. I am not naive enough to believe that colorism is no longer a part of our culture. I *am* a realist, as well as an honest man. I hear the comments made by *some* people who share my complexion when those with darker skin are not around. I hear the name calling, and off-color jokes. My head is not in the sand about this. I am also pretty sure that this is a two way street. But the truth is, this is a very rare occurrence. When it does happen, it is almost always frowned on. It is definitely not cool anymore. Colorism is still breathing, and it still has a pulse, but it ain't getting up anytime soon.

The odds of me seeing a return to the day when a "black" man can't vote, or ride in the front of the bus, are a million to one. So why are we still acting like people are being whipped for looking at a "white" woman? Why do we seem to be keeping the concept of colorism alive and well with ignorant liberal policies like affirmative action?

I know, you are still waiting for me to tell you about why affirmative action is not a good thing, as well as what it is in the first place. Forgive me for getting off track.

Affirmative action is a concept that was designed and put into use for the sake of good intentions. The idea was to get those who had been discriminated against out into mainstream society. That in itself was not a bad *concept*. What was to follow became a perversion of the original idea, as well as colorism disguised as equality. Simply, it was a method of putting people into the workforce, solely on the basis of their skin color or gender.

"Affirmative action" is when someone is forced to consider the color of someone's skin, rather than the "content of their character." This was the very concept that Dr. Martin Luther King fought so hard to defeat. It is based on the idea of giving a leg-up to people with a different shade of skin, or female organs. This alone implies that these people are inferior to others.

Affirmative action starts with the assumption that if you belong to a "minority", you need help of some kind. If you are a "black" man, you couldn't possibly get a job on your own, or get into a college by the same merits as anyone else. On the other hand, affirmative action also assumes that you are automatically qualified for a position simply because you have a certain color of skin.

This liberal policy first tells a person that he is not capable of competing, but then tells him that he can't possibly fail. Allow me to explain.

Let's say, for the sake of argument, that you are a person who wants to be a police officer. You also happen to have dark skin, because your great-great-great-great-great-great-grandfather was from Africa. You have a high school diploma, and a good grade point average. You were also on the football team, and have a spotless record.

At this point, you are already a good candidate for the Police Academy. You apply as soon as you graduate. You take the entrance exam, and pass with a 93%. Or so you thought. Later that week, you find out that you actually passed with an 88%. Considering that the test was very hard, and the average grade for the same test taken by the other candidates was 85%, you still feel that you accomplished something. But something is wrong; you don't feel right about the extra five percent you received.

After you look into it a little further, you find out that the other 5% was given to you because of the affirmative action policy that the academy had implemented years ago. It stated that "African American" applicants were *entitled* to an extra five percentage points on their entrance exam.

Suddenly, it all starts to make sense. You couldn't figure out why some of the other applicants were giving you the "hairy eyeball." You thought it was just your imagination, but it wasn't. Those guys were pissed. They knew about the affirmative action policy before the test was even taken.

So, here you are. You're not even at the academy long enough get unpacked, but you already have people wanting you to pull a hamstring, or flunk out. These are the same guys that you might be working with some day, and they already hold a grudge against you.

Yes, it's true. It's not your fault that the academy still uses this idiotic policy, and you always say "don't hate the player, hate the game." But this philosophy hasn't caught on with your new bunkmates.

The more you think about it, the more you realize that "the Police Academy didn't even know me, but they thought I needed help. They thought I couldn't compete against these other guys without a helping hand". Suddenly, you start to feel like they treated you like a "special ed" student. You didn't know the Academy, and they didn't know you. You never did anything to the Academy, and your tuition check cleared. But they decided to start things off by insulting you with a ridiculous liberal policy, based solely on the color of your skin.

As a "white" guy, I have led a very status quo life. I don't recall many bars being lowered to accommodate any of my special needs. After all, I don't have any special needs that I can think of. I am pretty healthy, and I don't know of any physical disabilities or mental impairments. It's hard for me to put myself in the shoes of someone who has been insulted on such a level. I can only imagine being told that I need to have things spelled out for me because I am just a truck driver. Being a truck driver automatically means that you are not all that bright, so people should always draw a picture when they want to explain something to me.

I'm Not Hitler!

I have to believe that if I were a "black" man, I would be insulted by affirmative action's assumption of my inferiority alone. But it gets worse.

What about the guy who gets hired for a job because of affirmative action? If we are talking about a file clerk position, it might not be a big deal. But how does affirmative action affect positions such as doctors, pilots, lawyers, policemen, or the military?

Let's use airline pilots as an analogy. Imagine that you are on a commercial airline flight to England. Let's call it P.C. Airways. The head of P.C. Airways was forced to adopt affirmative action in the hiring policy of his company. He was told that he had to hire a certain percentage of "black" pilots per certain percentage of "white" pilots. The only problem was, not enough "black" people were applying for the piloting job at that particular time. The one "black" guy who did apply was not as qualified as the two guys that happened to be "white" who also applied. But the airline owner was forced to hire the "black" man, in order to comply with the new regulations.

So here you are, thirty thousand feet above the Atlantic, and you are headed for a violent storm. Your plane just lost engine number three due to a faulty modulator valve, the same modulator valve that was manufactured by a company that hired ILLEGAL aliens for its assembly line.

How confident would you feel about your pilot, if you knew what circumstances he was hired under? How important would affirmative action be to you then? Would you be praying to God that the color of your pilot was of equal representation according to national statistics? Or would you be praying that your pilot was hired because he was the best man for the job?

This is just a basic example of how affirmative action works in reality. The same principle can be applied to any profession. Would you want the man who is going to do a heart transplant on your daughter to have been hired over a better-qualified doctor, simply because of how much pigment he has in his skin?

You see, affirmative action either assumes that a minority is incapable of failure or mediocrity, or its proponents are simply more interested in color than quality.

It is at this point that some of you are going to accuse me of asserting that a "black" man can't fly a plane, or perform a heart transplant. Sorry to ruin your day, but you are very wrong about that.

As I said earlier in this book, I hold no degrees, and I have only a basic high school education. But I do pay attention to what I have seen in my lifetime.

I don't claim to know exactly why some groups of people seem to gravitate to one type of job, while another group gravitates to others. But I do think that it is safe to say that it happens. It definitely happens in professional sports. How many famous "black" swimmers do you know? How many famous "white" boxers can you name? Does this mean that a "black" man can't swim, or a "white" man can't box?

I think back to when I was just a little kid. When me and my friends talked about what we wanted to do when we grew up, we didn't consult a focus group to make sure that our chosen profession matched a preconceived color demographic. We just knew what we liked. It was that simple.

When an affirmative action focus group gets together, I can only imagine what goes through their minds. Let's say that they think that an Olympic hockey team needs to be 35% "black" to represent a 35% "black" population. Does that automatically mean that you will be able to find that percentage of "black" guys that even *want* to play hockey at all? Does this mean that the hockey team is prejudiced against "blacks" because it has no "black" players?

When I got a little older, I was really into motorcycles. I rode dirt bikes all the time. I noticed that no matter where I rode, I never saw any "black" motocross riders. This always puzzled me. I knew that most of my friends were not prejudiced. I also knew that there was no physical reason for a "black" man's aversion to motorcycles.

Then after many years of trying to figure out why I never saw "blacks" on dirt bikes, it finally hit me. The reason is, that there is no reason. Not only that, if there was a reason, it wouldn't matter anyway. Sometimes, things are just the way they are. Do "blacks" *need* to start riding motocross? Is someone going to try to stop them if they want to?

I'm Not Hitler!

Like most other professions, or pastimes, the people who want to do it, do. Or at least try to. I truly believe that if there is a young "black" man who *wants* to, he could be the next Wayne Gretzky, Mark Spitz, or Jeremy McGrath. There is nothing stopping him. On the other hand, there should be nothing *forcing* him either.

No one, no matter what the color, wants to be *forced* to do anything. That goes for jobs, sports, and even recreation. This however, is exactly what affirmative action is all about.

HOLD EVERYTHING!!! Today is December 14, 2003. I just woke up and turned on the news. Saddam Hussein has been captured in his hometown of Tikrit by U.S. forces. He was hiding in a hole in some shack. He gave up without a fight. What a wuss. Some leader he turned out to be.

President Bush just gave a brief statement to the country. No gloating, no bragging, and no hype. Just a simple statement, with a reminder that the war against terror is far from over. To anyone who wants to know what a real leader looks like, check out George W. Bush.

Ok, now that I have finished imagining how the current Democratic presidential nominees will try to spin their way out of this one, I can get back to discussing how liberalism does more harm than good.

As I was saying, affirmative action presumes that you can fix the problems of discrimination just by putting people in jobs, or schools, according to the color of their skin, their gender, or where their ancestors came from.

Liberals seem to think that a person's attitude is found on the surface of the skin. They seem to assume that just because you aren't doing something, someone must be keeping you from doing it. They also seem to think that everyone wants to do the same things. They never seem to want to factor in a person's upbringing, environment, or beliefs.

Another downside to affirmative action is the fact that it actually *kills* diversity. How? Let me explain it terms of food. How long do you think real Chinese food would last, if the Chinese food industry were forced to hire a certain percentage of "white" people? I think that is a safe bet that pork lo mein would end up being turned into some kind of sandwich. Eventually, the staff might be a proper representation of diversity, but the food would suck.

This same concept applies to most things. If you want to make a pork lo mein sandwich, that's fine. But some people like traditional, original Chinese food.

I don't like rap music. I make no apologies for that. I do recognize that it is an art form, and that a lot of people do like it. What would happen to the quality of rap music if the industry were forced to employ a representative percentage of "white" males? The Wu Tang Clan might end up sounding more like Cold Play or Dwight Yoakum. Maybe affirmative action isn't so bad after all. That's a joke!

Diversity is one of those things that sounds good on paper, but has no practical purpose in life. I suppose in a perfect world, everyone would be where they want to be, and coincidently, all statistics would fall into place evenly. Somehow, I doubt that is very realistic.

The truth is, if someone wants to do something, we live in a country that will allow him or her to do it. If a 150-pound Jewish man wants to be Sumo wrestler, in America he is welcome to do so. No one will stop him. I can't guarantee that he won't get flattened, but he can still give it his best shot. If a "black" man wants to be a rodeo star, he has a constitutional right to go for it. If an ex-Hell's Angel wants to start a quilting school for elderly people, who is to say that he can't?

These are all decisions that are made by the *individual*, not by a government policy. Government has no right to tell someone who they have to hire, especially for the purpose of diversity. Unless you can prove to me that all "blacks" like the same things, and want to work the same jobs, or all "whites" like the same things, and want to work the same jobs also. Until that day, diversity has no relevance.

Now, what about discrimination? I am not a moron; I know that it still happens.

But just because a "minority" may not get hired, it doesn't always mean that it had anything to do with skin color. Maybe he is a jerk, or maybe he just isn't as qualified for the job as someone else. On the other hand, if it *can* be proven that he was turned away just because of his skin color, then there are laws designed to deal with that.

By the same token, you can't *force* someone to hire a minority, just because he is a minority. What if he is incompetent? What if he is a complete idiot? Just because you are a minority, doesn't automatically make you a genius. After all, your brain is in your head, not on your skin. A brain is the same color, no matter what color its owner is.

What makes a person hirable or fire-able is his or her attitude. What is his or her education? Do they have good communication skills? Do they work well with others? Do they have a shady work record? Do they show up on time? Do they have good references? Are they physically capable of the job? These are the factors an employer needs to consider. Not what color some person's skin is, or what genitalia they are carrying.

Yes, diversity and affirmative action applies to gender also. According to liberals who support this kind of idiocy, firefighters, military personnel, football teams, police departments, bodyguards, and lumberjacks should be about fifty percent female. After all, America is almost evenly split between male and female.

Affirmative action can also put a hurtin' on the economy. By it's logic, we should force people to hire a representative amount of females for all jobs. So picture yourself as a lumber company owner. You employ fifty workers. Imagine that you are forced to use affirmative action to hire women. Will you be able to find twenty-five women who can swing a twenty-pound ax, or run a chain saw? Will that many women even apply? Realistically, you might get two female applicants, so you are forced to hire them because they were the only ones who applied. Unless both of these women are built like the rest of your male employees, your production will suffer. You will need to make up the loss in revenue due to loss of production. How will you make up the extra costs? The same way everyone else does, you will pass the costs on to the consumer. Lumber prices will go up. This in turn raises the cost of construction, which is also an industry that is primarily a male domain.

Contractors, too, will lose production due to *their* new policy of affirmative action. This double punch will raise the cost of home ownership through the roof. This is only an extreme hypothetical scenario, but I think it demonstrates the economic effect of a bad liberal idea.

Money is one thing, but what about safety? Should a 110-pound female be allowed to join a fire department and fight fires? Liberalism says "yes," common sense says, "not in a million years." In a perfect world, men and women would all weigh the same and have the same physical ability, but in the real world this is not the case.

If an average-sized man gets injured in the middle of a fire, should he be put in a position where he and his children need to rely on a person half his size to carry him out of a burning building? If you were that injured fireman, would you be praying for a 110-pound woman to bust through the wall and save you? It is more likely that you will be praying that whoever comes to get you will be able to carry your 250-pound butt down those five flights of burning stairs.

Am I saying that all women are not capable of fighting fires? No. The problem is that affirmative action assumes that all women can do all jobs. To fix this problem is not very complicated. Common sense demands that a single high standard of physical ability be applied in certain occupations. If this standard is not met, you can't be a firefighter, policeman, government agent, or soldier.

This would also root out weak *males* in these occupations. There *are* weak men in these occupations too. Should a 110-pound *male* be allowed to join the fire department? Probably not. A single high physical standard would make these occupations much stronger as a whole.

The size differences between men and women are not the only problem with affirmative action. There are other physiological differences that liberals want to ignore. Females have babies. They also have menstrual cycles. I wonder how many man-hours are lost every year due to cramps? I also have to assume that there are a few man-hours lost due to childbirth. Should a woman who is two months pregnant be chasing down crack heads, or running into burning buildings? Is a woman on her menstrual cycle mentally prepared to pull her service revolver? What are the odds of a female American soldier fighting only other female soldiers in battle? Can an average size female soldier defend herself against an average size enemy male soldier? Do red-blooded American male soldiers really *not* lose focus on the tasks at hand when young healthy females are around them? Do these same people *not* get involved in "love triangles" or relationships on the job? Do these situations really *not* cause problems on the battlefield, as they do in the civilian workplace? Are there *no* enemies that are willing to exploit women for their own gain on the battlefield? What *really* happened to Jessica Lynch?

These are all questions that are never asked by the "mainstream media." But they are all questions that need to be asked, no, *shouted* from the mountaintops. The irony is that I think we already know the answers to every one of those questions. The problem is, few have the guts to ask them in public.

Women in general are not physically designed for some jobs. Whose fault is that? That's just how it is. It can't be changed, no matter how many liberal programs are forced down our throats.

You see, somewhere along the line, someone thought that it was a good idea to put "looks" ahead of "ability." Apparently, it was assumed that as long as we look like we are equally representing everybody, everything would be just fine. The only thing that seems to count is the outside of your body. Your abilities are only an afterthought to liberals. They don't care if you have an entire platoon of big, tough, focused men, ready to defend our freedoms (liberals freedoms too), they are more concerned with making sure that you have the proper representation of colors and genitalia.

If you thought that affirmative action only applied to skin color, hopefully I have cleared things up a little for you. Affirmative action is being applied to anything and everything that makes us different from one another. Affirmative action is held up by the "mainstream" as if it were some brilliant plan to redeem us for the sins of our forefathers. Unfortunately, it is just another sin. How is it a good thing to put people in situations or places based solely on someone else's concept of diversity or perfection? Back in the day, they called that "fascism" or "social engineering." There was a guy who was into that sort of thing a few years back. I forget what his name was. Oh yeah, Adolph Hitler!

Diversity is a result, not a plan. It needs no help from anybody. It happens on it's own. That is, unless you truly believe that a "black" man can't pass the same test that a "white" man can. Unless you truly believe that a "black" man needs special help to do the same things a "white" man does. Unless you really don't care if the person who is going to try to rescue your loved ones from a burning building is a 110-pound female who trained under "modified" standards. Unless you truly believe that Jessica Lynch's captors didn't treat her any differently than their *male* hostages.

The fact that there are so many factors that trump diversity keeps affirmative action miles away from common sense. Until the day that we are all raised by the same two parents, live under the same roof, go to the same school, have the same problems, have the same ailments, or have the same thoughts and beliefs, affirmative action is just a road block.

Now, if you thought affirmative action was wacky, another brilliant creation from the brain trust on the left is "reparations."

"Reparations" is a relatively new idea. It is basically the idea that people living in the United States who happen to be of African descent are entitled to compensation for the slavery that their ancestors endured. I have heard of the concept of "white guilt," but let's be realistic for a minute. Who suffers from slavery today? Nobody that I know. Maybe in other countries, but not here. Even if it is happening in some remote corner of the U.S., it is very illegal. Who owns slaves today? Again, nobody in this country. The last slave bought or sold in this country was over a hundred years ago. So why would anyone think that they are entitled to compensation for injustices that they did not suffer? Why would anyone think that someone should have to pay for crimes that they did not commit? That is exactly what "reparations" are all about.

Let's say, just for the sake of argument that somehow reparations got through the radar of common sense. Who would pay for them? My ancestors were not even here yet when slavery was happening, unless you count the Native American side of my family tree. I don't recall hearing too much about Indians owning slaves though. Does this mean that I would be exempt from paying reparations? How would they figure out whose ancestors owned slaves? How much would that process cost? How much would be paid to the ancestors of former slaves?

Would they go by the current going rate for a "black" man, or the rate at the actual time of slavery, (you know, more than a hundred years ago!)? Did I mention that slavery happened more than a hundred years ago? By the way, slavery happened more than a hundred years ago. Guess what, slavery ended over a hundred years ago.

According to the logic of reparations, if your great-great-great-great-grandfather robbed my great-great-great-great-grandfather, you owe me restitution for that crime. The reasoning behind reparations is supposed to be that a "black" person has been held back due to the fact that his or her ancestors were not allowed to succeed because of slavery. This in turn has held them back in modern day America. So does this mean that unless your ancestors are privileged, you can't possibly succeed? Does this mean that if my ancestors were held back because of the plague that I have no way to be successful, so therefore I need to be taken care of by my government? Does this mean that if I murder a man, my grandchildren's grandchildren will have to go to jail for *my* crime? Should the ancestors of the people burned as witches in Salem be compensated too? Can you imagine the can of worms this whole concept would open? What goes through the mind of a person who would promote such an idiotic idea? Worse yet, what goes through the mind of someone who would put an idea like this out in the form of a serious news story? I can see putting it in the "wacky story" file, but this has been reported as something to actually consider. I almost didn't include a mention of reparations here. It is too silly to take seriously. I only bring it up because lately it has been in the news. I really don't know why, but apparently some in the media are taking this seriously. That must mean that all other

Terry Leasure

news issues have been resolved, and there is peace and prosperity throughout the world.

One theory I have as to why stupidity like reparations, affirmative action, and forced diversity gets taken seriously by some people - is guilt. We know for a fact that our nation's history is spotted with evil deeds. No one in their right mind can deny this. It is simply a fact. We did allow and even promote slavery at one point in our past. We did burn "witches." We did treat the Native Americans pretty crappy too. But when the term "we" is applied to our history, it does not actually mean you and I. It refers to our nation's history, and nothing more.

I know that there are still people walking around out there who still dislike others just because of pigmentation, gender, or cultural ancestry. I also know that I am *not* one of these people, and I also know that I am not alone.

I know that assuming that one's pigmentation, gender, or cultural ancestry is a handicap that requires a crutch or helping hand, is no way to solve the problem, or even change a bigot's mind. Can you think of a more personal way to insult someone than to say that their physical appearance makes them inferior, needy of extra help, and incapable of cutting the mustard on their own?

I know that appearance and ability are two very different things. We are all equal in the eyes of the law. That is guaranteed in the Bill of Rights. This does not mean that we are all capable of the same things. I cannot play basketball as well as Michael Jordan. So the government should never be able to force an NBA team to draft me in order to make the team more diverse.

I know that there are differences between males and females. This was explained to me in elementary health class. Men and women have always had a volatile history. At the same time, they have always had an attraction that rivals any electro-magnet known to man. When men and women get together, things *do* happen. Jealousy, infidelity, love, lust, sex, pregnancy, flirtation, and menstruation all have a place in life, but not on the battlefield. If a soldier gets "twitterpated" people can get killed. If you have seen any old Disney movies, then you know what that means. Pretending that men and women are not different is to spit in the face of common sense. Pretending that an enemy would never rape a female soldier is just crazy. Isn't losing a son to a bullet bad enough? Do we now have to lose a daughter to a bullet, only after an enemy combatant has sexually abused her? Where is the dignity in that?

These are things that are a matter of fact, not opinion. There *are* still racists out there. Color *is* only skin deep. Women *are* different than men. And none of this is *my* fault.

It is for just this reason that I do not feel guilty about "racism." If I were to assume that I owe a man something just because his skin is darker than mine, then I would be a "racist" by default. That ain't gonna' happen.

I believe that you cannot judge a man by the color of his skin. This was one of the first concepts from our history that really made sense to me. I owe *that* to Dr. Martin Luther King. If his message did nothing else, it taught this "white boy" how childish racism is. He showed us all how precious freedom is, and how hard it can be to acquire. At the same time, he taught generations about dignity, perseverance, and strength. Non-violent civil disobedience was nothing short of brilliant. I believe that if Dr. King were alive today and could see how his message has been perverted by liberal policies, he would probably hang his head and cry.

I feel no guilt for speaking out against affirmative action. It is a bad thing for everybody, blacks, whites, males, females, Americans and foreigners. I also feel no guilt for the bad things that happened a long time ago. Unless I can build a time machine, there is nothing I can do about it, and it wasn't my fault. Until we all learn that people were not meant to be pigeonholed according to color (even for the sake of good intentions), we are just *pretending* to be civilized.

Chapter 6
Stop! Or I'll Say "Stop" Again!

L iberals seem to have a way of thumbing their nose at reality. As we have seen recently in Iraq and Afghanistan, sometimes you have to use force or violence in order to control a situation. There are times when words will not help you. The truth is that there are people in the world who do not understand the concepts of negotiation, cooperation or diplomacy. No matter how many real-life examples of this you show a liberal, they will usually dig their heels further into the dirt of denial.

Trust me, no one would rather live in a violence-free world than me. I have always done my best to get out of sticky situations without raising a fist in anger. I have always used diplomacy as a first response. Thankfully, I have never needed to use a firearm to protect my family or myself. The problem is, I cannot predict the future.

When I walk down the street, I can be *reasonably* sure that I am safe. On the other hand, as someone who lives in the country, I don't walk down the street very often. When I do, I see a wide berth between *reasonably* and *definitely*. If you get on a plane, you may be *reasonably* sure that you will not crash. If you had the power to increase your odds of survival, and boost your confidence at the same time, why wouldn't you?

This brings me to another concept that liberals have always had trouble with - responsibility. If you are just one person who lives alone, and has no friends or loved ones, you may not see a need to invest much time or energy in protection, or personal security. But what if you have a family? Who is responsible for the safety of your spouse or your children? A liberal would say that the government is responsible for keeping you and your kids safe. In a magical fantasyland where bad people do not exist, and every person has a federal marshal assigned to them, that might work. Here in the real world, though, YOU are responsible for the safety of yourself and your family.

Part of the deal when you decide to start a family (as I have) is that you need to be willing to do whatever is within your power to protect them. That responsibility is yours, whether you are the mother or the father.

Let's get back to that single person with no friends or family. Does he not have responsibilities? If he is walking down the street and sees two men mugging an elderly lady, does he have an obligation to help her? Typical liberals would argue that he should call the police and not get involved. How long does it take for two men to mug an elderly lady? How long does it take to find a phone, dial numbers, get through, explain the situation, then figure out where you are, and how to explain that to a 911 dispatcher? Then how long does it take for the police to actually show up? Police competency aside, factor in traffic, distance, construction, railroad crossings, or even car trouble. This is all assuming that you found the phone in the first place. After all this time has gone by, how do think the elderly lady made out using the "not my problem" philosophy?

What if the same single man (with no friends or loved ones) tried to help the elderly lady? What would he do against two big guys who happen to be on meth? Maybe the elderly lady will get lucky, and the lonely guy will happen to be a martial arts expert. But what if one of the muggers has a gun? Maybe she will get lucky, and the lonely guy will be bulletproof. After all, Superman is somewhat of a loner. Oh, I forgot, we were talking about the *real* world. The reality of this situation is, the guy would probably get his head blown off, then the lady would have to die too so there would be no witnesses.

We could argue that when faced with such a situation, you should just keep walking and hope that the elderly lady is let go. We could argue that the elderly lady should try to talk the meth-fueled muggers into letting her alone. We could argue that sticking with the "call the police first" plan is the way to go. Which of these options are the most realistic? Which of these options will most likely result in the elderly lady getting home in one piece? If you are even vaguely familiar with common sense, you know that the answer is none of the above.

Now, let's apply a *controversial* approach to this same scenario. What if the same single man, with no friends or loved ones, happened to be carrying a .45 semi-automatic pistol when he found the elderly lady being harassed? Keeping in mind that there are no absolutes in the real world, wouldn't the odds of the elderly lady getting home in one piece increase just a smidgen? Yes, it could turn into a shootout where everybody dies. That is a *possibility*. But if you recall the earlier options, you *probably* end up dead. When it comes to death, I'll take *possible* over *probable* every time!

Think about human nature for a minute. We all have a natural instinct to stay alive. It is this very instinct that could be used to help the elderly lady. Even a mugger wants to live to mug another day. Keep that in mind as I rewrite the elderly lady's story.

Imagine the lonely guy, with his .45 tucked in his shoulder holster, rounding the corner only to find the two muggers roughing up the elderly lady. Immediately, he pulls out the .45 and yells, "Let her alone!" They both see that the lonely guy has a gun pointed right at them. At this point, the mugger who is carrying his own gun is forced to make a decision. Can he pull his gun fast enough to shoot the lonely guy? Should he just run for it, or should he just freeze and take his chances in court? Instantly, he weighs his options and runs away, followed by his partner in crime. The elderly lady is unharmed. She and the lonely guy *then* call the police, give descriptions of the two muggers and return to their homes safe and sound. Later that day, the muggers are picked up and put in the pokey.

If you really want to go out on a limb, wrap your mind around *this* scenario.

What if the elderly lady had been carrying *her own* .45 semi-automatic pistol? Pearl handled, of course. A real lady likes to be stylish.

You see, the original situation put the elderly lady in a position where she needed to rely on an armed gentleman to be *coincidentally* walking by just before she was assaulted. What if the lonely guy had been running late that particular day? What if he never came by at all? If the lady had her own firearm, her odds of survival would increase ten-fold. She wouldn't be *guaranteed* to survive, but you can't possibly deny that she would have a tactical advantage. Before you try to look it up, "ten-fold" is just an expression. We are talking about a matter of common sense. Common sense requires no statistics.

We never really decided for sure whether or not the lonely guy had any real obligation to help the elderly lady. Legally, this can be a grey area. Some states require you to help a person in need, but who is to say what that means? Morally, I think it is a "no-brainer". If you can watch an elderly lady being attacked and not try to help her, then your parents "dropped the ball" somewhere along the line.

Put yourself in the lady's shoes for a minute. As the mugger is raising his fist to punch you, what would be of more help to you? A phone, or a gun? How many rape or mugging victims wished that they had a phone, one second before the first blow to the head? Can we assume that they might regret not having some form of protection to even the odds at that particular moment? Is that *really* so far fetched?

Hopefully, you are not thinking that I am putting down our "men in blue," or suggesting that involving the police is wrong. I just accept the fact that the police cannot beeverywhere, every time. The laws of averages, physics, time, and Mr. Murphy prevent most people from real police *protection*. If you apply common sense to this discussion, you will realize that in most cases the police show up *after* the crime has been committed. I would be willing to bet that statistics show that the police spend most of their time chasing criminals, but have few opportunities to *prevent* crimes before they happen.

I am no expert on criminal statistics, but it stands to reason that the first people who show up at the scene of a crime are the perpetrator and the victim. I also have to assume that not all crimes happen in front of a crowd of witnesses or a video camera. I am also reasonably sure that even with their advances in technology, law enforcement has not found a way to see into the future. *Minority Report* is only a movie. Here in the real world, we have to take care of ourselves from time to time.

Gun control has been a *controversial* subject for quite a while. At least we have been *told* that it is a controversial subject. Personally, I don't see the controversy. A typical bumper sticker phrase sums up my opinion of gun control; "Gun control is when you hit what you're aiming at."

Somehow, guns have gotten a bad rap over the years. As with many other important subjects, common sense has been flushed down the crapper on the topic of guns. This is just another thing we can thank our old buddy liberalism for.

We have been taught for years now that guns are bad, they kill people, and if you see one you should run away (with arms flailing for dramatic effect). We are constantly reminded about little Timmy, who blew his friend's head off while playing with daddy's evil gun. Gun control groups blast us with statistic after statistic. We are constantly told that if you get rid of your gun, a criminal can't steal it and use it against someone else. We are told that the Second Amendment was only meant for the colonists. Like all good sheep, first we accept it, and then we believe it. Rarely do we take the time to apply a little bit of "brain juice" to the subject.

Let's get those brain juices flowing. Liberalism seems to be all about having someone else fix your problems for you, usually the government. The problem is, even in the most socialist places in history, crime still existed. Even at the height of Stalin's rule, I would bet that there were still murders, muggings, and rapes. After all, we are talking about humans here. As long as there have been humans, there has been crime. Even Michael Moore would have to admit that.

So, what would the government be able to do for you, if it were *you* in the alley, face to face with a violent criminal? Can you expect a laser beam to come shooting down from a taxpayer-funded satellite, stunning but not harming the man who is about to cave in your skull with a crowbar? Can you expect there to be a policeman in every alley? Can you expect the educational system to have created only law-abiding citizens, making the scenario impossible in the first place? Do you assume that you would be issued a can of crime repellant from the federal government? Maybe you could hand the mugger a government pamphlet that would convince him to leave his life of crime (printed in Pueblo, Colorado, no doubt). Maybe a bill would be passed that would make it illegal to own a crowbar. After all, a criminal would never break the law, and possess an illegal crowbar.

Another irony of liberalism is the fact that liberals claim to be the protectors of civil rights. But when it comes to *my* civil right to protect my family or myself, they do a 180-degree turn. Do you not have the right to protect yourself? Do you not have a right to protect your family?

A firearm is a dangerous device. I would be the first to admit this. It requires a certain amount of discipline, skill and personal restraint. A firearm can kill a person in the blink of an eye, and should only be handled by someone who has had some kind of instructional training. All of these things can also be said for a car, boat, lawnmower, or chain saw. As with these devices, a gun does not have a mind of its own. In the entire history of mankind, a gun has never killed anyone without the help of a human being.

You can put a loaded 44 Magnum on a table in the middle of a crowded mall.

Until a human being walks by and touches it, it will never harm anyone. This is the theory behind the commonly mocked axiom, "Guns don't kill people, people kill people." Actually, this not a theory, I submit this as fact.

Another phrase that is commonly labeled as propaganda is, "When guns are outlawed, only outlaws will have guns." This has been a favorite among the bumper sticker crowd for years.

Unfortunately for the anti-gun crowd, this simple, backwoods logic has never been disproved. They have made fun of it, and belittled those who profess the common sense of it, but at the end of the day, the concept still stands on its own merit.

Pop quiz. Can you name a country where guns are illegal that has no firearm violence? Neither can I. England has banned guns for years. Do you really think they have no crime involving firearms? Do people never get shot in England? Who protects a Brit when there are no "Bobbies" around?

My favorite irony of "gun control" is the fact that *everybody* benefits from the right to carry a gun. "How?" you ask. Put yourself in the shoes of a rapist. If you are in an area where it is illegal to carry a firearm, you have little reason to believe that you are going to have a problem. After all, the police can't be everywhere, and you are big and strong. So you go out and do your thing, with little resistance from your prey.

What if you were the same rapist, in the same area, but six months ago, they lifted the gun-carrying ban? Would you be as confident in your success? How bold would you feel when walking up behind an unsuspecting young lady? Since you would have no way of knowing, would it really matter if she were actually carrying a gun? Would you not realize that now you have a 50/50 chance of going home alive? As I mentioned earlier, even criminals want to live.

The same goes for home invasions. If you are a burglar, and you know that everyone is free to own and carry firearms, aren't you going to think twice before opening someone else's window? Again, you don't know for sure, thanks to an absence of gun restrictions. So now, a burglary becomes a gamble on your life. I'm sure not *every* criminal would summon the intellect to figure this out, but common sense demands that *most* would.

By this theory, you can be a die-hard, anti-gun, anti-death penalty, tree hugging, vegetarian, hybrid-driving liberal, but you get to walk down the street with little chance of being attacked. All thanks to the fact that the same gun ban *you* fought so hard to have, has been lifted. You tried to stop the very thing that is now saving your life. Being protected from rape, murder, or robbery could be considered a benefit. This is just another example of why liberalism is so self-defeating, as well as frustrating.

Should everyone carry a gun? No. Should everyone drive a car? No. The truth is, there are some people in this country that I wouldn't trust to sit the right way on a toilet seat. The real question is; who has the right, or ability to decide who can or can't own a firearm?

Let's say that you are a law-abiding citizen of the United States. If liberalism were the law of the land, you would not be allowed to own a gun. Simply put, your government would deem you untrustworthy to own a firearm. At the same time, criminals too would be considered untrustworthy to own firearms. The only problem is, criminals do not usually pay a lot of attention to what the government has to say. After all, robbery is illegal, but people still get robbed. Selling illegal drugs is illegal, but there are still drug dealers. It is for this very reason that I have never understood the logic behind making it illegal for law-abiding citizens to own firearms, especially as a means of personal protection. This brings us back to the old "red neck" bumper sticker logic of "when guns are outlawed, only outlaws will have guns."

Maybe we should take a trip through fantasyland for a moment. Let's imagine that all crime has disappeared. There are no more rapes, murders, wars, robberies, or even illegal music downloading. All crime is gone forever. Some could argue that a there would no longer be a need for firearms. This may even be true. After all, without crime, the need for firearms would be minuscule at best. Here is where the rubber meets the road for liberalism.

Now that there is no *need* to own a gun, why should anyone complain if guns are illegal? After all, now you have nothing to protect yourself against.

There is one reason to justify owning a firearm that outweighs all others, even if there were no *practical* purpose for doing so. That answer is... I WANT TO. It really is that simple. Actually, this is what I consider to be the best reason to do most things. Before you label me an anarchist, keep in mind that I do not want to do things that would hurt me, or anyone else. It is this fact that separates me wanting to own a firearm, from someone else wanting to steal cars. If you have any form of "moral compass." you do not want to do harmful things. I consider myself to have a pretty good grasp of right and wrong. You see, some liberals would try to dismiss my wanting to own a gun by asking what the difference would be in someone else wanting to commit a crime. Reasonable people can see the difference.

"Wanting to" is the reason that *everybody* does most things. It is our morality that steers us between right and wrong. Stealing cars is wrong, doing illegal drugs is wrong, kicking a puppy is wrong. The things we want to do are what is up for debate. Is it wrong to own a car? Is it wrong to stab the mailman with a knife? Is it wrong to buy an ice cream cone? Is it wrong to mug an old lady? Is it wrong to own an ink pen?

Hopefully, you didn't have trouble answering any of those questions. If you did, please put this book down, and seek help immediately. So, when I say I want to own a gun, is that wrong?

Liberals commonly question the *need* to own a firearm. This has always puzzled me. *Need* will always be debatable, depending on the individual and their circumstances. What seems to get lost in the shuffle of liberal propaganda is the *right* to own a firearm.

Every human being on this planet has the right to protect themselves and the ones they love. This fact is hard to dispute; I don't care how purple you die your hair. Even if you don't believe in God, you could say that you were issued the right to protect yourself on the day you were born. Who gave you this right is really not relevant. Whether you believe you received your right to protect yourself from God, Buddha, or Elvis Presley, you *do* have it. The only prerequisite is that you be a human being.

Actually, you could make a pretty good case for the theory that even animals have a right to protect themselves. They just don't have the ability. Trust me, if a deer was able to, it would carry an M-16. With a little luck, the law of natural selection will make sure that the animal kingdom never arms itself. In the meantime, I will continue to enjoy thick New York strip steaks and deer bologna.

The point is, self-preservation is a natural instinct. Does a newborn baby not flinch if you toss a rubber ball to it? Will the same baby not try to push your hand away if you pinch him? Apparently, a liberal baby would just sit there and take it. Just another clue that liberalism is unnatural.

Even the most oppressed people, from the most remote parts of the world, are born with the right to protect themselves. They just don't always have the ability to exercise their rights. In some cases the concept of a *right* is completely foreign to them anyway. Even *this* does not diminish the fact that they were born with the right to *life*, *liberty*, and *the pursuit of happiness*.

If someone tries to kill you, they are infringing on your right to live. If someone tries to rob you, they are infringing on your right to liberty. Ironically, if they do either one, they are infringing on your right to pursue happiness.

While we're on the topic of *rights*, try this one on for size. The right to keep and bear arms. For some reason, liberals seem to have trouble understanding this right. Apparently, the founding fathers of this nation predicted that liberalism would haunt us for a long time. They must have known that our freedoms would come under fire, and require easily definable constitutional protection. For this very reason, they wrote the Second Amendment.

Read the Second Amendment for yourself-

a well regulated Militia, being necessary to the security of a free State, the right of the people to keep and bear Arms, shall not be infringed.

Why is this so hard for some people to understand? If you are one of these people, do you really need to have a panel of English professors sit down and diagram this sentence for you? What part of "shall not be infringed" do you not understand?

Luckily, our rights are protected by a little piece of parchment known as the Constitution of the United States. Notice, I said *our* rights. I was also referring to *your* rights.

Having never met you (the reader), I have no way of knowing what side of the "gun control" fence you stand on. This is not a problem. I only need to know if you are an American citizen. You see, even if you hate guns, even if the very thought of holding a firearm in your hand makes you want to vomit, you still have the right to own one. The same holds true for *my* right to own a bra. I have no desire to own a bra; I also have no reason to own a bra. This does not mean that I have no *right* to own a bra. It certainly doesn't mean that I should try to have *your* right to own a bra taken away.

If you are a skilled master in the art of liberal debate, you are probably saying to yourself, "Bras don't kill people, so you can't use that for an analogy." For starters, I refer you back to the earlier part of this chapter, where I explained that guns don't kill people either. Remember the gun on the table in the middle of the crowded mall? Whether it's a gun, a bra, or a nuclear missile, it can't hurt you without the help of a human being. I would also have to assume that I actually *could* use a bra to kill a person if I wanted to. I don't know if it has ever been done before, but I would be willing to bet that I could choke the stuffing out of you with a common Victoria's Secret product. If I was really demented, I could probably stab you in the neck with the underwire.

Relax, I don't usually sit around trying to figure out ways to kill people with everyday undergarments...as long as I don't go off my medication (that was a joke).

I am just trying to illustrate a few points: rights are something worth protecting, even if you never use them. A bra is not as popular as a gun when it comes to killing people, but it could be if it were marketed correctly. I think the last point I am trying to make is; they can have my bra, when they pry it from my cold dead hand.

The absurdity of using underwear to kill people brings me to another point. Why do we not have a "hand control" lobby? Do people never get choked? Do people never get beaten to death? Where is the "pillow control" lobby? Do people never get smothered to death? There must be a "knife control" group somewhere. I hear about people getting stabbed all the time. What about the "baseball bat, tire iron, or blunt object control" lobbyists? They need to get a little more airtime. Shouldn't there be a movement to ban or regulate the sale of ice picks? When will we finally have a seven-day waiting period for the sale of rat poison? Hopefully, someday we can have background checks for the purchase of gasoline.

Again, a *savvy* liberal would submit that guns are a more efficient way to kill people, and that is why they should be outlawed. I would remind this same lefty that the last time I checked, box cutters were a pretty efficient way to kill people, too. Does September 11, 2001 ring a bell? By his logic, you would need to register the box cutter in your toolbox to the "proper authorities."

I try very hard to see the points of the various "gun control" groups that try to chip away at the Second Amendment. I also have a lot of sympathy for them. I'm sure that many of them have lost loved ones to gun violence. Having never gone through such a tragedy myself, it is hard for me to imagine the pain that these people are feeling. Honestly, I can't even say for sure that I wouldn't be anti-gun myself, if I had lost someone close to me to a bullet.

On the other hand, I did recently lose a good friend of mine to a car accident. I didn't blame the car, the car's manufacturer, the road, or even the snow and ice that covered the pavement. His was the only car involved and he was the only one in the car. That means that there is a 99% chance that the accident was *his* fault. If his brakes were bad, it was *his* responsibility to have them checked. If he slid on the ice, he was going too fast for road conditions. If he fell asleep, or was drunk, he shouldn't have been behind the wheel. As hard as it is to say, unless my friend blacked-out because of an unforeseen medical condition, the accident was *his* fault.

I never mention my opinion to my friend's brother, who I see from time to time. I know that he might take offense and I don't want to cause him any more grief.

I think that when you lose someone close to you, grief and pain take charge of you for a while. This is natural, but that does not always make it a good thing. Some people can control and channel these feelings into motivation for a positive goal. Other folks seem to lose focus of the actual root of the problem that caused their pain to begin with. Though their heart is in the right place, their aim is way off.

Apparently, this is the problem of the "gun control" lobby. Rather than put pressure on our elected officials to put criminals behind bars, or make jail less comfortable, "gun control" advocates want to make it harder for law-abiding people like you and me to own firearms. The phrase "throwing the baby out with the bath water" was custom-made for this kind of concept.

Liberals like to throw around statistics about gun-related deaths. I could write a few chapters disputing these statistics, and it would likely help me to demonstrate the media bias against gun ownership. That would require research. I hate research. On top of that, I am notoriously lazy. If you want numbers and statistics about guns and gun violence, contact the National Rifle Association. If you think they are incapable of being objective, then contact the Centers for Disease Control. Both of these outfits will be happy to give you real numbers. Not just broad general statistics that are given out of context. They will break them down into the facts for you.

I challenge you to ask a "gun control" group how many lives were *saved* last year thanks to firearms. The next time you read about a violent crime that was stopped by an innocent bystander, ask yourself these questions. Why aren't they giving any details about the bystander? Why didn't they say *how* he stopped the crime? One catch phrase to look for is, "He (or she) was able to subdue the armed assailant." How did he (or she) "subdue" an armed assailant? You do the math.

If you really want to get ambitious, when you hear of stories like this, research it for yourself. Don't be afraid to call or write to the people you read about in the paper. Don't be afraid to call the police departments of the towns mentioned in these stories. You would be surprised what kind of facts you can pick up thanks to the Freedom of Information Act.

One thing I have learned over the past few years is this; that the press seems to be "fact-phobic." Apparently, when they report a story, vagueness is the priority, second only to sensationalism. If the truth in a particular story does not meet the criteria of their own agenda, then all bets are off. If a story happens to be about a *controversial* subject like media bias, ILLEGAL immigration, "racism," religion, or gun control, then you better start learning how to read between the lines.

In an age where everybody wants to sue somebody, the media has lost its ability to be objective. News sources would rather eat worms than be *controversial*. I don't know if they are afraid of some type of litigation, or if they think that they are the sole arbiters of right and wrong. Maybe they think we are all just too unstable to handle the truth. Maybe they think they can change reality, simply by misrepresenting it. Maybe they just think we are all stupid. Whatever the reason, I no longer trust the mainstream media, especially when it comes to stories that concern my rights as an American.

Nowadays, when I hear about a new controversy, one phrase seems to run on a continuous loop in my head: "Never let the facts get in the way of a good story."

If you take the time to set aside your misconceptions about guns, and apply a little common sense to the subject, you will start to get a clearer picture. Actually, if you do that, you won't *need* any statistics or research material.

Let's set the "way back machine" for the early nineties. I am sure we all remember a guy named O.J. and his lovely wife Nicole. I was not there, so I am not trying to say I know who killed O.J.'s wife. I will say that if I ever see O.J. Simpson in *my* yard, I will have a loaded .45 on my side (just in case). Who killed Nicole is not really relevant to this discussion though. She and her male "friend" were brutally murdered with a knife, apparently by someone who was physically strong enough to overpower two people, quickly enough to not wake the neighbors, or get caught.

My questions are very simple. When I ask them, I only request that you apply *some common* sense to the answers. What I want to know is, what do you think would have happened that night if Nicole or Mr. Goldman had been carrying a 9mm pistol? Do you really think that O.J. would still be searching for the "real killer" on those California golf courses?

Another famous news story in the early nineties was the Los Angeles riots after the Rodney King situation. I remember watching that display of savagery in the comfort of my Pennsylvania apartment. I watched as people's lives were ruined, thanks to their inability to defend themselves or their property. I remember watching that truck driver being pulled from his truck and beaten within an inch of his life. I remember wondering then, as I do now, how much rioting would have happened if people in L.A. were free to carry firearms? It seems to me that not knowing if you were going to come back alive, would take some of the fun out of any type of free-for-all, even a riot.

Throughout history, you can find situations that probably would have turned out a lot different, had the victim been carrying a firearm. I wonder what would have happened prior to World War II, if more Jewish folks had been armed? Would Hitler have had the testicular fortitude to conduct the Holocaust, if he knew that every household contained some type of gun? Even if he were still crazy enough to go for it, would it have been as easy for his henchmen to pull it off?

I wonder how successful Fidel Castro would have become, if the bulk of the Cuban population were armed?

If you look at history, there seems to be a common thread between most evil dictators, and tyrannical leaders...an unarmed population. After all, how do you think we were able to fight the British in the Revolutionary War? Do you really think that the only people who had muskets were the *proper authorities*? If it weren't for firearms, we would be saying "God Save the Queen" instead of "God Bless America."

The most recent, and the most powerful example of a "what if" scenario would have to be the terrorist attacks on September 11th, 2001. Hopefully, even if you are a card carrying liberal, you can face the realities of what happened that day. A group of men took over four passenger airplanes. They then proceeded to ram those planes into highly populated, strategically chosen facilities, killing thousands, and devastating our national psyche. The cost of this attack will be felt for years to come, both financially and emotionally.

How did this happen? How did these small groups of men take over these airplanes loaded with people? What kind of weaponry could allow them to gain access to the cockpit of an airliner, and then get them past a three-man flight crew? The answer is embarrassing in its simplicity. BOX CUTTERS!!!

The worst attack in recorded history, on our nation's soil, happened because of box cutters! Thousands of people are dead, because of box cutters! The entire American airline industry was almost wiped out, because of box cutters! The most beautiful city skyline in the world is forever ruined, because of box cutters!

How can you not ask the question; What if the pilots had been carrying guns that day? Even if the terrorists were able to breach the cockpit door, what would they do with three men shooting holes in them? Would they be able to take over the plane then? I have never flown a plane before, but it can't be easy, especially with your brain sprayed all over the food station. The last time I checked, your brain was considered to be vital equipment.

I hate to keep harping on the whole "common sense" angle, but somehow in the 21st century, we have traded our security for the hopeless idea that evil can be repelled by happy thoughts and well wishes. Arming pilots is just another example of this.

Surprisingly, there has been a lot less "primetime" discussion of this issue than I was expecting. After September 11th, I didn't expect much debate about giving pilots the ability to protect the nation from further attacks. I was naive. I truly underestimated just how ridiculous our leaders can be, even in a time of crises. This should have been a "no-brainer."

Theoretically, pilots should have already been carrying firearms on September 10th. Shamefully, as of today we are still debating the issue. This begs the question; "How many more people need to die, before we start taking this a little more seriously?" Apparently, more than 3000.

I am not an unreasonable man. I have tried as hard as I can to see the point of view of those against giving a pilot a fighting chance. I have heard the pros and cons. The pros seem to go on and on, but I have only heard a few cons, and they don't make any sense to me.

I have heard people express concern over the damage that a stray bullet *could* cause. At first that seemed to be a reasonable argument. Then our leaders decided to allow pilots to carry stun guns. It was at this point that my interest in all things mechanical was applied to the issue.

I started to visualize a bullet going through the instrument panel of a 747. I imagined the worst-case scenario of a plane going down due to a bullet-riddled control panel. I started to get all caught up in the frenzy of anti-gun propaganda. Then I thought back to a day in high school when I tried to hook up my friend Scott's car stereo for him. The wires were marked wrong and I ended up putting 12 volts directly into the wrong wire. The stereo started to smoke, and then sizzle and it was fried for good. So I can only imagine how much carnage a high voltage stun gun could do to the sensitive electronics of a jet airliner.

Then I remembered how much damage those box cutters did, and damage to the plane seemed to be less of a risk than a dead pilot. The truth is, there are no perfect options when you are dealing with madmen. As responsible human beings, we are left with figuring out the most *effective* way to handle any given situation. History has taught us that when it comes to stopping a person, bullets are very *effective*.

In keeping with the "stray bullet" theme, another concern is a passenger getting shot accidentally instead of the terrorist. Putting myself in the shoes of that passenger, would it really matter to me if I get shot, or if I'm rammed into a skyscraper at 500 miles per hour? Yes, it would. You see, people get shot and live to tell the tale all the time. Very few people have ever survived a plane crash. On September 11th, no one did. At least if you get shot, you might have a chance. As long as at least one of the other bullets finds it's way into the terrorist, I'll take a bullet over a skyscraper every time.

I'm sure that someone less understanding than myself would probably sue an airline if they accidentally get shot on an airplane. By the same token, airlines are still being sued today over the events of September 11th. This negates *litigation* as a reasonable argument against arming pilots, especially in an age when you can be sued over hot coffee, anyway.

Another popular excuse to keep an effective tool out of hands that could use it the most is *training*. This is laughable for two reasons. First of all, a large majority of pilots are former military personnel. Where do you think military pilots go after they leave the service? Do they go to work for McDonald's flipping burgers? No! They enter the private sector as commercial airline pilots.

As former members of the military, your typical pilot has already had formal firearms training. A course in how to use a firearm in a terrorist takeover of an airplane may be in order, but I have to assume that most pilots would be familiar and comfortable with the basic operation of a common side arm.

Second, an average gun has very few moving parts, and is mechanically pretty simple to operate. I don't think that the same can be said for a Boeing 747. Of course, I have never flown an airplane, so maybe I am being too presumptuous. I have however fired quite a few firearms in my time. I still think a jetliner is probably more difficult to operate. This must be the case, because a gun does not take a three-man crew to use.

My point is, if a pilot is capable of flying something as technically advanced as a jet airliner, I would bet that he could figure out how to pull a trigger, even if he had never been in the military.

I wish that I could recall where I heard this next excuse, because it is my personal favorite. I actually heard a "talking head" question the *competency* of pilots in handling firearms. They were asserting that pilots might not be able to handle the pressures and responsibilities of carrying a gun. When I heard this, I nearly drove off the road, I was laughing so hard.

Let me get this straight. The same guy who is flying a JET AIRLINER over countless towns and cities, loaded with hundreds of people, may not be able too handle the pressure of carrying a gun? After September 11th, it seems to me that flying *without* adequate protection would be a bit more stressful. It also seems highly *irresponsible* to force pilots to take off, knowing full well that they would not have a good way to protect the innocent people in the plane and on the ground in the event of a terrorist takeover.

I have even heard people say that a pilot is *too busy* to effectively use a gun in a terrorist takeover. My question is; "Too busy doing what, bleeding to death from a box-cutter slash to the throat?" Am I to believe that between three men on a flight crew, one of them won't have enough time to reach over and push the auto pilot button?

I don't know what is more ridiculous, the fact that someone came up with these ridiculous, time-and-life wasting excuses, or the fact that the press is willing to give them ink and airtime. It is as if common sense has no practical purpose anymore.

I also wonder why we don't waste as much time questioning the reasoning behind arming the police, bodyguards, federal agents, or the U.S. military? The irony here is, Al Qaeda is not rushing to take over a police car, and drive it into a skyscraper.

Before September 11th, I would have never thought about the concept of arming pilots. On the other hand, I would have never thought that someone would want to crash an airplane into a skyscraper, either. Now that we know for a fact that this can happen, why are we dragging our feet on preventing it from happening again?

Earlier I used the scenario of a rapist in a city that had recently lifted a ban on carrying firearms. I suggested that he would be less sure in his ability to attack a woman, not knowing if she might be armed. This same theory applies to air travel. Even if there were a pilot who refused to carry a gun, would a terrorist know that? So even *thinking* that a pilot was armed would throw a serious wrench in a terrorist's works.

Admittedly, after we were attacked, I was angry. I was also prone to snap judgments on the topic of arming pilots. I have been quoted as saying; "I think they should let everyone carry a gun on an airplane". At first this seemed like a good idea. After all, who would be brave enough to hijack an airplane loaded with armed passengers? Then, after giving it some thought, I realized that it would not be impossible for a large group of terrorists to charter a plane. Just for the record though, I'll never get on a plane until I can take my .45 with me. Any plane I get on then *will* land safely at its destination. A box cutter won't impress me.

It is a sad commentary on our society that when I started to write this book, I knew I would have to include a chapter about gun control. After all that our nation has had to go through to gain its independence, some people still don't get it. I guess it was this fact that forced me to write to begin with.

I still don't understand how so many people can be so rabidly against the very thing that helps them live in a free society.

I always get a kick out of the liberal view of firearms, especially if the liberal happens to be wealthy, or famous. You see, if you have enough money to be able to afford armed bodyguards, private jets, bullet proof windows, security alarms, and an iron fence surrounding your estate, you may have less *need* to carry a gun. Unfortunately for the rest of us, affordable protection may need to come in the form of a revolver.

Trust me, if I could afford a personal bodyguard to stay with my family and me, I wouldn't care so much about my right to carry a gun. I wouldn't need to take the time to clean and maintain it either. I would just let my bodyguard deal with all that.

If I lived in a gated community, and had an expensive security system, I probably wouldn't have to worry about keeping my wife and child safe from burglars and rapists. The problem is, a truck driver's paycheck does not allow these luxuries.

What really fries my bacon, though, is when a famous wealthy liberal uses his (or her) access to the media to try to take away *my* ability to protect *my* family. Consequently, *your*

ability to protect *your* family. Do they have the right to say what they want? Absolutely.

Ironically, men who carry guns protect this right. Unfortunately, liberals with media access have no respect for the rights of others. Worse yet, their message gets out, and people eat it up by the spoonful. For a lot of the young people in our country, anything that Joe

Schmo movie star has to say is accepted as gospel. A one-line sound bite, with no basis in fact, can erase any previous common sense logic that someone may have possessed, as long as the right actor or rock star said it. The media can't seem to get enough of these uninformed opinions. They seem to assume that we care what Rosie O'Donnell thinks about guns. As if she ever needs to worry about someone getting past her security staff. I wish I had a security staff.

The word "elitist" comes to mind when I hear rich liberals speak out against people owning firearms. If they are able to protect themselves or their loved ones without picking up a gun, then more power to them. I take my hat off to them, and hope to be able to do the same someday. Until that day, I may need more than foul language and a scowl to defend my family. Why do these people fight against our most basic of freedoms? Where do they get the nerve? How does the media not ridicule them? Why do we listen to them? Why do we pay them to entertain us, when they use that same money and fame to hamstring us?

Again, this situation is chock full of irony. As a gun owner, if I was walking down the street and saw one of these liberal anti-gun whackos getting mugged, I would use my gun to help them. That is the nature of a civilized human being.

As an expectant father, I want my kid to grow up to be happy and healthy. At the very least, I just want him/her to grow up. I plan to make sure my child has access to all the inoculations that are available. I am going to make sure that my child is kept warm. I am going to make sure that my child is educated. I will be putting my child in a safety seat. I will be installing safety latches on the cabinets, and childproofing the entire house. After going to all this trouble, why would I (why would anybody) not take effective measures to protect my family from the bad people that we *know* exist?

As far as children and gun safety, it would be irresponsible of me to tell you how to handle that subject. I am only a truck driver, and my child is not able to play with my gun yet, because he or she has not been born yet. I can tell you that a good source of information about firearm safety is the National Rifle Association. They would be more than happy to point you in the *right* direction (no pun intended). If you are afraid to associate yourself with such a *controversial* organization, contact your local Sheriff's department.

If you are still against the right to own a firearm, even after having read this chapter, I hope and pray that no one ever tries to undermine one of the freedoms that *you* care about.

Chapter 7
Crimes and Misdemeanors

When I decided to write this book, I didn't really have a plan of attack. I just decided to start writing and see what happens. The closest thing I had to a plan was the idea that I wanted to keep it simple. I didn't want to bog the process down with statistics. I have been trying to go one chapter at a time, keeping things very general. I have also been trying to relate each chapter to one topic at a time.

I thought it would be appropriate to move on from a chapter about gun control, right into a chapter about crime, and the liberal approach to it. At first, I was going to write separate chapters relating to morality, illegal drugs, the judicial system, and prison reform. Then it dawned on me that crime covers a lot of ground. For me to write a legitimate chapter on crime, I would have to cover all of these topics at the same time, plus a few others.

I am going to try to demonstrate how crime relates to liberalism. I am also going to offer some time tested, good old-fashioned common sense solutions.

Keep in mind that I am only a truck driver. I am not a lawyer, and I am not a social worker. Everything that you are about to read is based on opinion and personal experiences.

For the sake of argument, let's just create an imaginary person to use as an example. We will call him Joe. This morning at nine AM, Joe was convicted of murder and sentenced to death. It is at this point that you can tell if you, yourself, have liberal tendencies. If your first instinct was to assume that the death penalty is too much of a punishment, this is a clue that you may lean a little to the left. Relax; it's not the end of the world. Capital punishment is not the easiest thing to reconcile in anyone's mind. We *are* a civilized society made up of human beings. However, a non-liberal would wait to hear the particulars of Joe's case before they automatically rule out "the Chair".

Another way to tell if you are afflicted with liberalism is if your second instinct was to ask yourself if Joe was abused as a child. I intend to do my best to demonstrate just how irrelevant that is, too.

Not that I am trying to rip off Jeff Foxworthy, but if you need to know if Joe is black...you may be a redneck, or a liberal. Hopefully, you can find the irony in that.

So just what happened to Joe that put him in such a pickle? That was a trick question. A non-liberal would not assume that something happened to Joe, they would assume that *Joe* happened to someone. We also don't use phrases like, "in a pickle".

So, without further ado, let's hear the troubled story of a man named Joe. Joe was arrested for the murder of Mr. and Mrs. Smith. They were a typical couple who lived in a typical house, in a typical neighborhood. They were not rich, but they paid the bills, with enough left over to put their daughter through college.

One night, while they were sleeping, Mr. Smith heard a noise. He got out of bed, and grabbed his flashlight and a golf club. He thought a golf club would be a pretty good way to get the drop on a burglar. Besides, he was against the use of firearms, and had recently written his Congressman, asking him to kill a bill that would make it illegal to sue firearms manufacturers when someone gets shot.

Mr. Smith walked out into the hallway of *his* two-story colonial, where our new friend Joe met him. Before he could say a word, Joe hit Mr. Smith over the head with a piece of steel pipe. Mr. Smith fell to the floor with a dull thud. He was killed instantly.

Mrs. Smith was not as lucky. Before she was bludgeoned to death with the steel pipe, she was brutally raped. Thankfully, their daughter Jane was away at college, where she was a freshman majoring in finance.

Before he left the Smith residence, Joe pocketed all the money he could find, as well as Mrs. Smith's jewelry. He climbed out the back window with $53 in cash, and $38 worth of costume jewelry. As he made his way across the back yard, he was met by Mr. Wesson, Dan Wesson. The .357 Dan Wesson with walnut grips was being held by the Smith's next-door neighbor, Bob Jones.

Bob had lived next door to the Smiths for about three years. He had always tried to get to know the Smiths a little better, but they weren't very sociable. So, after three years of being next-door neighbors, Bob didn't even know the Smith's phone number. Unfortunately for Joe, Bob happened to be out in his back yard looking for fishing worms when he heard Mrs. Smith scream. He ran back inside and called the police. He didn't know what she was screaming about, but he thought somebody should check it out. Sadly, the nearest squad car was thirteen minutes away at this point.

Unsure of what was going on, Bob went to his bedroom and got his gun. He went back outside, where he saw a man climbing out of his neighbor's window. He didn't recognize him, but he knew it wasn't Mr. Smith. Bob walked around an adjoining rose bush, where he stood directly in the path of Joe the murderer. He drew his gun and pointed it at Joe's head. Needless to say, Joe froze in his tracks. After all, he had brought a pipe to a gunfight. Bob still didn't know for sure what was going on, so he told Joe to lie down on the ground while they waited for the police to show up. Joe had no choice.

When the police arrived, they took Joe into custody, along with the bloody pipe and the Smith's stolen property. The evidence was overwhelming. DNA on Mrs. Smith confirmed the rape, and the crime scene was self-explanatory.

So, what went wrong here? This is where liberalism usually starts to come into the picture. At this point, a liberal will usually start whining about Joe's childhood. Yes, what type of environment you grow up in does have a serious role in what type of person you turn out to be. It does "make or break" you. No one could ever argue against that.

The problem is, according to the *wisdom* of liberalism, a person's upbringing relieves them of responsibility. Joe's father *did* run out on him, and his mother, at age ten. His mother *did* drink a lot and she *did* slap him around from time to time. Even when his lawyer brought this up at Joe's trial, the jury never questioned the validity of his claims of childhood trauma.

Common sense dictates that studying what makes a man do evil things *does* have a place in the cause of justice. This place is well *after* guilt has been proven and sentences have been given out. To do it any other way would be putting the cart before the horse, but this is exactly what liberalism calls for.

Just for the sake of argument though, let's take a look at Joe's bumpy childhood. Joe was the son of teenage parents. Oddly enough, so were *their* parents. One night, years ago, the combination of hormones, beer, and poor parenting resulted in the birth of a little boy named Joe. At birth, he was the picture of health. Physically and mentally he had the raw materials for greatness. What he *could* have turned out to be is really not the point of this story though. In the real world, the only thing that matters is what you actually *do* turn out to be. Reality is the only consequence that the rest of the world has to deal with.

Where Joe's troubles started could be a topic of debate for years to come. It could have been the fact that Joe was never taught about respecting others. It could have been the fact that his parents were more interested in hanging out with their *friends* than teaching him how to spell. Maybe it was the fact that he was conceived too early, thanks to the fact that his grandparents never even tried to explain the concept of abstinence to *their* children. It may have been the fact that at the most confusing time in his life, Joe had no father figure to guide him through the forest of puberty and adolescence.

Morality is one of those things that few people give enough credit to. Worse than that, some people try to beat up on morality. These people would have others believe that morals are just vague guidelines. They would tell you that no one can say for certain what the real difference is between right and wrong. They like to tell you how there are always "grey areas" to consider. Those who do recognize "right and wrong" are considered to be arrogant, or self-righteous. People with this attitude sometimes go as far as referring to criminals as "free spirits," or even "heroes." These people can be easily spotted by their "Free Mumia" bumper stickers.

Heaven forbid if you have any religious upbringing, especially if you happen to be a Christian. The Ten Commandments are commonly treated as "right wing propaganda," but after thousands of years, their logic is hard to debate. Not that Christianity is the only port in the social storm, but Joe had been drifting out to the stormy sea for a long time. His parents had no moral compass at all. They were not Christian, Jew, Catholic, Buddhist, Hindu or even Scientologists.

From day one, Joe knew nothing of morality. He grew up learning by example, as we all do. The examples from which he learned were taught by the people he looked up to the most, his mother and father. At age three, he knew what smoking looked like. Joe learned early on how to treat women by the example his father had shown him before he left.

School was no source of guidance for Joe either. Discipline was not a priority of his school district. Of course, nowadays discipline is not the priority of *most* school districts. Thanks to new liberal policies, most public schools are afraid to discipline students who act up. They are afraid of damaging their "self esteem." Today, the popular way of dealing with rowdy children is to pump drugs into them. If your kid has trouble concentrating, you are told to send him to a doctor (who is recommended by the school). Not that I am an old geezer, but "in my day," if I wasn't paying attention, I was the first to be called on to answer the question. If I was staring out the window, the teacher closed the blinds. If I talked in class, I was made to stand in the corner. I even remember getting paddled! To try that today would result in a class-action lawsuit.

Joe grew up in a time when causing disruptions in class was considered "expressing yourself." He grew up in a time when teachers were under the thumb of teacher's unions. Anyone who has ever dealt with unions knows what that means. You are entitled to what the union says you are, regardless of whether you actually *deserve* it or not. So there is no motivation for a teacher to do his or her job any better than anyone else. It is the best kind of job security, but it breeds mediocrity. If a child is lucky, he or she will get that rare teacher who actually cares about teaching. Using the powerful force of unions to promote stupid policies has always been a favorite tactic of liberals.

Joe grew up in a time when schools frowned on stern discipline, claiming that it is the job of the parent to control the child. Never mind the fact that the parent is not actually in the classroom, but other people's children are. The irony is, these are the same people who have no trouble taking over the job of parenting when it comes to sex education, and handing out birth control.

When you couple the fact that children are being drugged instead of disciplined, with teacher's unions having so much control over the teachers, you really have to wonder just how chummy the unions and the pharmaceutical companies are.

As a child, none of this had ever entered Joe's mind. He was just a kid. His *parents*, on the other hand, had no excuse. If they had taken the time to go to a PTA meeting, or even read a newspaper, they might have been able to stop the inevitable chain of events that was about to start Joe on his journey to the electric chair.

(On a personal note, today my wife enters her third trimester of pregnancy with our first child. As I write this chapter, I realize that I am tampering with my own karma. Sometimes I wonder if I have the right to criticize the parenting of others when I have yet to change a diaper. I guess I will find out if I knew what I was talking about in about 18 years. I could be setting myself up for some serious embarrassment. That just means I will have to work a little harder when I try to raise my child.)

Enough about me, let's get back to Joe. Even if the liberal policies of his school were not going to ruin him, his attitude surely would. Joe was never a mean or violent kid, but he did have a temper. That is really not a big deal, because we all do. The problem was, he didn't know how to control it. The closest thing he had to a role model was whoever he was watching on TV. That's OK if you're watching C-Span or the History Channel, but Joe rarely watched anything but MTV and football. His role models became "gangsta rappers" and overpaid athletes.

At age thirteen, Joe's father was long gone, while his mother was spending most of her time at the local watering hole, trying to find a new sucker (boyfriend) to mooch off of for a few weeks. Joe spent most of his time at the mall or at his friend's houses.

One day after school, Joe made a decision that would set the tone for the rest of his life. He smoked his first cigarette.

You may be wondering how smoking a cigarette has anything to do with murdering two people in their own home. Realistically, one may have nothing to do with the other. But someone once said that a journey of a thousand miles begins with the first step. I believe that Joe's "first step" happened to be that first cigarette.

You see, Joe made the same mistake that many people make in their teenage years. He misplaced his priorities. Being "cool" was more important than being intelligent. Joe's formal education was nothing to brag about, but he was no moron. He knew that smoking was bad for his health, but having no respect for himself, he didn't really care. He just wanted to look cool. The irony is, very few people who are considered to be "cool" in high school, ever stay "cool" in their adult years. This same logic would lead him to the next natural step of alcohol abuse. From there, he moved onto smoking weed. After all, if it was OK for a President to smoke pot, it had to be OK for him. Even if Bill didn't inhale, a precedent was set.

After a few years, Joe basically became nothing more than a houseplant. He stayed inside all day, rarely left the front of his television, and did nothing but eat stale pizza and smoke weed all day. Then one day, one of his *friends* came over to watch Speed Racer and get stoned. He brought something new for his old buddy Joe to try. Cocaine.

Thanks to four years of beer and weed, Joe's decision-making processes were too far gone for him to give any rational thought to the road he was about to travel. He was hooked instantly.

From here on, Joe's life became a cliché. He was the lead character in every after-school special that you ever watched. He lived for his next high, and not much else. He moved on to crack, and heroin. That wouldn't be so bad, if he were filthy rich and could afford his next fix. But he was not the son of a rich man, so he had to find a new way to pay for his highs.

He started stealing from his grandparents, and then he moved onto robbing vending machines. After that, he started getting a little bolder. He began breaking into garages to steal tools and car parts. Two weeks after his eighteenth birthday, he decided to branch out into the exciting world of home invasion. This would be the last decision that he would ever make on his own.

Joe was still not a violent person by nature, but he had lost all ability to make rational decisions. His brain was fried. In fact, the only reason he needed the steel pipe with him that night was to be able to break into the house. He didn't intend to hurt anyone, he just needed some cash. The only reason he hit Mr. Smith was because he was scared. When Mrs. Smith started screaming, he knew he would have to kill her, too. Raping her was just a spur of the moment thing, driven by cocaine and adrenalin.

So here we are, finally getting to the point of this chapter. What is the best way to deal with Joe's situation? Actually, that is a trick question. It is not Joe's situation that needs dealt with; it is Joe himself.

According to the laws of the state he lives in, Joe will be sentenced to death. Is this fair? Is this reasonable? Who can say?

The fact is, two people were killed, and a young girl will never see her parents again. Whose fault is that? Is it the fault of the educational system that refused to discipline Joe as a young boy? Is it the fault of Joe's parents, who had a child long before they were able to do the job right? The answer to both of these questions is *Yes*. After a lifetime without guidance or education, Joe was a ticking time bomb.

Now that we have established how Joe turned into the man he is, why are we punishing Joe? After all, he was a victim of society. This is what liberalism would have you believe. The irony is, they are probably right. The problem is, Joe is the one who did the deed. *He* is the one who made the decision to enter another man's home on that particular night. *He* did that on his own. There were no teachers or alcoholic mothers there when *he* broke that window. Why he did it is incidental to the crime itself. Society may have created the man who would eventually murder two innocent people, but Joe himself was *solely* responsible for the death of Mr. And Mrs. Smith. Therefore, he, and he only, will have to take the punishment.

As for the questions of "fairness" and "reason," they are only parts of the capital punishment equation. There is also "deterrence." I have no idea what the statistics on deterrence are (nor do I care), but speaking for myself, I know that I will probably never risk murdering another human being, especially in a state that has the death penalty.

Fairness is something that will always be up for debate on the topic of capital punishment. But then again, fairness is debatable on a lot of topics. *Reason* is another favorite "grey area" of the left. Is it really reasonable to kill Joe for his crimes? After all, Joe only killed *two* people in cold blood. It's not like he was Adolph Hitler. Simple folks like myself have a hard time understanding that logic, especially as I watch the liberal media's current day outcry for the "reasonable" treatment of Saddam Hussein, another mass murderer. Liberals have been speaking out against the death penalty for him too. They did the same for Timothy McVeigh after he killed all of those people in Oklahoma City.

This brings me to the one word that trumps all others in the death penalty debate. It is a little used word, but in my uneducated opinion it is the word that most supports the idea of capital punishment. That word is *recidivism*.

Recidivism is defined by Webster's as; A tendency to slip back into a previous, esp. criminal, behavior pattern. The justice system keeps track of recidivism rates of all criminals. They use this information to come up with statistics, and to try to figure out what punishment works best for changing criminals' behavior after they are released back into society.

As of right now, the recidivism rate of people who were found guilty and sentenced to death is exactly zero. Until murderers find a way to come back to life, I expect the rate to stay the same for a long time.

Of course, we all know that it is impossible for anyone to break out of a prison, so I'm sure that life without parole would be just as effective. I must admit, I did feel a little sense of relief when one of Jeffery Dahmer's prison mates took him out of the gene pool. Admittedly, Jeff Dahmer was probably not a real threat to my family or me, but a recent criminal case hit a little more close to home. I am referring to the D.C. sniper case. Coincidently, as I am writing this chapter, John Mohammed and Lee Boyd Malvo's sentences were recently handed down.

This case was a little more personal to me because for those few weeks that Mohammed and Malvo were terrorizing the D.C. area, my coworkers and I were delivering groceries there. I remember the fear in my wife's voice when I told her where I was going on my deliveries. I remember her relief when I got home.

I do realize that given the population of the D.C. metro area, and the fact that I was only there for a few hours at a time, I was probably not going to catch a bullet. At the time though, that is not what goes through your mind, especially when you are passing the places where people are being killed, and knowing that the killers are still on the loose.

Thankfully, the killers were caught. Ironically, the man who originally called in the location of blue Chevy (that the snipers were in) happens to be a friend of mine. The rest area where the killers were caught happens to be only thirty miles from my home; I pass it all the time. This definitely added to the "relief" factor when they were caught.

When the sentence for John Allen Mohammed was handed down, there was little controversy, at least in the local northern Virginia area. He was sentenced to death. A fitting punishment for such an evil crime. Justice was served. After the sentence is carried out, no one will ever have to worry about being shot by John Allen Mohammed.

I'm Not Hitler!

Prior to Mohammed's sentencing, Lee Boyd Malvo was sentenced to life in prison. In case you have forgotten, Malvo was an ILLEGAL immigrant. Oh, I'm sorry, he was an "undocumented worker." I think I may have mentioned this earlier. This sentence was not as well received by the local population. You see, Malvo was not "technically" an adult when he was a partner in the killing of all those innocent people. He was old enough to operate a motor vehicle, but not receive justice.

Liberals would argue that justice *was* handed out in Malvo's case. I whole-heartedly disagree. I started to think about what the rest of Malvo's life would be like. That's when it occurred to me. The operative phrase here is... "Rest of his life." Lee Boyd Malvo will have *a* life. Not a *great* life, but a *life* nonetheless. This is much more than can be said for the people that he helped kill.

Under different circumstances, I might feel differently. If Malvo were eleven years old when he committed his crimes, I would probably be more lenient. If prisons were a little less comfortable, I would not care as much about murderers being put there for life. Unfortunately, here in the real world, these situations are just wishful thinking.

The victims of John's and Lee's "road trip of terror" will never be able to do the following; read a book, call a lawyer, write a letter, work out in a gym, watch cable TV, have friends, be popular, eat a meal, sing, talk, joke around, have visitors, brag, draw a picture, get a haircut or breath fresh air in the summer sun. As a prisoner in the modern day American penal system, Lee Boyd Malvo is guaranteed to be able to do all of these things for the rest of his life. To add insult to injury, his new life as an American prisoner is probably an improvement over his life in the slums of Jamaica. In my mind, justice has yet to be served.

Justice aside, can anyone say for certain that Malvo could never possibly escape from prison? If he does, should we assume that he would turn over a new leaf and become a model citizen on the outside?

Even if he never escapes, can anyone guarantee that Malvo will never be able to kill someone in prison, another prisoner, or maybe a guard?

Liberals seem to hold onto the idea of "rehabilitation" as if it were the "be all-end all" of justice served. In principal, I have no problem with attempting to rehabilitate *some* criminals. If someone has been found guilty of shoplifting, or possession of illegal drugs, they may have a shot at being rehabilitated. Furthermore, due to the nature of the crime, it is probably a good idea to at least attempt to show small-time criminals a better way to live. After all, it would be unreasonable to execute, or imprison someone for life, for such minor offenses. It stands to reason that eventually, a shoplifter will be back on the street. It may be worth the investment to give them a few other options while they are in the slammer.

The problem is, liberals tend to get a little carried away with ideas such as rehabilitation. They see it as something that should be applied to *all* criminals. This brings me to a few questions. What's the point? If someone has been put away for life, rehabilitation seems to be a waste of time. It strikes me as being "too little too late." How can you tell for sure when someone has been rehabilitated? Aren't there some people who just can't be rehabilitated? If you were in charge, would you be willing to roll the dice on whether or not a child molester has been rehabilitated before you send him back into the world? Why is so much emphasis put on rehabilitation, instead of incarceration?

You see, liberals tend to forget that incarceration is supposed to be a punishment, not an opportunity. This brings me to what I believe is the root of the problem. Years and years ago, someone invented the first jail. It was not designed to be comfortable; this was done on purpose. It was designed to be miserable and uninviting. It was designed this way so that if you ever had to be put in a jail, you would go the extra mile to make sure you would never have to go back.

Of course, back in the old days, the justice system itself was not always fair or accommodating to true justice. There was a lot of "mob rule" and DNA testing was not even an idea yet. Today, things are much different. As Americans, we are all considered "innocent until proven guilty." This is exactly how it should be. Unfortunately, when we rebuilt our court systems, we went a little overboard revamping the penal systems. We have gotten too far away from the idea of incarceration being "uninviting." Today, criminals no longer go the "extra mile" to not get put back in prison. From what I have seen, who can blame them?

Having never been to prison myself, I do not claim to be an authority on prisons or prison reform. My knowledge on this particular subject comes from what I have seen in television documentaries, and newspapers. So after all the dust has settled, if it turns out that I have no idea what a modern prison is like, blame the Discovery Channel. I am not dedicated enough to writing this book to have myself thrown in the pokey, just for the sake of research. I think you will find that I am not too far off in my estimation of modern prison life, despite never having been there myself.

For starters, what is a prison supposed to do? It seems reasonable to me that a prison is meant to be a place to store criminals. Prisons are supposed to be a place where people who have been found guilty of a crime are sent as a *punishment* for that crime. In addition to punishment, prisons are supposed to be a place designed to separate the *bad* people from the good.

There are certain responsibilities that prison officials have to those who are being kept there. They are responsible for keeping a prisoner healthy and safe. They are responsible for making sure that a prisoner has everything he or she may need to proceed with legal processes. Every prisoner has a right to legal council, as he should. After all, the system is not perfect, accidents happen, mistakes are made. The American justice system deals with this by giving a prisoner the right to appeal his or her case. In addition, prisoners are even allowed to write letters.

Liberals have decided that these things are not enough. Today, for some reason prisoners are entitled to cable TV, weight rooms, conjugal visits, and cherry pie. *I* didn't have cable TV until I was in my mid-twenties. I still don't have a weight room, and I rarely get a cherry pie. I do have conjugal visits pretty well covered though.

My point is, I don't think that this is what they had in mind when they invented jail. Don't get me wrong, we are a civilized society, and even criminals have some rights. I am not suggesting that prisons revert back to the days of abuse and neglect. I do think we need to make prison life a little less inviting though.

Keep in mind that we are talking about criminals here, not patients in a hospital, or students in a school. These people have committed some type of despicable act, and have lost their right to live in a free society. We are talking about robbery, rape, child molesting, murder and even terrorism. These are people who can no longer be trusted to live peacefully among the rest of us. They are no longer capable of living unsupervised.

There are some people who subscribe to the theory that if you keep an inmate happy, he will be more agreeable, thus less dangerous. If you keep a prisoner occupied with TV and weight rooms, he will be more likely to be manageable. Another part of this liberal equation is the idea that if you give an inmate something, you can take it away if he gets out of hand.

At first, these seem like pretty solid ideas. They almost sound like common sense. In fact, the principals behind these concepts are pretty good ways to raise children. If you catch your child doing something wrong, take his TV privileges away and he will have to work harder to get them back. As opposed to a spanking, which is over within a matter of minutes, and is easily forgotten.

As I look back on my childhood, I remember *some* of the spankings I got, but none of the reasons I received them. I do remember what I did to have my favorite things taken away. Usually it was something simple like forgetting to do the dishes, or picking on my brother. I would always have to behave and convince my parents that I had learned my lesson before they would allow me to watch TV again.

I believe that one reason this type of discipline works on children is because they don't know any other way to be. They are born, and then life is a series of trial and error. Error results in some type of punishment, then they grow into maturity. From then on, if the parents have applied themselves, the child is likely to become a civilized human being. Unfortunately for the cause of liberalism, these same theories do not apply to prison inmates.

A convict enters prison for something he or she did as an adult. No matter what type of upbringing the inmate had, the damage is already done. At this point in their life, it is not impossible for them to grow or mature, it's just not likely. Children, on the other hand, are automatically presumed to move up the maturity scale, unless neglected.

This does not mean that I think trying to teach a prisoner a "better way" is a lost cause. It just means that if you apply some common sense to the subject, you should not be surprised if a convict robs a liquor store two days after his release from prison. So this would make a normal person ask..."Why would you rob a liquor store two days after you get out of prison?" My question would be, "Why not?"

Let's say you just did ten years for armed robbery. You pulled a knife on some guy in a parking lot, and stole his wallet. That part was easy. After all, you knew he wouldn't be able to defend himself. You knew that it was illegal for him to carry a firearm, so all you needed was a steak knife from the local diner to gain a tactical advantage. Oh, I'm sorry, we covered that in the last chapter. Maybe now you are starting to see how liberalism tends to create these vicious little circles.

Anyhow, you get out of prison. In prison, you were a popular guy. You had friends, and you knew how to work the system. You were fed, and clothed, as well as having healthcare. You got into a routine of watching your favorite shows on cable and you even had laundry service. Now you are sent back into the real world. Your new life becomes a series of bills, responsibilities, and hassles. Now, if you even have laundry, you are forced to do it yourself. You don't even have a TV, let alone a cable connection.

Since patience and self-respect have never been your strong suit, you are easily frustrated. After a few weeks of being treated as an ex-con, and having few friends around you, your subconscious will probably start missing the predictability of prison life. After all, you are still living in a violent neighborhood whether you are in prison or not. At least in prison, you knew the guards would probably break things up, or your friends would have your back.

In your head, you start to do the math, and decide that you will get back into the crime game, and if you get caught, so what. You look at it as a "win-win" situation. As for the public at large, if they are lucky, you won't kill any of them in the process.

So, what is the solution to this? Liberals would tell you that the convict needed more rehabilitation and understanding. As for me, I would say that he needed "hard time." Not "extended time", "HARD time."

What ever happened to the "chain gang"? Where are the striped uniforms? Where are the crew cuts? Who says that the food needs to taste good? Who says that the food needs to taste at all? Why do inmates need to watch TV, in order to keep them under control? What ever happened to "the box"? Why are inmates allowed to smoke?

The "chain gang." The very words conjure up memories of a better time in our history. For me, they conjure memories of movies like "Cool Hand Luke", or "Brubaker." In the

movies, prison inmates are usually portrayed as the poor downtrodden victims of society. The guards are usually portrayed as the oppressing abusive tyrant. Call me crazy, but when I watched Paul Newman in "Cool Hand Luke," I never saw anything that I would consider *abusive*. The

characters in that movie didn't look they were having fun, but they were being fed and were

providing a valuable service to the community. Luke only got put in the "box" when he tried to escape. I even thought the scene when they made him dig and re-dig the hole looked like a good way to teach an unruly inmate a valuable lesson. It seemed cruel, but think of it from another perspective. After it was over, ol' Luke probably lost a few pounds, and slept like a baby. Digging holes is a great cardio workout. Unfortunately, liberals look at sweat as a sign of physical abuse. Never mind the fact that some people pay good money for a comparable workout.

"Brubaker" is a different story. Murdering and beating prisoners is not what I would consider a reasonable punishment. Before you say it, the old guy that was killed in the movie was not sentenced to death by a jury of his peers. He was sentenced to time in prison. Then when it was discovered that he knew too much about the corruption there, he was murdered. This was after he had spent more time in prison than he was sentenced to, of course. Robert Redford's character was hired to reform the prison. The changes he proposed were meant to end corruption and prisoner abuse. He ended up getting fired when he realized that the corruption went too far up the food chain.

Here in the real world, prisons seem to have been *over* reformed. We have gone from not abusing inmates, to not punishing them. So what do we do? If we are to pay any credence at all to *common sense,* we need to make some drastic changes in how we punish criminals today. Actually, we should have started yesterday. We need to strike a balance between the movie world and the real world. Here are a few suggestions from a simple truck driver from PA.

First, remove all television sets from every prison. Donate them to the public school system, or hospitals. This will save money as well as make time in the "big house" a little less comfortable. This of coarse will result in riots and protests, but that should not be problem. Why? You ask. The answer is simple...RUBBER BULLETS.

Over the years, we have developed some of the most advanced "non-lethal" weaponry known to man. What's the point of having it, if we don't use it? As soon as the riot starts, break out the tear gas, rubber bullets, stink bombs, and beanbag guns. Or, if you really want to get radical, let the riot go. Before you assume that I have lost my mind, hear me out.

If a prison was operated on the grounds of common sense instead of political correctness, a prison riot would not be as big of a deal. A prisoner should not be allowed to smoke, but he is. This gives him constant access to the fire starting devices used in riots to set the prison on fire. Solution; no smoking = no fires in a riot. This would also stop the concept of "prison currency." Cigarettes have been used as a substitute for money for years. No cigarettes = nothing to buy weapons or drugs with = less crime and safer inmates and guards. The phrase " I killed him for a pack of Luckys" would no longer exist. Consequently, you would be improvingthe health of the inmate, which is the exact opposite of cruel and unusual punishment. After all, keeping a prisoner healthy is one of the first responsibilities of a prison warden.

Another problem with prison riots is when the inmates start

throwing tables, beds and chairs. So I would naturally ask the question... "Why are these things not cemented into the floor?" How can you throw a chair, if you can't even pick it up? Where is it written that a chair needs to be mobile? If a prisoner decides to throw his mattress, let him. After the riot, pick it up and put it in storage for a few weeks. When the *next* riot erupts, the inmate might remember those few weeks of sleeping on springs, and opt to keep his mattress where it belongs. If not, so what? Take it away for a month; eventually he'll get the picture. If I throw *my* mattress out the window, should I expect someone to buy me a new one?

Probably the most dangerous part of a prison riot would have to be hand-held weapons. The odd thing about this is, anytime I have ever seen a documentary about illegal weapons in a prison, they are always made of things that a prisoner shouldn't have to begin with. Why are there hard plastic toothbrushes that can be made into shivs in prison? A softer plastic would be tougher to stab with. Other items that should be nowhere near a prisoner include; lighters, metal eating utensils, shop tools, razor blades, and glass of any kind.

This leaves "hand-t- hand" violence. To remedy this, I would refer back to RUBBER BULLETS, and TEAR GAS. These time-tested little gems are self-explanatory. When a liberal hears the words "tear gas" or "rubber bullets," they react the same as if you had said, "mustard gas" and "real bullets." Again, with no regard to the fact that we are talking about hardened criminals who would slash your throat if given the chance. It is assumed that inmates react the same as any other citizen if asked by the authorities to "stand down."

Another luxury item that should be considered for retirement is food. No, I'm not suggesting that we starve prison inmates. I am suggesting that food is something that is enjoyable. Sometimes, food is the best part of your day. I am not the one who coined the phrase, "comfort food." My point is, food is something that is capable of putting a smile on the face of a prison inmate. I believe that if you are smiling while you are in prison, someone has dropped the ball on your punishment.

At the same time, a prison is still responsible for the health of an inmate. They are required by law to make sure an inmate is fed a nutritious meal. The solution is to create some kind of cheap, nutritious, vitamin fortified, potato-based food. Something that has all the benefits of a five course meal, but no taste whatsoever. This would make life in prison much less enjoyable, and save millions of dollars at the same time. All you would need is a can opener and a scoop. An inmate could serve it, eliminating the need for a large serving staff.

Using desserts as a substitute for money would be a thing of the past. As with the banning of smoking, after the first few months an inmate's health would certainly improve. This would make the whole "cruel and unusual" concept hard to swallow (no pun intended).

The great thing about the concepts that I have just suggested is that they kill many birds with one stone. They improve the health and well being of the prisoner. They eliminate the need for making sentences longer. They keep the inmate from wanting to return to prison. They save tons of money. Last but not least, they take the fun and glamour out of prison life, making it more risky to get into the crime business. Consequently, all of the above would put a serious dent in the prison overcrowding problem.

Though I have a whole list of other ideas on this subject, this is not a book about prison reform. For the sake of trying to keep this book simple, I would like to end this chapter by looking at probably the biggest problem with our justice system; liberal judges.

Most of the counter-productive, criminal-accommodating concepts that we have addressed so far have come from the minds of liberal judges. Whether it is done out of fear of public opinion, or failure to recognize common sense, when a judge turns to liberalism for answers, we all lose.

The irony is, a criminal does not check to see if you are a liberal or conservative before he puts the knife in your ribs. So the next time the guy that robbed your mother gets off due to the ruling of a liberal judge, or you can't defend yourself due to the anti-gun rulings of a liberal judge, ask yourself these questions. Did I vote in the last election? Did the Senator I voted for help to keep these liberal ideas "in play" by blocking the nomination of a more conservative judge? What kind of justice does liberalism offer? Will the liberal brand of justice make my family and me safer in the long run, or even in the short run?

I have heard people try to defend liberal justice (oxymoron) by saying that Mother Theresa, the Pope, and the Dalai Lama were all liberals. This may or may not be true, but the last time I checked, none of them had a wife or kids.

Chapter 8
From Tea Party to Twinkie Tax

F rom the point of view of a regular guy like myself, liberalism always seems to be akin to shooting yourself in the foot on a daily basis. In previous chapters I have mentioned that liberalism is self-defeating. Sometimes I can almost see how a person would lean to the left on some of the more *scary* issues, and sometimes it takes a big set of cohones to be a conservative. But the one thing I would have assumed everyone could agree on is money. Apparently, I have been very naive in my thinking. In my opinion, nowhere is the concept of liberal self-defeat more evident than the topic of money. In particular, taxes.

For some odd reason, I have always been under the assumption that money was something that you *wanted* to possess. Maybe it's because they don't *give* things away at the mall. Don't get me wrong, there may be something to the old saying..."Money is the root of all evil." On the other hand, money is the only thing that pays my mortgage. So anytime someone tells me that I need to give up some of my money, I expect to have some sort of explanation, and I also expect to see some sort of return on the investment. I believe the root of all evil is not money, it's ignorance.

Terry Leasure

Money is a funny thing. Actually, it's not money that is so amusing, it's some people's concept of it. There are people out there who believe that anyone who has money, must be a selfish jerk. The irony of this is that these same people whine about not having money themselves. There are also people who would punch their grandma in the face for a buck, but I have to believe that these folks are in the minority.

Lately the news has been full of people who had a lot of money, but were not satisfied. So, they tried to take money that did not belong to them. Of course, I am talking about Enron, Tyco, and WorldCom as well as a few other big companies who have tried to "double dip," but got caught. These are classic examples of greed gone unchecked.

The sad thing is, instead of giving "the hairy eyeball" to only those who have committed the crime, liberals (including the media) seem to have taken the position that ALL company executives are evil. To hear the left speak, you would think that anyone who has become successful is a low-down snake-in-the-grass who fires people and steals pensions for kicks. Even in the movies it's always the "rich guy" who turns out to be the villain. Somehow, in the most prosperous nation in the world, having money has become a sin. Thankfully, being a truck driver allows me to live "sin free."

I see a lot of irony in these wacky liberal theories. The same people who scream about the lack of employment opportunities have nothing good to say about the people who own businesses. Who do they think provides jobs...homeless people? I'll have more to say about the "homeless" later. For right now, I'll try to stay on topic. Besides, I'm already a little "all over the map" with this subject; it's a big one that covers a lot of ground.

Apparently, liberals believe that a job is something that is created from thin air. They also seem to believe that every man, woman, and child on the planet is entitled to one. If you have money, and are not providing a job for someone, you are wrong. It does not matter if you actually *need* to hire someone or not. It also does not matter what type of "work ethic" a person has, he should just be issued a job regardless. The irony here is the fact that liberals always like to talk about what's "fair." Hopefully, in this chapter I will be able to demonstrate how liberalism has a negative effect on all of our wallets.

I guess the best place to start is on the level of the "common man." After all, that is the level on which I currently reside. I think that would make me an authority on the subject. Most of my "common man" associates (friends) don't pay much attention to politics or who's in charge of the national purse strings. They do, however, pay attention to their paychecks. I am no exception. And we all have our own opinions about how best to spend *our* money. The problem is, there is a good chunk of *our* money that we have no control over. This is the part of our paychecks that go to good old "Uncle Sam". This is known as "taxes."

Taxes are a necessary evil. Anyone who says otherwise is just not being realistic. We do need roads, bridges, police, firemen, and a strong military. These things do not pay for themselves. Can you imagine what our military would be using to free the Iraqis if we had to rely on the generosity of the masses? Saddam would still be slaughtering people well into his golden years. The list of things that are needed for a free, democratic nation to function is pretty long. Everything from the stop sign on your corner, to the aircraft carrier that protects your freedoms, costs money. Considering that we all benefit from the common stop sign as well as the aircraft carrier, it is our responsibility to pay for a small portion of each of them. This is where taxes come in.

Taxes are our way of paying for the services that our government provides. Here is a tiny example. A small portion of your paycheck this week may have gone to replace the broken headlight on the truck that plows the main road that you drive on when you go to work. Last week, a portion of it went to pay for a can of beans that will be eaten by soldiers who are defending our country. In principal, this is a pretty good system. We have been using it for a long time, and I doubt that it will be changing anytime soon.

Common sense demands that we *all* accept the burden of taxation. The problem is that *some* have a bigger burden than others. Liberals will tell you the same thing. Unfortunately, they seem to be a little fuzzy on who is carrying the bigger load.

Currently, I am watching two guys battling for the office of the President of the Untied States. They both have very different views on the subject of taxes.

One guy wants to raise taxes, the other wants to lower them. After my earlier explanation of taxes, you might think that if taxes were increased, the government would have more money to use for snowplows and aircraft carriers. At first, this seems reasonable. Unfortunately, that is not how it works. Have you ever heard the phrase; "You can't get blood from a stone"? Keep that in mind as I try to sort this all out for you.

People pay taxes. All people spend money differently, but there are always a few constants...food, clothing, and shelter for example. No matter who you are, you need these three things. When you get your paycheck, Uncle Sam takes a good chunk of it, and *then* you get the rest. You take what's left, and provide food, clothing and shelter for yourself and your family. After that, you take care of the secondary necessities; medicine, telephone, transportation, and cable TV. Anything left after that is gravy. From this point on, remember; more taxes for Uncle Sam = less gravy for you.

Here is where you need to pay attention. Liberals always "boo-hoo" about how "the poor" are never given a tax break, and the "rich" are given some sort of free ride. This has never made much sense to me. I can never get past this question, "Who pays more taxes, Joe the mechanic, or Donald Trump?" I have no idea how much "The Don" pays in taxes every year, but I'm willing to bet that he pays a few dollars more than the "poor" guy. So when it comes time to hand out a tax break, who should get it? Liberals would submit that the mechanic should get the tax break, while Donald should have his taxes increased. The truth is, *both* should get the break.

The logic is pretty simple. If Joe the mechanic has a few more dollars in his pocket, he will probably spend them on something. Let's say, an air compressor, for example. Like most Americans, Joe received a tax break last year. He got enough back to finally by the new air compressor that he has needed for a long time. His old one had been leaking, costing him more in lost productivity and electricity. Rather than put his tax break under his pillow, he spent it on the compressor. That money went to the Acme Tool Company in Anytown USA.

Coincidentally, other tradesmen across the country also received tax breaks, allowing them to purchase tools from Acme, too. Suddenly, orders were coming in for air compressors, pneumatic drills, hammers, and all sorts of tools. The Acme sales staff was ecstatic. They increased their commissions, and added them to *their* tax breaks, allowing them to buy things that *they* had been putting off. One bought a car, another a house. The house purchased by the salesman allowed a building contractor to hire back three men that had to be laid off earlier that year. He too needed to buy some tools to complete the house, purchased by the salesman, who sold the air compressor to the mechanic, who received a tax break. Those three men who had been laid off were back to work, earning money to purchase toys for their kids, and hair spray for their wives.

As with the air compressor, the other tools, the toys, the hair spray, and the house (including furnishings), the car purchased by the other salesman had to be manufactured. Who manufactures these things? Other companies. These other companies also benefit from the chain reaction of tax relief, continuing the cycle. People are hired back to jobs in order to meet the demands of other people who had been hired back to other jobs who all have received tax breaks, creating the demand for products, made by companies who supply the demand.

As with new furniture for the one salesman's house, you can't buy a new car without buying fuzzy dice to go with it. Someone needs to make the fuzzy dice. The cycle continues. New toys means more skinned knees. Someone needs to make the bandages and iodine. The cycle continues. New tools means a new tool shed. The cycle continues. More hair spray means happy wives. A happy wife means an extra brownie in your lunch box. Someone needs to make the instant brownie mix. The cycle continues.

If you have been paying attention, you see just how simple growing an economy can be. Back in the day, the press dubbed this economic theory "trickle down economics." Liberal economists also commonly referred to it as "Reaganomics," and always with a crooked smile. Having never taken an actual economics course, I am left with only my basic understanding of how money flows throughout our society. This means that I have a very simplistic way of looking at our economy. If I am not mistaken, the actual term for "Reaganomics" is "supply side" economics. Whatever you call it, it makes sense to me. Unfortunately, liberals tend to ridicule "supply side" economics as being too simplistic. My question has always been, "Why does economics need to be complex?" This brings me to another question. What's wrong with simple?

For those of you diehard liberals who would love nothing less than to be completely dependent on government, allow me to point out some more irony. Liberals like government programs. Actually they *love* them. To be exact, they are hopelessly addicted to them. If you can name a problem, liberals would love to see a government program to deal with it. Never mind the cost effectiveness, logic, or just plain silliness of the problem, Uncle Sam is expected to take care of it for you. I bring this up because these programs cost money. This money comes from, you guessed it...taxes. So anytime a liberal hears the words "tax" or "cut" in the same sentence, you can literally see the panic in their eyes. They see a tax cut as a reduction in the money that is used to pay for their beloved government programs. Here is where the irony of liberal economic theory is pushed kicking and screaming into the spotlight.

I am going to explain this as condescendingly as possible. Not because I assume that you are stupid, but because breaking something down into its simplest form is the best way to explain it to anyone. I actually prefer people to "draw me a picture."

Tax cuts actually make *more* money for the government than tax increases. End of story. It's just that simple.

That's right. More money for government programs is a direct result of cutting taxes. If you are a liberal, you are probably under the assumption that I have been spending too much time indoors. Please give me a chance to explain. I will demonstrate this to you, the same way it was demonstrated to me. To do this, you will need six coffee cups and eighteen pennies.

I'm Not Hitler!

Put the six coffee cups on the table in front of you. In each cup place three pennies. The six coffee cups represent a product, let's say cars. The pennies represent the amount of taxes attached to the price of each car. Pick up one cup, and set it aside. This cup represents a car that was purchased by a consumer. This one cup also represents the weekly average of cars sold at the *current* tax rate. This one car purchase netted the federal government exactly three pennies. Due to the current tax rate, no more cars will be sold this week. After all, the consumer is only going to pay so much for a car. Now, let's lower the tax rate in the other coffee cups. Take one penny from each cup. Now the cars are more affordable, as a result of this, more cars are sold. Let's say that only one more car is sold this week than last, a grand total of two cars. This week, the government has received four cents in revenue, as opposed to the three cents last week. That extra cent is probably going to be headed for some idiotic entitlement, but it is profit nonetheless.

To compound the "car/coffee cup" theory, you can go ahead and figure an extra set of tires (which are taxed), an extra air filter (which is taxed), an extra set of spark plugs (which are taxed), tags, plates, fuzzy dice, and so on. All of these things need to be manufactured, which brings us right back to the earlier example of the chain reaction of an economy not held down by excessive taxation (the air compressor theory). In short, the government makes less money per coffee cup, but more coffee cups are sold = more tax money for...well, whatever.

My belief in the concept of limited taxation does not come from some blind loyalty to a particular political party (I'm an independent), or even a deep hatred for another. It comes from the things I see in my every day life. It also comes from my old friend; common sense. The long and the short of it is, I call them as I see them. Though you may not accept this as proof, please allow me to submit a personal analogy to show you why I am all for cutting taxes.

Bear in mind that I have an annual income in the lower five-figure range. Also remember that I have a mortgage, and a baby on the way (as of this writing, six weeks to go). Anyway, two years ago I received a check from the federal government for a little over three hundred dollars. After the attacks of September 11th, our national economy took a major dive. These checks were sent out to help boost the economy that had already been floundering from recession. I had heard this check was coming, but being a die-hard pessimist, I was not camping out beside my mailbox. Lo and behold though, it actually showed up.

Rather than bury this money in the back yard, I did a wacky thing with it. I spent it! I didn't put it all on "red" at the roulette table. I didn't give it to gypsies. I didn't donate it to Michael Jackson's defense fund. I purchased something with it. To be exact, I bought bricks to build a retaining wall in my back yard, and I used what was left over to have my chimney

inspected and cleaned. Both of these helped to raise the value of my home, which will benefit my family in the long run. Not to mention the fact that my back yard and chimney are a little bit safer now.

I have been trying very hard to not let this book turn into just another Republican

vs. Democrat propaganda piece. There seems to be no shortage of those. I do need to point out a little bit of irony though. It is no secret that liberals tend to vote overwhelmingly Democratic, (Green party notwithstanding). It is also no secret that Democrats have always hailed President John F. Kennedy as the "be all, end all" leader of our nation. Even with my conservative leanings, I too have always thought he was a great leader. He was definitely not perfect (Bay of pigs, Vietnam, Marilyn Monroe, etc.), but he was a good guy nonetheless.

The irony lies in the fact that J.F.K. was on the "right" side of the issue of tax cuts. He knew that putting more money in the hands of the people was the best way to fuel a national economy. Liberals never seem to bring this up. Either they believe that he was not so bright after all, or they know he was right but refuse to admit it.

An excerpt from John F. Kennedy's Speech to the Economic Club of NY

"The final and best means of strengthening demand among consumers and business is to reduce the burden on private income and the deterrence to private initiative which are imposed by our present tax system: And this administration pledged itself last summer to an across-the-board top to bottom cut in personal and corporate income taxes to be enacted and become effective in 1963. I'm not talking about a quickie or a temporary tax cut, which would be more appropriate if a recession were imminent; nor am I talking about giving the economy a mere shot in the arm to ease some temporary complaint. I am talking about the accumulated evidence of the last five years that our present tax system, developed as it was in good part during World War Two to restrain growth, exerts too heavy a drag on growth in peace time: That it siphons out of the private economy too large a share of personal and business purchasing power: That it reduces the financial incentives for personal effort, investment, and risk-taking".

John Fitzgerald Kennedy

Over forty years after his speech to the Economic club of New York, liberals still rail against cutting taxes, but tax cuts still boost the economy. Recently, President Bush applied the Kennedy doctrine by cutting taxes to boost the economy. You would have thought the world was coming to an end by the way some on the left were talking. The "go to" complaint was that these tax cuts were only going to the rich.

So, for the sake of argument, let's say that was actually the case. Let's imagine for a moment that George Bush cut only the taxes that were paid by "rich" folks. What's so wrong about that? Some would say that it isn't "fair." I would argue that "fairness" has nothing to do with it; it's irrelevant. You see, as the son of two small business owners, I learned early on that taxes are a part of "overhead." "Overhead" is just the cost of doing business. If you have a lot of overhead, your profit is smaller. If you have little overhead, your profit is bigger. Keep that in mind for a bit, as I try to hash this out for you.

To a businessperson, paying taxes is no different than having to buy a tool, or heat the office. It's just part of the "overhead." Business people don't like to pay taxes, but they do. They accept it as part of the process. It's just another bill. So when that bill comes, what happens? Do they exempt it from the "overhead"? No. They pay it. So where does the money come from to pay that tax bill? You guessed it...the consumer. It's added onto the cost of whatever they are selling or producing.

So, the irony here is that every liberal who wants "the rich" to pay more taxes, will be shooting him/herself in the foot when it comes time to go to the check-out counter. That liberal is paying the taxes of "the rich" and they don't even know it. The liberal solution to this is to make this practice illegal. OK, let's say that it is now illegal to recoup the tax burden by raising the price of the service, or product you provide. Now staying in business has become too costly. Most of your profit is going to the government, so why bother. The doors are locked, and another business is closed, or relocated. California is experiencing the aftermath of excessive taxation. They actually recalled their Governor because of their failing economy. They made it unprofitable for businesses to stay in their state due to over regulation, and excessive taxation. The businesses that couldn't keep up simply moved to other states. Arnold will need more than big pecs to lure them back.

I have heard people say that "the rich" should pay more taxes simply because they can afford to pay more. OK, so let me get this straight. If you have a cake, and I only have a cookie, you should be forced to give me a portion of *your* cake? On top of that, the fact that I was *given* the cookie, and you baked the cake yourself should have nothing to do with it? I guess the fact that you baked the cake for your children has nothing to do with it either. What is the name of that system of government that makes all of your personal decisions for you? Oh yeah...communism.

Income redistribution is one of those things that look good on paper, but here in the real world, it just doesn't make any sense. Actually, it don't even look that good on paper.

Liberals commonly cry about the plight of the underprivileged, or "the poor." Ironically, it's a rare occasion when they actually do anything about it. There are those who operate homeless shelters, and make donations to the Salvation Army, but that's not who I'm referring to. I'm talking about the die-hard liberal. The bullhorn toting, protest participating, S.U.V. hating liberal.

At first, these folk's hearts seem to be in the right place. They see a poor person, and they feel bad about it. They want to help. This is where things start to go down hill. Rather than actually help this person by buying them some groceries, or paying a month's rent, they look at someone else...you and me. They start by making assumptions about how this person got into such a predicament in the first place. They never question the poor person's attitude or aptitude. They never question his or her work ethics or temperament. It always seems to be the fault of the "rich" guy who laid him or her off, or the wealthy businessman who refused to hire him or her. To blame the rich always seems to be the "default" tactic of liberals.

So, to remedy the situation of the "poor" guy, they turn to you and me. They lobby the government to help out by handing things out. Welfare, shelters, unemployment, etc. are among the most common handouts. Of course, these things cost money. That money comes from taxes. You and I pay those taxes, and I'm not rich. Unfortunately, these handouts are still not enough to satisfy a true liberal. Some of these people actually want to create something called a "living wage." This is where you get paid just for waking up in the morning! Your reaction to that is a good test of your liberal or conservative leanings. If you are a liberal, you probably think getting paid just for existing is a great idea that would end poverty. If you are a conservative (like me), you know that this is the basic premise of a communist society and has never worked at any time in the history of man. Don't take my word for it, though. Ask any immigrant from the former Soviet Union over the age of forty. Ask any immigrant from China (any age).

A living wage will keep you alive, but nothing more. It would rob you of any ambition you may have had, as well as the will to succeed. After all, if you don't have to work, why would you? As a nation, we are already fatter and lazier than ever. Can you imagine what would happen to us if we were just given a check for no particular reason? As long as we had a TV and a pizza, we would just sit around and expand. As a culture, we would stop trying to excel at anything. We would stop inventing and creating the things that have made us the leader in modern advances. We would do just enough to get by, just like the Russian people used to do. Just as one example of this, have you ever driven a Yugo? There is a reason that Cadillacs, Porches, and Ferraris are made in free countries. That reason is AMBITION!

With a living wage, what would motivate you to go the extra mile? With no threat of starvation or poverty, why bother trying to succeed? A Yugo isn't a great car, but as long as it gets you to the bread line, it's good enough. For the Soviets, it was vodka, for us it would probably be porn or Playstation. As long as we have something to keep us occupied, we would never ask any questions.

At this point, you may think I am getting way off topic. I'm really not. The "living wage" concept is just one of many that is being tossed around as a way to combat poverty. Combating poverty is just one of many problems that our government is asked to deal with every day. For the government to fix this or any other problem, they require money. This brings us back to taxes.

Having a discussion on taxes pretty much demands that the excesses in government spending of any type be brought up, too. A "living wage" would be the ultimate example of excessive government spending. Unfortunately, there are a lot of people who would support such a thing, especially in today's culture of entitlement. The "slacker' crowd dreams of the day when having a job is no longer necessary.

As an example of just how self-defeating a "living wage" would be, just look at our minimum wage. Stick with me on this one. Currently, in America, we have what is known as a minimum wage. This is the least amount that someone is allowed to pay an employee for a particular job. The government mandates this. The exact figure and how they come up with it is not relevant to this discussion. Well, maybe it's a little relevant, but only in one sense. In my lifetime, I have seen the minimum wage raised more than once. I don't recall it ever being lowered. This only makes sense because who wants to *lose* money? This begs the questions; where do you draw the line? If the minimum wage is $7.00 an hour, why not make it $7.50? In fact, why not make it $10.00? Would that be *fair* enough? The problem is, a wage of any kind is not pulled from thin air. Nor does it grow on a magical tree in the back yard of some mystical elf.

Wages are paid by the employer as part of their "overhead." An employer has a need that must be filled by an employee. The amount of money that the employer pays out to the employee is based on the skill and productivity of that employee. At least, that's how it is supposed to be. The minimum wage demands that an employer have a limit as to how little he/she pays someone, regardless of his or her skill level.

Let's say you own a small company. You happen to know a man who has a learning disability and as a result, he has a very low level of skills that you could actually use at your company. You know he is reliable and you would like to hire him to sweep the floors and empty the trash in your offices. This is typically a $4.75 an hour job, but the minimum wage you are allowed to pay is $7.50. You can choose to overpay him for a medial job, or just not hire him. In order for you to be able to pay your taxes, you are forced to make sacrifices. You don't hire him, and opt to empty the trash yourself, or delegate it to other employees.

The harsh truth of the matter is, some people's skill level (for whatever reason), is not worth $7.50 an hour, let alone $10.00. As a matter of fact, some people's skills aren't worth a nickel. Somehow though, the government says that they are. I have worked with some of these people. I know guys who I wouldn't trust to sit the right way on a toilet seat, but they still make the government mandated minimum wage. It's a similar principal to the spoiled rich kid that we all knew in high school, always getting something for nothing. Beyond that, some jobs just aren't worth the rate of typical minimum wage.

I have also heard people say how great it is that the minimum wage eliminates competition from people willing to do jobs for less money. The irony there is, these are usually the same people who think ILLEGAL immigrants should get a free pass for doing jobs for less money. Of course the answer to this little conflict of interest is to give ILLEGAL immigrants a minimum wage too.

Taxing the rich is always a favorite "go to" of the typical liberal. They usually justify this by asserting that a rich guy would just buy another yacht or country club membership if he were given a break on his/her taxes. That is probably even true, but I don't understand why this is a bad thing. You see, yachts are a "durable good", and country clubs are a "service." Until yachts, speedboats, and sports cars magically appear by rubbing a lamp, someone will have to manufacture them. The same goes for country clubs and the services they provide. A liberal looks at a yacht or a Leer jet and sees personal excess, or gluttony. As a "blue collar" conservative, when I look at those things, I see manufacturing jobs.

So, let's say you were filthy rich. You could buy and sell Trump ten times over. One day you wake up and decide to buy a new 150-foot yacht. Your old buddy from college (who happens to be a liberal) talks you into giving the money to the less fortunate instead. You donate the yacht money to homeless shelters all over the city. Thinking that you have done the right thing, you feel a sense of personal satisfaction for doing such a good deed.

What you don't see is the fallout on the other side of town. The yacht manufacturer that was counting on your purchase was forced to lay off five workers. The marina where you would have docked and maintained your boat also lost money. The captain you were going to hire to pilot your ship had to look elsewhere for work. All of these people have families, and financial responsibilities. Lots of people were counting on the sale of that yacht, but lost jobs and revenue instead, thanks to the instant gratification of liberal "feel-goodism."

"But look at all the homeless people who were helped," you say. OK, how were they helped? Did they get jobs? Certainly not at a yacht factory. Did the drug addicted among the homeless finally put down the crack pipe? Did anyone go back to school? No. A new homeless shelter *did* get built, but the homeless stayed homeless.

Basically, after the extra funding trickled down to the individual, each homeless person got a new blanket, and a bigger helping of baked beans for a few weeks.

I am not saying that helping the underprivileged is a waste of time, far from it. I am just saying that throwing money at a problem is not always the best way to fix it.

This is the whole problem with our system of government finance. Whenever there is a problem, we assume that throwing money at it will take care of everything. Then, when there is not enough money to take care of every little sniffle that the population has, we give the government the ability to *take* it from those who happen to have some. The battle cry of "TAX THE RICH!" is shouted from every rooftop. We have a very "Robin Hood" way of dealing with problems in this country. Maybe that's part of the problem. As young children, we were taught that Robin Hood was a hero, someone to look up to. Whenever your job description has anything to do with *stealing*, that is a clue...you're a thief.

Should the "rich" be taxed? Of course, just no more or no less than anyone else. They certainly should not be looked at as the safety net for our government's financial problems. As I watch the current race for the presidency, I see that there is a certain political party who is running on a platform of doing just that. I won't say who they are, but the name of their party starts with the letter "D", and ends with "emocrats."

I don't mind paying taxes, until I start to think of just how many taxes I pay. Right out of the gate, before I even get my paycheck, taxes are taken. Notice I didn't say, "Taxes are paid." They are <u>taken</u>. Without even so much as a thank you. Chris Rock said it best (I'm paraphrasing), "We don't *pay* taxes, they *take* taxes. That's not a payment, that's a *jack*!" For those of you who are not up to date on hip-hop lingo, "*jack*" is slang for steal or rob. After I actually get my paycheck in my hands, I look at it to see just how bad I got *jacked*. Then I get in my vehicle - on which I pay taxes - and head for the bank. On the way I stop for gas - for which I pay tax - and fill my tank. As I go to the counter, I pick up a Pepsi - for which I pay tax - and proceed to pay my bill. Then I go to the bank and deposit my paycheck.

I go back to my house - for which I pay taxes - and sit on my couch. You guessed it; I paid taxes when I bought the couch too. The beer I decide to drink also required a little gratuity to Uncle Sam. After that, my wife walks into the room. Believe it or not, even she came with a tax. You see, you have to pay taxes to get married. That's called a "marriage penalty," as if getting married should be regarded as some sort of violation for going out of bounds.

Even the ground that my house sits on is taxed. This has always puzzled me a bit though. I pay property taxes every year, and usually a little *more* every year. The funny thing is, my land never grows an inch. When I buy a wrench at the hardware store, I pay the sales tax and that's it. No matter how long I own that wrench, I only pay taxes on it once. For some reason though, I pay taxes every year on my land.

They say that the only two things you can count on in life are death and taxes. The irony there is, you even get taxed when you die. Yes, there is actually something called a "death tax" ("death penalty" was already taken). As if death isn't enough of a penalty already. That's right, even after you pay taxes on your burial plot, casket, and funeral services, Uncle Sam puts his hand in your pocket expecting your family to pay taxes on anything you have left after you die.

As a big fan of stand-up comedy, I like to watch HBO specials from some of my favorite comics. Last night, I was watching the latest televised special from one of them. Part of his act was a routine about how President Bush's tax cuts were not going to work. He asserted that the Bush administration was to blame for a multi-trillion dollar budget deficit. He failed to mention the fact that Sept 11th itself dealt a major blow to our economy. He also failed to mention the effect that corporate scandals, a war on terror, and a recession had on our economy.

He scoffed at the fact that parents were awarded approximately $400 in tax relief. He joked as to how this was a paltry sum of money to most people. This may even be true, but it beats the NOTHING sum that they got the year before. Apparently, Lewis Black believes that every one of these parents had put their $400 in a jar, and buried it in the back yard. They didn't. Instead, they bought stuff...lots of stuff. Judging by my trip to Wal-Mart this morning, they're still buying stuff today.

I don't know exactly how many people actually got this $400, but for the sake of argument, let's say five million people received this particular tax credit. According to my elementary teacher Mrs. Kendall, that's 2 billion dollars. BILLION, not million. All going back into the pot. That's just one tax cut, one time. Let's not forget, taxes were collected on nearly everything purchased with this money. So here we end up right back to the "air compressor" theory I mentioned earlier. The irony to this is...it was *our* money to begin with.

Lewis' brilliant solution to the deficit problem was one I have typically been hearing from liberals for some time now. He proposed a massive public works project. He called it "the big f#%*ing thing" project. He said that the government should design a "big f#%*ing thing", and pay the people to build it. He theorized that this would create jobs and wipe out the national debt. At first that sounds reasonable, and the way he worded and presented it, it *was* hilarious. He forgot one important thing though; he said that the government would PAY people to build it. Pay them what? Money. Money from where? Exactly...you and me. Then what happens when the "big f#%*ing thing is finished? Will there be enough "big f#%*ing things to keep the economy afloat forever?

Granted, Lewis Black is only a comedian. It is his job to make us laugh, and he does that very well. The sad thing is, the "big f#%*ing thing" concept has been a mainstay of liberalism for years. The Soviet Union was built on this type of economy...I sure do miss those guys. More irony to Lewis' routine; claiming that Bush's tax cuts were stupid while in a national deficit, but at the same time claiming that they were too small.

Lewis recorded this particular concert in the winter of 2004. At the time of this entry in my book, it is early summer 2004. Currently, all economic numbers for our country have revealed that our economy is recovering even better than we could have hoped for. Housing starts are way up, unemployment is down, Wall Street is up, and the gross domestic product is *way* up.

Terry Leasure

It was not my intention to single out Mr. Black when I started this book. I only mentioned him because he happened to be the only comic I have heard lately who included taxation in his routine. Coincidently, the chapter I am writing today is about taxation. Lewis suffers from a very common affliction among today's comics - *easy laughitis*. Like many other pop culture icons today, he goes for the big laughs via the simplest possible route. Their jokes are based on impeccable timing, not factual accuracy. Another *easy laugh* is the personal insult. It's easier to bust on Bush for still not being able to pronounce *nuclear* right, than it is to rip on his economic policies. Don't get me wrong, these tactics make me laugh too, but they still lack imagination and require little skill. To be fair to Lewis, in his act, he did say he flunked an economics course.

OK, enough about liberal comedians, let's get back to one of the more important things in life, like money. I like money, I happen to think that money is a good thing. After all, without it, I couldn't eat. Well, I could...but not without upsetting animal rights activists. Liberals seem very conflicted when it comes to money. To be a modern day liberal, you are supposed to support raising taxes on the rich, but you are also supposed to be against unemployment. As if jobs grew on trees, and not from businesses belonging to "the rich." You are also supposed to be for helping the poor, as long as it's not *your* money that does it. A true liberal will always want to throw other people's money at every problem that comes down the pike, but if a "rich" guy spends any of *his* money to solve his own problems, he is wrong.

Liberals will also assume that every problem that comes down the pike is the result of a lack of money. Liberals also seem to believe that the purpose of businesses is to employ people. This is not the case. I have never met anyone who started a business so that they could hire people. Businesses are started for the sole purpose of making money. People are hired only if it is necessary to increase the profit margin, not for the sake of employing them. If your business is started for any other reason than making money, it will probably not make much of a profit. Ironically, if that happens you probably won't be able to hire anyone.

I'm Not Hitler!

As we are currently getting closer to the Presidential election of 2004, the economy is a popular topic, as it always has been in an election year. As the economic numbers keep looking better, the liberal wing of the Democratic Party keeps harping on the fact that there is a big budget deficit facing our government right now.

I say, "So what!" Right now, our national debt is pretty big. Don't ask me how big, because I don't care. Let me tell you why. As the son of two business owners, I learned a few things about running a business as I was growing up. The first thing I learned was that sometimes, you have to spend money to make money. The second thing I learned was, you get what you pay for. These are both simple concepts, but important nonetheless.

You see, America is basically just one big business. Just as a successful garage may require the purchase of a new floor jack to remain competitive, America may need to buy a new aircraft carrier from time to time.

To use a more personal analogy, let me tell you about a recent conversation I had with my mother. We were talking about how hard my stepfather works every day (he is also a business owner). I asserted that he would have more time to spend relaxing or running one of his businesses, if he would buy better equipment. I told her that I knew how he spent so much time and energy fixing his junky old trucks and tractors. And I know from experience just how stressful that can be. Coincidently, as we were talking, we were looking out the window at a construction project that was being built (thanks to an economy made stronger by cutting taxes) across the street from her shop. We watched as the new, still shiny, heavy equipment moved back and forth, shaping and contouring the earth.

I told her that her husband could use some equipment like that. She agreed, but then went on to explain how my stepfather was taught to save money and not spend it. But as we watched the equipment gouge into the ground without missing a beat, we were both picturing the same thing in our minds...my stepfather out there, trying to patch together one of those machines with duct tape and bailing twine.

I am not naive enough to believe that my stepfather has so much cash lying around that he could just pick up one of many piles and go buy a new excavator. Like most of us, he might have to take out a loan. I take out loans to buy things all the time, we all do. I have taken out loans for every thing from motorcycles, to the house I currently live in. As for my house...though it is a good investment, I will be paying for it for the next 28 years. In short, I have a *budget deficit*. Strangely enough though, no one nags *me* about the fact that I am in debt. That's because my wife is smart enough to know that you have to spend money to make money. So I wonder why people are griping about our nation's *budget deficit*?

Running a nation is slightly more involved than operating a farm or buying a house, but the economic principles are still the same. Sometimes a country may need to buy things, even if it doesn't have the cash lying around at the time. Especially when unexpected expenses happen to pop up.

Let's say for instance, your country's economy goes into the crapper due to over inflated market numbers from the "dot com" industry or corporate scandals that were not addressed soon enough, both resulting in a national recession. Maybe a terrorist threat is allowed to go on for eight years without serious attention, resulting in a terrorist attack which cripples the entire air travel industry as well as shaking consumer confidence for months on end. Perhaps an evil dictator who has been allowed to go on murdering his own people, all the while defaulting on agreements to disclose his weapons collection, needs to be dealt with.

If one of these things were ever to happen to our country, we may need to spend a little cash to fix it. Oh yeah...one of these things *did* happen to our country. Come to think of it...*all* of these things happened to our country. So, what were we to do about it?

Well, according to everything I am currently hearing from the left side of the aisle, we were supposed do *something*, as long as didn't involve spending any money. Because after all, going into debt would be bad, and terrorist attacks are "no biggie." And who needs an airline industry anyway? Why did we need to bail *them* out? It's not like they are an important part of our national economy. It's not like anyone depends on the ability to travel by air. We could all just take the bus, or ride bicycles.

As it turns out, we decided to take some action on these things. Unfortunately, no one came up with a way to do it for free. We were forced into a war on terrorism, so money needed to be spent. Apache helicopters and night vision goggles don't grow on trees. The good news is, you don't have to be an economics major to see the long-term benefits of our actions.When liberals look at what we did for Afghanistan and Iraq, they see people who have had their way of life interrupted by an imperialist foreign power. When a conservative looks at Afghanistan and Iraq, they see people free for the first time to make their own decisions. We also see some of those same people as future business partners and customers. Granted, we are still early in the running on this whole "Iraq" thing, but my money's on Iraq getting a Wal-Mart within the next few years. Since I have always believed that most of the people living in the Middle East are "crazy from the heat," air conditioners at an "extra low price" would have to be a good thing.

So when it comes to our national debt, I just don't care. I see it as a necessary evil that will go away in time. That is, as long as the people of this nation are allowed to go out there and make some money without having to fork over half of it to the government every week. Just as my personal debts will eventually disappear, so will this nation's. In the meantime, we still need to take care of business. It is also *because* of my personal debts that I don't care about our nation's debt. Referring again to the "coffee cup" theory, I know that the government makes more money when I pay fewer taxes. That extra money could go to the national debt. When my taxes go up, I don't buy squat! Beyond that, if the government is "in the hole," I can't use that for an excuse not to pay my bills.

Now, getting back to "spending." You see, our government is no different than anyone else. It likes money. The only trouble is, it likes *our* money. In fact, our government is so helplessly addicted to money, that it would make a crack addict say "Man, you need to get some help for that!" Apparently, our nation's leaders have long forgotten the fact that the money they use belongs to you and me (assuming that you are an American citizen). Instead, they spend it as if it comes from a magical faucet in the men's room.

When I started this chapter, I considered writing a laundry list of stupid things that our government spends money on. I decided against that, because with a little luck this book might actually get published, and such a list is always in a state of flux. A few years ago, we all heard about the $400 toilet seats for military aircraft, and the $300 screwdrivers. Today, we might be hearing about $400 toilet paper holders and $300 screws. The point is, we will always have to keep an eye on what our government does with our money, so a list today will be different tomorrow. Besides, I still hate research.

Just for the sake of current example though...When people come up with brilliant ideas like national healthcare, or college tuition for ILLEGAL immigrants, do they consider who is actually footing the bill? No. That's not a problem though, because if we can't afford it, we'll just get more money from the magic faucet, AKA taxpayers. If the taxes we already pay aren't enough, they'll just make up new ones. Currently, there is a push to institute a tax on junk food. It is disguised as a tax to promote healthy eating and weight loss. That sounds good at first, but since when did I start letting the government decide what I am going to eat? This little gem has been affectionately dubbed "the Twinkie tax."

Sadly, we now seem to accept these things. Most of us don't even bother to look at our paycheck stubs anymore. We pay so many taxes, so often, that we don't even seem to care anymore. We don't ask any questions, and we rarely even complain. This is both sad and ironic when you consider the fact that at one time, a simple tax on tea started a war between two countries.

You can be sure that our nation's leaders are fully aware of our apathy. We have become a nation that knows only one answer to every problem...throw money at it. If the education system is failing, throw money at it. If Joe Blow can't get his own healthcare, throw money at it. If someone else's country has an AIDS crisis, throw money at it. If someone else's country is in poverty, throw money at it. And to what end? America is still going to be considered a bully, or imperialistic. Meanwhile, back at the ranch...I've got bills to pay.

As a conservative, I look at the government as a necessary evil. I also see it as a bureaucratic obstacle that gets in the way of real progress. A necessary evil in the fact that we all need, as well as benefit, from things such as military protection and a fair but efficient justice system, but a bureaucratic obstacle in the fact that excessive taxation and regulation only keeps the average entrepreneur or parent from reaching a set goal.

The liberal view of government is to be dependant on it to survive. The whole "teach a man to fish" thing goes right out the window when liberalism enters the picture. So I end this chapter by asking the tough questions. Do you look to government to provide a safety net? Do you believe that the government should provide you with the basic necessities? Where does the money come from to pay for those? If you believe that the government "giveth," doesn't it stand to reason that they could "taketh away?" If they have the power to "taketh away," do you trust them to know when to stop? If Bob needs a car, does the government have the right, or better yet, should they have the power to make John pay for it? Is this fair to John? Why shouldn't John just say "the hell with it," and make George buy *him* a car too? As this escalates, where do you think it would end? Who benefits? How does this make America stronger? What if the Wright brothers were liberals?

Chapter 9
Mother Nature is a Right-winger!

O ne of the great things about liberalism is the fact that there is no shortage of conflict or irony to point out. As a guy who loves to argue with people, this is always a good thing. One of the best examples of this is the topic of "the environment." This particular topic is also constantly providing a steady stream of laughter to those of us on "the right." After all, the terms "tree hugger" or "greenie weenie" are bound to pop up eventually in a typical conversation about the environment.

As a mammal, I too have a stake in the future condition of our home planet. As an air-breathing biped, I too want to make sure that there is plenty of clean air and water to consume for generations to come. As a conservative, I just want to make sure that we do this in a way that actually makes sense. Unfortunately, as with most other issues, liberalism usually complicates and delays the process.

Being a truck driver allows me to see a pretty wide cross-section of our natural habitat. One day I may be delivering to the city, the next day I may be in the mountains. I consider this to be a "perk" of my chosen occupation. As they say, variety is the spice of life. Does this make me an expert on environmental matters? No, though it does give me some "street cred" on the subject. Besides, from what I can tell, there seems to be a pretty even divide between scientists on the left side of the environmental issue, and those who reside on the right. One "expert" will tell you that the sky is about to fall, and then another will tell you that we'll be fine. To me, this means that they cancel each other out. It is for this very reason that I am not going to spend a lot of time quoting anything from the scientific community. Instead I am just going to use a little deductive reasoning, and yes...common sense.

So where do you start on a topic like the environment? Since it seems to be a hot topic as of late, let's start with everybody's favorite paradoxical issue, oil. Oil is a paradox in the sense that we have a love/hate relationship with it, but we all know that we can't possibly live without it...yet. I say "yet" because even though I am a conservative who routinely makes fun of environmentalists, I am optimistic about our chances to find a better and cleaner way to fuel our way of life. That being said, I am still a realist, and understand all too clearly that that day is probably a long way off. So in the meantime, I have to live in the "here and now."

Here and now, we use oil for pretty much everything. I touched on that fact back in chapter three. The conflict of interest of the left, when it comes to oil, is just plain staggering. Some of the same people who are against the war in Iraq are also against the idea of us drilling for oil in Alaska, which may have made "George Bush's war for oil" unnecessary. Ironically, that is why we bought Alaska in the first place. Or am I the only one who remembers what "Seward's Folly" is all about? Just in case, here's a short history lesson. Back in 1867, then-Secretary of State William H. Seward arranged the purchase of Alaska from the Russians for two cents an acre (7.2 million dollars). Everyone thought he was an idiot. They thought 2 cents an acre for a frozen wasteland on the other side of Canada was a waste of money. They dubbed the purchase "Seward's Folly." Five years later, Seward died.

Call it a hunch, or call it foresight, but Seward knew that there were valuable resources to be found in Alaska. At the very least, he recognized the fact that they quit makin' land a long time ago.

Unfortunately for Seward, he didn't live long enough to see the Alaskan gold rush that followed a few years after his death. He probably didn't understand the *strategic* importance of the purchase either. You see, to look at it on a map, you'll notice that Alaska is basically a giant bridge from Russia to North America. Now we own that bridge. That came in very handy in WWII, as well as in The Cold War.

Basically, Seward was a genius. Unfortunately, at the time, he had too many critics who refused to see the big picture or understand what he was trying to do for America. He had to wait for history to judge him correctly. I bet President Bush knows how that feels.

So now we flash forward to the year 2004. Apparently, there is supposed to be a big ol' pile of oil sitting in Alaska. This may or may not be true. If I were a betting man, I would put all my money on this to be true. My reasoning is this; oil companies are no different than any other profit-driven organization. They want to make money. They probably wouldn't care about Alaska if they didn't have good reason to believe that there is "oil in dem dar hills." I would have to assume that they have better things to do with their time than spend millions of dollars to drill holes in ice for no reason. Beyond that, the technology being used today to hunt for oil is so much more dependable than in the old days. At the very least, it's worth a look.

So what are we waiting for? Funny you should ask. Enter A.N.W.R., or Arctic National Wildlife Refuge. This is a section of Alaska that has been set aside for the protection of the environment. Protection from what? People who want to live in a habitat that closely resembles Mars? I have seen pictures of this place. I don't see a future there for the real estate industry anytime soon. So protection from industry would be my next guess. OK, that makes sense...to a degree. Even though I am a conservative (we are stereotypically out to get Mother Nature) I still would not like to see Alaska turned into something that resembles a frozen Detroit. Though I have never been to Alaska, I know it is a beautiful state. I also know that there are large parts of it that are not exactly post card material.

On the other hand, as a realist, I think we all need to step back for a second and look at the big picture here. As I said earlier, we all need oil. In fact, I may say it a few more times before the end of this chapter. Not to be repetitive, but to drive that fact home to anyone who may forget it. Furthermore, when I say "we all," I mean WE ALL need oil.

So where do we get this life affirming liquid? Well, currently we get it from a lot of places. We get some of it from right here in America, and we get some of it from other countries all over the world. That's fine except for one thing; some of these countries don't like us. In fact, some of these countries are currently helping people who are trying to kill us. Dictators and thugs rule some of these countries. Technically, we are currently financing the same terrorists that are trying to kill us every time we pull up to the pump. That doesn't change the fact that WE NEED OIL!

Right now, I could turn this into a discussion of who hates us and why, or whose fault it is. At this point in the game though, I don't think that really matters. The only thing that matters right now is, WE NEED OIL! That presents us with a problem. A lot of the people who have oil hate us vs. WE NEED OIL! We do have options, but the hard part is deciding which option is the most realistic. Actually, that is not the hard part after all. The hard part is working around those who refuse to see the most logical options; you guessed it...liberals.

The liberal answer to the problem is to conserve energy and develop cleaner ways to fuel our existence. Funny thing is, they are actually right about that. The problem is, that is where they stop. To them, these are the only two options. In a perfect world, these may be the only two options necessary. Unfortunately, this is not a perfect world. In the *real* world, we still have the dictators and thugs to deal with. Since a lot of these shady countries are more than willing to hand over their oil profits to terrorists, that kinda means that this is a race against the clock now.

Our country was built on the concept of independence. It's what we're all about. Except when it comes to oil. Granted, it may not be a "slam dunk" that there is oil in Alaska, but given our circumstances, I think it would be a wise move to check it out. Just the possibility that we have the opportunity to be free from depending on terrorist states and oil cartels should be enough to make it worth our while.

I'm Not Hitler!

Here is where we take a "no-brainer" and make it complicated, thanks again to liberalism, this time in the form of the so-called *environmentalists*. Don't get me wrong, on this particular subject I can sympathize with liberals...to a point. That point is the exact moment when we throw common sense out the window. Here are a few examples.

Oil needs to be transported, one way or another. This is because WE NEED OIL. The two most important questions about oil transportation are how? And from where? You can't exactly send a large amount of oil through the mail. This leaves us with the options of pipelines and tanker ships. A pipeline from Iraq to America is really not an option; this leaves tanker ships. That is how we've been doing it for years. I don't know how many of these tankers are floating around out there, but judging by the amount of oil we use, there must be a whole mess of them. Speaking of "messes," does anyone remember the Exxon Valdez? I do. I remember the environmentalists "having a cow" over that one. Actually, so did everyone else. Wouldn't it be nice if we could eliminate the need for some of those floating ecological time bombs? How do we do that? Maybe we could drill our own oil right here in America. Whether it be in Alaska, or downtown Philadelphia, we need to drill some holes. Another option that I have always wondered about is Mexico. What if we were to buy oil from them? That would work out pretty good considering the fact that they are right next-door. It's true that this is not the *best* idea as far as energy independence goes, but I think it is a pretty good "Plan B." Another bonus is the fact that Mexico is not trying to kill us, unlike a few Middle Eastern countries that I know of. We could actually build a pipeline right out of Mexico to California, Texas, and New Mexico.

Or we could work out a deal with Mexico that we will accept all ILLEGAL immigrants who cross the border, providing that they are carrying at least one barrel of oil. That should be good for a few million gallons a week. Oops! That was a politically incorrect joke. Pardon me.

Before September 11th 2001, I had always thought of myself as an environmentalist, not in practice, but at heart. I did recycle, and I still do, but I was a lot more likely to side with the left on matters of Mother Nature. At one point in my life, I actually took Ralph Nader seriously. Believe it or not, I still have the Green Peace T-shirt that I used to wear in high school. Today I have a very different outlook. After I witnessed what a handful of highly motivated, well-financed nut jobs can do with their spare time, I changed my tune real quick. Do I know for a fact that our own oil money funds the terrorists? No. I do know that money does not grow on trees in the desert though. Unfortunately, none of this changes the fact that WE NEED OIL!

Today, I am a very different person. Now that I have woken up from my liberal slumber, I see the "big picture." Honestly, if someone discovers that there is oil under Mt. Rushmore, I think George Washington's forehead would make a great base for a drilling rig. I believe that George would be proud to know that we were securing our nation's independence by eliminating our *dependence* on foreign oil. OK, I may be going a bit overboard, but we do need to loosen up a bit on the whole "oil is evil" trip. If for no other reason but to buy us some time until we can invent a car that runs on sewage. That seems like a logical strategy, but the environmentalists don't even want to hear it.

Since I have never had the time to meet every person who has walked the earth, I am not afraid to use generalities and stereotypes to make a point. Keeping that in mind, stereotypically, a lot of liberals tend to smoke weed. Not all, but a good percentage of them. I dare anyone to dispute that. One of the favorite arguments of the "legalize it" crowd is that marijuana is *all-natural*. I mention this because stereotypically, these same folks tend to resent the oil industry, and oil in general. If you want to have some fun, the next time one of these "hippies" tells you that weed is OK because it's all natural, just say, "You mean...like oil?" You will almost be able to hear the gears grinding in their pot-clouded heads. The password is *hypocrisy*.

I wonder if the word "hippy" comes from the word "hypocrisy?"

One of the biggest gripes that your typical "greenie weenie" has is the building of offshore drilling rigs. They fear that they are dangerous because they could spill oil into the ocean. At first, that doesn't seem too unreasonable. But during the process of writing this book, I came across a little-known tidbit of information that I thought was very interesting. Did you know that oil actually seeps up from the ocean floor naturally? Not only that, but it happens all over the world, all the time. I guess this makes sense, because I *did* know that it seeps up from the ground on dry land in some places. Apparently, this is not a problem because there are enzymes in the ocean that actually eat oil. Does that mean that Green Peace will have to launch attacks on Mother Nature? Does she need to hire a lawyer?

So, am I saying that we should treat oil as a resource that could never run out? No. Am I saying that the oil industry can always be trusted to do the right thing? No. I'm just saying that we need to start using a little common sense on the subject. I am also saying that we should not let our safety or sovereignty take a backseat to irrational fear.

A recent example of liberals putting safety in the back seat is the Sport Utility Vehicle. The SUV has become the "Dr. Evil" of the automotive world. As the owner of two of them, I have to believe that if you are in the anti-SUV crowd, you have probably never owned one, and you probably have no children. The rest of us however, understand their many pros and few cons. (Oh yeah, speaking of children. As of my last update, my wife has given birth to our beautiful little daughter. I am officially a father. That makes me an authority on everything.) I'll have more to say on parenting later, but right now we need to get back to the evil SUV.

As I am completely addicted to watching the news, I often see a story that just makes me shake my head. Recently, I saw a story about a group that calls itself "the Earth Liberation Front." They were in the news because they were taking credit for the firebombing of car dealerships that were selling SUVs. If I remember correctly, they were mostly targeting Hummer dealers. As I watched the footage, I wondered if these E.L.F. goobers had ever heard of *insurance*. Then I watched as the burning Hummers bellowed toxic gasses and smoke hundreds of feet into the air. I bet it would take one of those Hummers a half-a-million miles to put that much pollution into the air had it been left alone. Then I thought of the pollution that all the fire engines would add to the mix. Compound that with the extra industrial waste after all those replacement Hummers are built. Then I thought to myself, "If I could afford one, I would go buy a Hummer right now, just to spite those idiots." I am willing to bet that there were a few people out there who *could* afford one, and bought one for just that reason. As if anyone is going to give up buying a Hummer, just because some moron is threatening to burn it. I have to assume that if you can afford an SUV, you probably have it insured. I wish someone would burn my Toyota. So, just what are the pros and cons of the SUV? Environmentalists say that the SUV is bad because it uses too much fuel, which is bad for the air. They may even be right about this, but I just don't care. Let me tell you why. As a new member of the "Fatherhood Society," I have a whole new set of priorities. First on the list is my daughter. She enters the discussion due to one undisputable truth...S%#* happens. When it does, I want my family to have every advantage that I can provide for them. In case you haven't figured it out, I'm talking about the most common of tragedies...the car crash.

Before you mention it, I know that typical SUVs are prone to "rollover." I also know that this usually happens because people don't know how to drive them. For a country boy like myself who has been driving pick-up trucks, jeeps, and eighteen-wheelers for years, this is pretty clear. For the typical city boy or soccer mom whose last car was a BMW, this may not be as obvious. So what happens is, you put the soccer mom in the Escalade, and now you have a ticking time bomb. Does this mean that the SUV needs to be outlawed? No. Does this mean that the soccer mom may need a short tutorial on the physics of driving a top-heavy four-wheel drive? Yes.

Now that we have that out of the way, let's get back to my daughter getting home in one piece. Liberals say that the SUV has an unfair advantage over the sub-compact car in the event of a crash. I agree, and that's exactly why I don't put my family in a sub-compact car. They propose that we outlaw the SUV, and make all cars the same size. That's fine if you happen to know that the only thing that will ever crash into you is a car that is the same size as your own. Here in the "real world" though, we have these things called trucks, and trains. I guess you could say that the eighteen-wheeler has an advantage over the sub-compact in the event of a crash too, so I guess we should outlaw the eighteen-wheeler as well.

It is not my place to make decisions for anyone other than myself. So if a liberal enviro-nerd is more concerned about the *possible* future effects of a few less miles to the gallon, than the crash stability of the vehicle he puts his family in.that's his business. But when he tells *me* that I have to do the same thing, that's when I get my panties in a wad.

Another factor that is commonly forgotten, when the SUV is the subject of liberal scorn, is *snow*. There are large portions of this country that get big amounts of snow on a regular basis. Most SUVs are four-wheel drive...you do the math. Moms all over the country are finding that it is much easier to put 2.7 children, a dog, and six bags of groceries in an SUV, and then drive home in a snow storm, than to pull it all off in a Volkswagen. Have you ever tried to pull a boat, or a camper, with a Honda? All things considered, the SUV is just a practical mode of transportation.

I read a T-shirt once that read, "What would Jesus drive?" My guess is he would have driven an SUV. He could have hauled a lot of disciples and still had room left over for stone tablets. The desert sand would have been no problem at all with four-wheel drive.

As for fuel efficiency, that is largely up to how the SUV is used. Which is more efficient, eight people car-pooling in two cars, or one SUV?

For liberals, fuel equals air pollution. So just how big of a problem is air pollution anyway? As I said earlier, for every one scientist's theory, there is another's counter theory. So I have done my own test (I looked out the window). The air looks clean to me. OK, it may not actually be that simple, or is it? What is clean air? My understanding is that it is air that is free of pollution. Nobody wants to breath air that has been polluted. If you disagree, I defy you to breath the air in a port-a-potty. Now that's pollution!

So what causes air pollution? Of course, liberals will tell you that pollution comes from the internal combustion engine, and the evil industrial establishment. At this time, I would like to expose another bit of liberal hypocrisy. The same people who cry about the pollution caused by engines and industry (two things that are necessary for our survival) are currently crying about the fact that we took Saddam Hussein out of power. This is the same guy who set hundreds of oil wells on fire at the end of the first Gulf War. This was an air pollution nightmare of biblical proportions. I'm sure we were wrong to overthrow him; he was such an environmentally conscious kinda guy.

Another source of air pollution that liberals seem to forget about is volcanoes. Just one of these little mountains of mischief can put more junk in the air than an American factory ever will. Not only that, but they create rivers and lakes of acid, as well as destroy trees by the thousands. I guess that means yet another lawsuit for Mother Nature to fight off. Let's not forget forest fires. We know how much damage they can do, because they keep happening out west. They too lead to air pollution, as well as soil erosion. Who would have thought that Mother Nature was so environmentally irresponsible?

Environmentalists not only have a problem with oil, but they also hate the process by which it is produced. To them, the sight of a drilling rig is a blight that destroys the horizon. They don't seem to care much about the New York City horizon, which was destroyed on September 11th. That attack was also an ecological disaster. I remember the smoke and fumes that went for miles, and the dust and debris that blanketed downtown Manhattan. Again, I have heard no cries for Bin Laden's head on a platter from the "enviro-jerks". They seem to be too preoccupied with making it harder for America to become less dependent on the Middle East.

They spend so much time putting down the oil industry, that they don't take the time to see that in a lot of cases, they are actually doing more harm than good. As an example, I refer again to the fact that environmentalists have been railing against any further drilling in Alaska, due to the effect on wildlife in the area. At first, this doesn't sound so unreasonable, until you start to apply some brainpower to the topic.

Supposedly, these self-proclaimed saviors of all things cute and fuzzy assume that any change in the natural habitat of any given animal will automatically cause the extinction of that species. I submit that even if this were true, it's not the end of the world. A shame maybe, but not the end of the world. Thankfully, the law of common sense prevents this from being the case. Sure, if one species is hunted out of existence, then there is a problem. This almost happened to the buffalo right here in America. That's not were talking about, though. We are talking about industry vs. nature. That's a whole different thing. For starters, industry in America does not set out with the intent of wiping out any species. In fact, our nation leads the rest of the globe in environmental protection. The point is, when an "enviro-nerd" starts whining about industry wiping out a species of animal, remind him/her that there is a difference between oil exploration in America, and the ivory trade in Africa.

Back to Alaska and common sense. Though I am not an expert on the migration patterns or mating habits of any creature that might be living in Alaska, I do know about two things...bullets and human nature. Bullets tend to have an adverse effect on pretty much all living things. One shot to the head will greatly reduce the plans of any animal to migrate or mate. It's very hard to do either when you are dead. How do bullets end up in the heads of animals? Human nature.

It is human nature that drives a man to provide for his family. He is charged with the task of making sure that there is food on the table, and heat in the house. In Alaska, this is not the easiest thing to do for most guys. For centuries the Eskimos of Alaska have provided for their families by (you guessed it) hunting. They still do today. Eskimos hunt everything from seals to caribou for food and money. What does this have to do with the oil industry? Well, you see, Alaska is not exactly a happening place to be if you need a job. That is why so many people there hunt for a living. It stands to reason that if an Eskimo had a job on the new oil rig down the road, he may not have as much time or need to hunt the cute little fuzzy creatures. That's right, you can't drill oil without employees. That too is ironic, because liberals are the first to cry about unemployment rates, especially in an election year.

Another benefit to the local animal population is the fact that today's industries do more to help the environment than ever before.

From the fish ladders that the hydroelectric industry has been building for years, to the deer whistles that my company puts on their trucks, American industry is not out to destroy the earth as liberals would have you believe.

Some credit also needs to be given to the wildlife itself. For thousands of years the animal kingdom has learned how to do one thing very well...turn. Of all the animals I have ever seen, I don't know of any that stand in one place all its life. I can't even think of any that stand in one place all day. Imagining myself in the place of a wild caribou, I can only wonder what I would do if I was walking across the frozen tundra and happened upon an oil rig or a pipeline. I would probably turn left. Actually I would be a conservative caribou...I'd turn right. Then I would keep on walking. Except in the world of Dr. Seuss, I don't know of an animal that can only go straight. Basically, I would do what every other living thing has been doing for the past few million years...ADAPT.

You can also be assured that along with oil companies come the employees who love animals. If a polar bear breaks it's leg, it's out of luck. If a *human* sees that it has broken its leg, it has a chance at getting some help. A polar bear is just an animal, but a polar bear near humans is an animal with a health care plan. Besides, most people are good at heart (I have to believe that in order to get out of bed in the morning). That means that you can bet that any industrial expansion into Alaska would be accompanied by large amounts of contractually obligated money to be used for feeding and caring for the surrounding wildlife.

Even though I shun research like a wayward Amish teenager, I did happen upon this interesting little nugget of information. After the completion of the Alaskan pipeline, it was discovered that some animal species actually increased in number. Apparently, the oil that flows through the pipeline is heated in order to flow better. This makes the pipeline itself a source of heat for animals living near it. That in turn stimulates the mating process. After all, it's hard for me to "get *my* groove on" unless it's at least above fifty degrees in the house. Imagine trying to mate when it's below zero. I would be hanging out by the pipeline too.

Don't get me wrong; I am not saying that the oil industry is a group of perfect little angels. They are no different that any other group. You are always going to have a bad apple. I am also not trying to say that there is *no* risk of environmental accidents caused by oil exploration. I *am* saying that the risk of becoming any more dependent on foreign oil is much greater. The destruction and loss of life caused by our dependence on terrorist funding, infidel hating, oil embargoing, Middle Eastern countries has far surpassed any oil spill or oil fire that *could* ever, or *has* ever happened. This fact is what is known as "the big picture." Oddly enough, as simply as I just explained it, I am willing to bet that a large majority of liberals would still not see it. Of course there are those who do see it, but have too much pride to admit it.

Ironically, most of the things that should be important to liberal environmentalists have already been the industry standard for years. The oil industry is now one of the most watched and regulated industries out there. Technically, the left won the environment war a long time ago; they just refuse to see it. The days of companies being able to do whatever they want without repercussion are long gone. This is the time of "real time" digital satellite video. This is the age of the Internet, and cell phones. The technology that exists today would make it nearly impossible for companies to get away with things as easily as they could have twenty years ago. Today we have multiple government agencies solely devoted to making sure that companies don't get out of line when it comes to protecting the environment. Keeping that in mind, there is just one thing left to do...DRILL! After all...WE NEED OIL!

As usual though, the fact that environmental protection has become a multi-billion dollar a year bureaucracy is not enough for the liberal elite. Now they are trying to go "global" with their overreactions.

Back in the late nineties, "global warming" became a front-and-center issue. For those who don't know what global warming is, I'll try to explain it. Basically, it is the warming of the globe. Yes, being a smart-ass is a full time job. On the other hand, that is exactly what it is. The controversy is found in the debate over whether it actually exists, and if so, what causes it. This is another chance for some to decide if they are a "glass half full" or "glass half empty" kind of person. Since most of us are not climatologists, we are left to decide for ourselves which theories make the most sense.

Those who believe that global warming is a real factor, that could someday kill us all, tend to get a lot of press. After all, scare tactics sell a lot of papers. These folks tell us that the earth is warming at an exponential rate, and will someday not sustain our natural habitat. The "fear" factor tends to make most people take a second look at this as a real problem. Naturally, people then want answers. So who do they turn to? The same people who made the original claim...the scientific community. Unfortunately, as I wrote earlier, for every theory, there is a counter theory.

For the sake of argument, let's assume that global warming is a real threat. There are many theories as to what causes it. The most popular theory is that global warming is caused by the depletion of the ozone layer. This of course happens because of everybody's favorite scapegoat...industry. Not just any industry though, American industry. Apparently, the United States pollutes the air, and this pollution eats holes in the ozone layer, which protects us from the sun. This causes the air we breathe to be hotter, which will kill us all!

Another popular theory is "the green house effect." Apparently, these pollutants that the U.S. routinely poisons the air with accumulate in the atmosphere. These same pollutants act as an insulator, trapping the heat, as in a green house. This causes the air we breathe to be hotter, which will kill us all!

Recently, I read an article in The Washington Times, which asserted a new theory. According to their article, scientists have found that the sun is getting hotter. This could be a problem, unless we can figure out a way to turn the sun down. After all, the sun radiates a lot of heat. This causes the air we breathe to be hotter, which will kill us all!

Then there is the theory that I have decided to put all of my chips on. The theory that the Earth's climate changes all the time, and there is nothing you can do about it. I like this one because it makes the most sense to me. It makes sense to me for a couple of reasons. Even if there had never been an internal combustion engine, there will always be volcanoes and forest fires. The other reason is, rain. If you have ever walked outside after a rainstorm, you know what I mean. The air is crisp and clean. When it rains, the water droplets fall to Earth, picking up all those little pollutants along the way. I also choose this theory to believe because it does not involve the thought of me dying.

The heart of this matter is, no one knows for sure what causes global warming, or if it even exists. Am I saying that I know for a fact that global warming is not real? No. Am I saying that we should not check into it a little further? No. The problem is, there are a lot of powerful people who are buying into this silliness hook, line, and sinker, before it is proven to be a fact. Not only that, but they are treating it as a crisis. These folks are generally found sitting on the *left* side of the table.

At one time, environmental extremists were little more than a fringe group that was usually not taken very seriously. Today however, these same folks have moved from the basements of college science buildings, into the international limelight. This is due in part to our good friends at the United Nations.

In an effort to combat the *alleged* crisis of global warming, the United Nations came up with a brilliant plan to force industrialized nations to reduce all "green house gasses" by a predetermined time. This was called "The Kyoto Protocol." At first, you might wonder why someone would have a problem with reducing green house gasses. That's not the issue though. The issue is cost.

America is the most industrially productive nation on the planet. This also means that we produce the most waste. According to the Kyoto Protocol, America would be paying the lion's share for Kyoto compliance, while developing nations get a free ride. That is all well and good except for one thing...we are <u>not</u> the United States of The United Nations, we are the United States of America. Oh yeah, and we're not stupid.

You see, as I mentioned earlier, our nation *does* lead the world in waste production, but we also lead the world in waste management and regulation. For America to meet the Kyoto standards would cost us billions of dollars. These standards would have meant waste and emission standards would be tightened on every single thing in America that produces some type of green house gas. Every new car, lawn mower, train, plane, or boat would have to be checked and modified to meet the Kyoto standard. That alone would be akin to shooting ourselves in the foot financially. All for the sake of a *theoretical* problem.

In my opinion, the worst thing about the Kyoto debacle is the fact that it undermines our national sovereignty. America did not fight for its independence, just to give it to some organization of foreign countries.

Apparently, I was not the only one who felt this way about the Kyoto scam. Early in his presidency, George W. Bush made it clear that he was not going to sign our country on to this economy-killing program. The environmental community on the left practically had a cow. To this day, they continue to say that President Bush is out to destroy the environment. The irony here is that the Kyoto Protocol had already been struck down by the United States Senate under the Clinton administration (almost unanimously). It was dead before Bush was even a candidate. It is also not widely reported that many of the other industrialized nations *also* refused to join the Kyoto silliness. Not even Russia signed it. They saw it for what it was, a convoluted snow job by the U.N., designed to take money from prosperous nations and give it to poor ones. This is income redistribution on an international scale.

The left still refuses to see Kyoto for what it is; they still believe that President Bush refused to sign it because he hates the environment. Let's not let a few facts get in the way of some good old-fashioned Bush bashing. After all, that seems to be the most popular way for the left to kill time lately.

Conservatives always get a bad rap when it comes to the environment. Of course, we usually get a bad rap on most controversial topics. I guess that is why I decided to write this book. I'm just tired of being misrepresented and misunderstood. The fact is, conservatives are usually very "pro environment." The first clue is in the root word; *conserve*. There is no law that says you cannot be an environmentalist and a conservative at the same time. I would even go so far as to say that most conservatives *are* environmentalists. The only difference is, we don't accept liberalism as a way to help the environment...we try things that actually work.

As one example of a way to save the environment that actually works, we only need to watch the news. Every summer, for I don't even know how long, I have watched as forest fires tear through the western portions of America. These fires are caused in a number of different ways. Some are started by natural causes such as lightning. Others are started by the carelessness of campers and hikers. I even heard of one that was caused by a squirrel that ran across a high-tension power line (do yourself a favor, don't try to picture that one in your mind). The point is, forest fires happen.

Preventing them is always worth trying, but they're still going to happen eventually. The problem is, there is a big debate on the best way to prevent them, and control them. Liberals will tell you the best way to prevent forest fires is to remove the human element. This means keeping man out of the forests. After all, forests are all natural, and humans are...well, I guess humans are made in some factory somewhere. So liberals spend lots of money, and grease a lot of palms to get legislation enacted to close off large chunks of forest to man. Some of this legislation prevents people from using the land for recreation, while others prevent it being used by the lumber industry.

At first, this doesn't seem too unreasonable, until you look at the big picture. To buy into the liberal method of forest fire prevention, you first have to believe that until man came along, forest fires didn't happen. Since many forest fires are caused by lightning strikes, you would also have to believe that lightning never happened until man came along either. I am willing to assume that you (the reader) are smarter than this.

So, now that we have established that man is not always to blame for every bad thing that happens to nature, let's move on. Oh yeah, I almost forgot...lightning is a natural occurrence. For those of you keeping track, that's lawsuit number three against Mother Nature.

Some of you may remember your childhood. If so, think back to the first time you went camping. Maybe you were a Boy or Girl

Scout. Maybe a parent or relative took you on a camping trip. If not...sorry about your luck. You'll just have to use your imagination for this one. If you went camping, you probably had a campfire. If you had a campfire, it is a good bet that you may have been allowed to help build it.

When you were told to get firewood, were you told to get the "green" wood? No.

You were told to get the dry, dead wood. You were told this for a reason. Green, live wood is hard to burn. Dead wood burns very well. Some of you, who have never gone camping, may have used a fireplace before. The same principal applies. It also applies to forests.

This brings us to the concept of "healthy forests." Hopefully, we can all agree that a burnt, charred wasteland is not considered to be a "healthy forest." Forests are made of trees. Trees are living things. Just like every other living thing, trees eventually die. After they die, they decay. So, when you go to a forest, you will notice that along with the living trees, there are thousands of dead ones. Some are on the ground, and some are still standing. These dead trees also go by another name...fuel. That's right, nothing feeds a forest fire better than dead trees and underbrush.

It is at this point where liberals and conservatives part company. Libs would have you believe that man's intervention has a negative effect on the natural forest environment. It disturbs the natural habitat of the forest creatures. Conservatives realize that forest fires have a slightly more *negative effect* on the natural habitat of the forest creatures. After all, if your house burns down, you might consider that to be a "negative effect." If Joe Blow drops a gum wrapper in the woods, a chipmunk will probably get over it. If that same chipmunk burns alive, it may not be able to "get over it."

Conservatives have known for a long time that in order to reduce the risk of forest fires, humans need to get in on the act. After all, it is humans that are capable of identifying and correcting any situations that might pop up in the forest. It's *how* we do this that always gets the "enviro-weenie's" panties in a bunch.

The problem is, these guys never offer a better way of doing things. For example, a conservative would assert that we should be clearing the dead wood and brush out of the forests, essentially removing the fuel that drives a wildfire. This would be a travesty in the eyes of the "run of the mill" liberal. They would argue that man has no right to tamper with the forests. Yet they have no better way to remedy the wildfire problem.

This brings us to the dreaded logging industry. For years, liberal environmentalists have been trying to put an end to logging. In the early days, they may have had a point. Years ago, logging companies commonly utilized the practice of "clear cutting." Basically, they stripped the land of all trees, and left very little behind. Like most other industries, the methods that the logging industry uses today have evolved and improved by leaps and bounds.

Today, lumber companies have their own "tree farms." They actually replant entire forests after they have been logged. More modern equipment has made "clear cutting" a thing of the past. Thanks to lasers and computer technology, more usable lumber can be cut from a log than could have been just twenty years ago. That means that fewer trees need to be cut to provide the same amount of lumber.

You see, lumber companies wised up a long time ago. They realized that trees are a renewable resource. They also figured out that an unhealthy forest is an unprofitable forest; if a forest is full of trees that have diseases or fire damage, then they are no good to the industry. This means that it is now more sensible for a lumber company to invest in the care and well being of a forest. So, they do just that. After all, they have a financial stake in making sure that forests don't go up in smoke.

In my opinion, it's not like we have many environmentally sound alternatives to lumber anyway. Wood is used in the building of too many things to put handcuffs on the lumber industry. It is very likely that the roof over your head and the floor under your feet is made of some type of lumber. The demand for wood and wood products is always growing. This is not because human beings get their rocks off by watching the destruction of defenseless oak trees. It's because even after years of technological innovation, wood is still the most logical material to build with.

New building materials are being developed everyday. Some are made from recycled products; others are composed of man-made chemical compounds. Someday, these materials will probably blow wood right out of the water when it comes to durability, dependability, environmental effect, and cost effectiveness. When that day comes, lumber companies will be able to put down their chainsaws and reminisce about the good old days of logging. After all, wood will then be obsolete. Until that day comes though, wood will remain the material of choice.

The irony of the "wood vs. other material" debate is that other materials are not yet as environmentally friendly as wood. You see, wood is basically as simple today as it was at the dawn of mankind. Using it hasn't really changed that much either. Wood needs to be cut today just as it did hundreds of years ago. The only real difference is the quality of the cutting process; the mechanical principals are still the same. We used saws then, we use saws now...bigger, faster, better saws, but saws nonetheless. Once the wood has been cut to its desired form, that's pretty much the end of the story. Beyond the harvesting, and cutting process, very little energy is used in making usable lumber. The same cannot be said for metals, concrete, or plastics. To create any of these materials, tons of energy needs to be used. Do you know how much energy it takes to mine minerals from the ground, then melt them into steel? Neither do I, but I know it's a heck of a lot more than it takes to cut a few two-by-fours out of a log.

Another commonly forgotten concept; there is a difference between "recyclable" and "renewable." Although metals *are* recyclable, the existing raw materials for making metals cannot be grown again after they have been harvested. Whatever raw metal materials exist today is all there will ever be. Wood, on the other hand, is *renewable*. That means that it can exist indefinitely. You see, when one tree is cut down, another is planted in its place. This process can be repeated forever if necessary. Assuming of course that we mind our P's and Q's and act responsibly, there should be no reason for us to ever run out of trees.

Recycling is another technique that has become a mainstay of environmental protection. Over the past twenty years or so, recycling has become a very normal way of doing things. This is a good thing, as well as being a victory for environmentalists. I don't say that begrudgingly, because being an "environmentalist" is not what makes someone a liberal. It is when you refuse to acknowledge common sense that you stake your claim on the "dark side." Recycling is a good example of this. Recycling is just a good idea; it really is that simple. Why would you throw something away to rot in a landfill and take up space, when you could turn it into something useful instead? This is a classic example of common sense. Even us "right wing extremists" see the value of recycling. You see, whether an idea comes from the left or right is irrelevant...a good idea is a good idea.

Trust me, I am not trying to sound naive about problems that plague our environment. I know that there are a lot of bad things going on out there. I know that the rain forests are being destroyed, and I know that pollution is still happening all over the world. I just think we need to take a deep breath and look at some of the progress we *have* made in protecting the environment. I also think we need to be realistic about our needs as a society. Right or wrong, we still need oil and wood. Right or wrong, we still need to build things to accommodate our existence. In other words...we still need to build a lot of stuff to live. Right or wrong, we still need cars, trucks, planes, trains, houses and factories. Right or wrong, it is not realistic to expect any of us to revert back to the lifestyle of primitive man. I will never trade in my house for a grass hut or a cave in the mountains. I will never trade in my car for a pair of moccasins. I think it is safe to say that I am not alone.

The point of this chapter was not to discuss the entire laundry list of environmental issues. After all, I have barely scratched the surface. I wrote this hoping to point out the fact that environmentalism and liberalism are not mutually exclusive. Hopefully, I have demonstrated the difference between an environmentalist and an environmentalist wacko. I would even be willing to bet that your typical conservative is as much, or even more of an environmentalist, than an average liberal. The only difference is, one who truly cares about the environment will take the time to see what the real problems are, instead of scaring people into thinking that the world will end if you use oil and lumber. I also wanted to show how liberalism, applied to the environment, has much the same results as liberalism applied to anything else. These results are; wasted time, wasted money, distraction from the real problem, prevention of progress, and even death.

Chapter 10
Fool's Court Press

W hen I started writing this book, I only had a vague idea of the format I wanted to use. I knew that I wanted to get my points across in the simplest of terms, and I also wanted to reach the broadest cross-section of people as possible. I also didn't want to bore everyone to death with the legislative process of dealing with any given subject. In my opinion, as important as the political process is, it makes for some very boring reading. Besides, politicians come and go every day...morals, ideals, and values are constant. What was wrong yesterday will be wrong tomorrow. You see, this is supposed to be a book about one man's interpretation of the conservative philosophy, not a who's who of politics. Maybe my next book will be geared more toward dissecting individual politicians and their moronic ideas. But let's face it, that market has been pretty well covered anyway.

Ranting was also something I wanted to avoid, but then I realized that there was really no way for me to write this book without passionately spouting my opinion; after all, that was the whole point of this book. The trick has been to not *sound* like I'm ranting.

All that being said, some things have been happening lately that have really "burnt my ass," as we say in the trucking business. So if this chapter seems to turn into an angry rant...TOO BAD!

Every subject that I have covered or will cover in this book is one that means something to me on a personal level. Whether the topic is immigration or war, my opinions and theories are nothing more than that...opinions and theories. Right or wrong, I make no bones about my ideology, or beliefs. I am firmly dug into my warm, cozy bunker of conservatism, and I'm very comfortable there. Consequently, I am sure that most of those who live in "the land of the left" feel the same way about *their* ideology. As frustrating as liberalism is to me, I can still have *some* respect for a person who embraces liberalism...until they're dishonest about it.

This brings us to a very hot topic as of late...media bias. I touched on this subject a little earlier. Originally, I had not planned to write an entire chapter about liberal bias in the media. After all, I knew it would come up on its own at some point. Then something happened that made me so angry that I knew the subject would have to get more than a few casual mentions.

The Abu Ghraib prison scandal hit the airwaves and newspapers with the force of a fully loaded Mack truck. Having driven a fully loaded Mack truck myself, I can tell you that *that* is a lot of force. For those of you who have just arrived from your long journey from Mars, I will try to bring you up to speed with a brief overview of the controversy.

Well along into the war in Iraq, it became necessary to find a home for captured Iraqi POWs. Coalition forces utilized a former Iraqi prison to house the prisoners. Unfortunately, like most government operations, this prison didn't exactly run like a well-oiled machine...as far as we know. I say "as far we know" because I was not there, and most likely neither were you. Whatever we know, or *think* we know, about this or any other news story is largely dependant upon what the media tells us...hence, this chapter.

According to the *media*, it was discovered that U.S. forces in charge of the Abu Ghraib prison in Iraq, were routinely *torturing* and *abusing* the prisoners. For weeks, we were bombarded with pictures and stories of abuse from all corners of the press. And what controversial pictures they were. Every night for weeks, my TV screen was plastered with images of naked Iraqi men being humiliated by female American soldiers. I figure that there is a 99.9 % chance that you too have seen the same pictures.

When I first heard of this story, I thought to myself "this is terrible, how could Americans do such terrible things to other human beings?" I wondered how the rest of the world would react to this. Then I started to (you guessed it) *think* about the subject. I started to realize that questions I had about the Abu Ghraib controversy were not being answered.

One of the first things I noticed was the repetitive use of the words *torture* and a*buse* by the press. I searched the Internet for as many pictures as I could find (and there was no shortage), but one thought kept popping into my head - where is the *torture*?

Maybe it's just me, or the fact that Hollywood has desensitized me to excessive violence, but no matter how many pictures I saw, I couldn't find any that I would classify as torture. I saw some that I would classify as controversial, unusual, puzzling, intimidating, and even embarrassing, but putting the "torture" label on them really didn't seem to fit right. You see, when I think of *torture*, I picture beatings, rapes, breaking bones, red hot irons to the feet, tongues being cut out, hands being cut off...you know, the stuff that *Saddam* did to his people. Somehow, pictures of naked dudes in provocative poses really don't make the cut with me. The most questionable picture that I could find was one of a female American soldier standing over the dead body of an Iraqi soldier packed in ice; she was smiling and giving the "thumbs up" sign. This I would happily file under "tasteless," but not *torture*...after all, he was dead.

Still, the media spun the story out of control. Every time they would refer to what happened in Abu Ghraib as torture, I found myself wanting to climb through my TV screen and *torture* the newscaster. "Where are the thumbscrews? Where is the whipping post? Where are the cigarette burns? Where are the wounds?" I would scream.

Don't get me wrong, the stacking and posing of naked enemy soldiers is probably something that should be looked into by the proper authorities, but calling it *torture* is a bit of a stretch.

The more thought I applied to the issue, the angrier I would get about it. It was disturbing on so many levels, but not because of the actual *abuse*. The media playing "fast and loose" with the English language was just the icing in the cake. There was the fact that this story was being treated as the most important thing since the moon landing, too. If you didn't know any better, you would have thought that nothing else was happening in the world at the time. Even with the excessive coverage of the story though, no one was trying to get to the heart of the matter. For instance, no one seemed to be interested in *why* a group of soldiers might do this to begin with. There were a few theories thrown around, but not much *investigation*. Ironically, the theory that made the most sense to me got the least amount of attention.

I am certainly no expert on the cultural norms of the Middle Eastern male, but in the past few years, more light has been shed on the subject. According to sources that an average truck driver could have access to (Internet, magazines, TV, radio, and books), it is common in Middle Eastern culture for females to be treated like the dog doo that might be on the bottom of your shoe. For a woman to be put in a position of authority over an Iraqi man is *not* acceptable. Coincidentally, it is also said that one of the most shameful things you can do to an Arab male is to photograph him naked. You also have to keep in mind that it is very likely that the guys being held in Abu Ghraib are probably there for a reason. Allegedly, these were some of Saddam's nastiest boys. We're talking about dudes who are used to dishing out *real* torture, as well as murder, extortion and rape. This, in addition to being trained to endure conventional methods of interrogation themselves.

Now that you have a general idea of what kind of people we're talking about, is it possible that the U.S. soldiers at Abu Ghraib (or their superiors) realized early on that sleep depravation and threats of violence were not going to impress the Iraqi soldiers? Is it possible that this incident was not soldiers running amuck after all, but actually an attempt to exploit an enemy's weakness in order to get information that might save someone's life (ironically without actual violence)?

Granted, this is just a theory. In *my* mind, it seems to be the most logical of all the theories that I have heard so far. But that is incidental. The real problem is the way the story was covered, and of course...why. This brings us back to the concept of liberal bias.

For whatever reason, President Bush has been in the cross hairs of the media since day one of his term in office. This was made painfully obvious during the Abu Ghraib scandal. Of all the people who could be blamed for the incident, the press was all too eager to put the blame on Bush and his administration. Any talking head that was willing to go on the air and point the finger at George Bush or Donald Rumsfeld was given prime time coverage. Of course, no direct link could be made from Bush to those running Abu Ghraib, but that didn't stop our buddies in the media from advancing *that* theory. From day one, I got a chuckle out of this. I see it as blaming Donald Trump personally for a dirty bathroom at the Trump Tower. There is quite a long chain of command between the two. Does this mean that no one should be accountable? No. I just don't see *any* President having enough time to go out and personally check on *every* aspect of the government. Is it Bush's fault when a jet fighter crashes because of a part that was improperly installed? Is it Bush's fault if a soldier gets a rash on his rear because the toilet paper he was issued wasn't hypoallergenic? Where do we draw the line? Now, if there was evidence that Bush or Rumsfeld *knew* about, and either condoned or ordered the mistreatment of POW's, then you would have a story. That has not happened yet, and probably won't. Probably the most disturbing aspect of the press' coverage of the Abu Ghraib scandal was the *other* story that was being poorly covered at around the same time.

Nick Berg was a young man who was working in Iraq, trying to help rebuild the infrastructure. He was a civilian, and apparently just a regular guy trying to help a struggling country get back on its feet. He was taken hostage by what the press referred to as "a group of *militants.*" In reality, these *militants* were actually TERRORISTS. I guess calling them what they really are might offend them, and we wouldn't want that. This is akin to calling a used car *pre-owned.*

Though it may not be a false description of the subject, it hardly drives the point home.

When the TERRORISTS realized that their demands were not going to be met, they beheaded Mr. Berg. As if that weren't bad enough, they videotaped it and rushed the tape right over to an Arab news organization and downloaded it onto the Internet for all to see. It seemed to me that giving publicity to terrorists was a very bad idea, but in the age of the worldwide web, I accepted the fact that putting that genie back in the bottle was not going to happen. Instead, I tried to find solace in the idea that these gruesome images would strengthen our national resolve to kill the terrorists...I was wrong.

In true pacifist/liberal form, the press decided to focus on possibly the least important points of the Nick Berg issue. They decided to run the beheading video, minus the actual footage of the beheading. At first, I understood their reluctance to showing the violence of a public beheading, but then I remembered...oh yeah, we're at war. Don't get me wrong, I have not seen the video, and I don't want to, but I *do* believe that there is a lot to be said for showing those who do not yet "get it" just what the war on terror is all about. In fact, the word *terror* seems to go hand in hand with the concept of *beheading* someone. What could be more terrifying than that?

On my list of worst ways to die, beheading is in the top three, right between burning to death and falling from a tall building. Ironically, the people we are at war with are guilty of killing thousands (possibly millions) of innocent people by using all three of these methods, plus many others. For the press to use the terms *militant* or *insurgent* fails to paint a mental picture of TERROR. In fact, according to the definition of the word, the U.S. and coalition forces (the good guys) are *militants*. Until *we* start cutting off the heads of innocent civilians for the sake of evil, I doubt that we could be called TERRORISTS.

By the way, just a little nugget of information that might help drive the point home; I read once that the human head can live for up to six minutes after being severed from the body. Try to imagine this happening to you. Try to imagine being able to see, hear, taste, and feel for those six minutes. Not being able to breathe, talk, or scream. What would be going through your mind? Imagine being able to see your bleeding, twitching, headless body adjacent to you. I mention this not for shock value, but to try to make you understand what a terrorist *truly* is.

So when it came time for the press to cover this story, I guess I shouldn't have been surprised that none of this would be mentioned. Instead, like the good liberals they are, the press decided to question whether the war in Iraq was worth the killing of innocent people like Nick Berg. This was the *real* "kick in the nuts" in my opinion. After all, isn't that why we are at war in the first place? We were not in Iraq *or* Afghanistan on Sept 11, 2001. This did not stop these crazy bastards from killing thousands of "innocent people" on *that* particular day. We were not in Iraq when the same crazy bastards kidnapped and beheaded journalist Danny Pearl. It is still being assessed as to how many "innocent people" Saddam Hussein killed *before* we got there. All the estimates I have seen are six digit numbers, and thought to be a million plus. Keep in mind that these are *people* we are talking about, not inanimate objects.

I heard a phrase recently that really struck a chord with me; "To a liberal, one death is a tragedy, but a million deaths are a statistic."

To further harp on the point, the most ridiculous word the press used to describe what happened at Abu Ghraib was *atrocity*. The simple fact that this word was given the green light by the editorial staffs of so many *respected* news outlets, says a lot about the motives of these editors. Don't get me wrong, I like a good "fish story" as much as the next guy, and I am no stranger to exaggeration either, but these jerks have taken *hype* to a sinister level. It's as if the press actually wants us to *lose* the war on terror. They have gone from reporting a story, to hyping propaganda. To accept the premise that the press was just *reporting the news* about Abu Ghraib, I would have to be convinced that 90% of the major media outlets have no access to a dictionary.

A few years ago, I saw a story that got a good bit of attention in most of the news outlets. It was a story about college fraternities and their excessive hazing practices. For a few days in a row, we were shown actual videotape of these hazing techniques. The things I saw on *that* video would certainly have warranted a lawsuit or at least a letter to my congressman. They were disgusting and violent acts, and the *alleged* violence was even worse. There was even a story of a student being beaten and having a pinecone shoved into his rectum. In my opinion, *these* stories were worse than anything that I saw coming out of Abu Ghraib. After all, those guys were bloodthirsty terrorists, not college kids trying to make a better life for themselves. But my opinion aside, the word *atrocity* was never used to describe what those college kids were going through.

The Abu Ghraib scandal was embarrassing to me as an American. Not because of what happened at the prison, but because of how it was covered by the freest press in the world. As a news *consumer*, the most important aspect of a story (right behind *truth*) is *perspective*. If you can't keep a story in some kind of realistic perspective, then you become nothing more than a sensationalist, or a tabloid huckster. The Abu Ghraib story was so far out of perspective, that I am still amazed that anyone bought into it, but they did. That too is a sad testimony to the gullibility of some people today.

In my simple black and white world, it comes down to this. As juvenile as it may seem, even at age thirty-three, I still think that one of the funniest parts of the human body is the ass. I still laugh at fart jokes to this very day. When I finally saw the pictures from Abu Ghraib, my first reaction was a chuckle. The first picture I saw was the one of the naked terrorists piled on top of each other. Even now that all of the cards have been put on the table, I still laugh every time I see that one. The ones with the female soldier pointing and laughing at the enemy troops are always good for a laugh too. I can also safely say, that if the shoe were on the other foot, and I were in the pile of naked guys being laughed at, I would probably *still* think it was funny...lame, but funny.

Granted, some of those pictures were a bit over the top, but I defy *anyone* to find the humor in the beheading of another human being. You also have to keep in mind that there are people out there who would pay good money to be photographed under a pile of naked dudes. I have heard that in New York City, there are actually clubs devoted to that sort of thing. I have yet to meet someone who would pay good money to have his or her head sawed off with a dull blade. That's *perspective*! The press would do well to look that word up, if they ever find their dictionaries.

As the war in Iraq goes on, Abu Ghraib has become just one of many news stories that have been misreported. The liberal media is no different than any other media...they want to make money. Unfortunately, their only theory of how best to do this seems to be, "if it bleeds, it leads." Consequently, only bad news comes out of Iraq. If a roadside bomb is detonated, killing two Americans, that will be the lead story. The fact that *that* happens to be the chosen lead story is not the real problem. What chaps my ass is the fact that this is all too often the *only* story.

The two dead American's story should always be told, even it happens every hour on the hour. No reasonable person would argue that point. *My* issue is the fact that just like the Abu Ghraib story, the liberal media reports without proper context or perspective. If you were to take the current reporting from Iraq at face value, you would think that the only thing happening over there is death and destruction. You would probably think that the war in Iraq was a big waste of time, money and lives. Things like newly built schools, or modernized infrastructure, get little to no mention. There are few reminders of the new freedoms and rights that the Iraqi people now have thanks to the efforts of the coalition forces. There is very little prime time discussion of how a free democratic Iraq will affect the rest of the Middle East.

It is the American people, as well as our allies, who are making the sacrifices in the war on terrorism. You would think that the press would have enough decency to let us see the return on our investment. After months and months of being constantly bombarded with bad news, I think it's safe to say... "OK, we get it, war is hell." Where are the prime time exclusives about the reasons *why* we're in this war to begin with?

Am I to believe that Saddam's years of torture and atrocities wouldn't be worth a few shares in the ratings? Would it kill the media to give us a little reminder every now and then as to *why* we had to take Saddam out? Why do *I* have to use *my* personal time to play "junior cub reporter?" Why do *I* have to scour the Internet, read actual transcripts, or go to five other sources before I can get the *rest* of the story? Why is there no real *perspective* or proper *context* woven into news stories today? I have a theory.

The reporting of the war in Iraq has led me to a conclusion. I can think of only two reasons that the press has so poorly covered Iraq. The mainstream media is either biased to the left, or grossly incompetent. Either way, they are of little use to me.

Assuming that they actually *are* biased to the left, you still have to wonder why they seem to want *us* to lose the war in Iraq. My theory is that they don't want us to *lose* the war as much as they want us to lose our will to *go to* war in the first place. I think we have become so conditioned to believe the concept of war never being the answer, that we don't even question the motives of those running the media. "Make love not war" became the battle cry of the left in the sixties, and the same people who believed in that grew up to become the movers and shakers of the mainstream press (as well as college professors, as I mentioned earlier).

Unable to outgrow or contain the ideology that lost the Vietnam War, these same clowns now control what we see and hear before we go to bed at night. Add to that a Republican in the White house, and now you not only have a "peacenik" media, but now you have a *highly* motivated peacenik media.

As for the possibility of gross incompetence, I have already modified my theory. You see, you can't have liberalism *without* gross incompetence; therefore the media must be *both*.

My job puts me in contact with a lot of people; it also allows me to listen to a lot of news on the radio. I spend countless hours listening to call-in talk shows from both sides of the political aisle. Though this does not qualify me to be an expert on pop political culture, I *do* believe it qualifies me to make my next assertion. If the news media in this country were truly doing their job effectively, objectively, and honestly, there would not be so many people out there who *still* don't know why we're in Iraq.

I was willing to give these people a pass in the first few weeks leading up to the war in Iraq because it was a new concept to a lot of people for us to be going to war, and a lot of people don't pay much attention to world affairs. At this point in the game though, after all that we know about the history of Saddam Hussein and his two psychopathic sons, you would think there would be no question about the integrity of this war. Unless of course the news source that you assume is telling you the whole story is trying to push an agenda without being obviously biased. Couple this with a population that won't take the time to actually watch a State of the Union Address or a political debate because Snoop Dogg or John Madden aren't involved, and you end up with an uneducated public that just doesn't understand the situation.

As a professional instigator, I am always on the lookout for a good argument. Talking to people who agree with me actually bores me to tears. So whenever the subject of politics comes up, I come out of my shell and jump in headfirst. As you would expect, the war in Iraq comes up pretty often out on the road (truck drivers *are* the most opinionated people on the planet). Inevitably, the loudest guy will usually start by saying that he doesn't even know why we are there in the first place. I take that as my cue to ask him where he has been for the last twelve years. That is usually met with some mumbling and light Bush bashing, then after he collects his thoughts, he pulls out the "Where are the weapons of mass destruction?" card. "Bush said we were there because of weapons of mass destruction!" is the common reply. It's then that I ask the telling question; "Did Bush say that, or did someone *say* that Bush said that?" At this point, I usually get a "What do you mean?" Then I ask the questions that I already know the answers to; "Did you actually *see* him in a speech or a debate saying that? Have you actually *read* the transcripts of any of Bush's speeches, interviews, debates, or press conferences?" The answer is usually; "No, that's just what I heard on the news."

Just for fun, I then ask, "Hey, who won the big game?" or "Hey, who won the big race?" Then I just sit back and listen to the barrage of detailed "play by play" commentary. For the grand finale, I ask him if he actually *watched* the game/race. The answer is always yes, at which point I ask him why he didn't just listen to what they *said* about the game/race on the news. Gotcha.

Moving on from one unpopular war to another, *Vietnam* has become quite a hot topic lately. This moldy oldie of the left wing bias charts has been resurrected, compliments of the Presidential race. That's right, old school bias with a modern day twist.

By the end of the Vietnam War, *my* greatest accomplishment was learning to spell my last name. The most important thing to me at the time was my big box of Crayolas. You know, the one with the built-in sharpener. So today, anything I know (or think I know) about Vietnam comes from what I learned in school, or what I see on the History Channel. It is for that very reason that I am not *even* going to try to assume that I know *anything* about what happened over there. My opinion of Vietnam is nothing more than that...an opinion. After piecing together bits of information over the years, I have come to this conclusion; we were *right* to go into Vietnam. After all, we were trying to stop the spread of communism. It seems to me that we ran into trouble when we stopped letting the *warriors* fight the war. Apparently, politics got in the way, and the soldiers got caught in the crossfire.

Add to *that* the pacifist *geniuses* in the press fueling the anti-war sentiment, and the troops never had a chance. Winning that war was just not going to happen.

The Vietnam War was something that I never would have expected to be very relevant in life today. I know it was a bad chapter in American history, and I know that a lot of people who fought in that war are still walking around today. I have a personal connection to three of those people. One is the father of my best friend, another is one of my uncles, and the last is my own father. One thing that all three of these people have in common is the fact that they rarely (in fact almost never) talk about their time in Vietnam. I never gave much thought to this, until the year 2004.

For my money, 2004 will always be the year that I decided that if you can't see the bias to the left of mainstream American media, then you just don't want to. This was the year of the 2004 democratic primary election and campaign for the Presidency of the United States. What a can of worms this opened up.

I'm Not Hitler!

Since Vietnam, America has been able to "get by" without having to get involved in an all out *war*. We have had a few skirmishes, and Desert Storm was a big deal for a few weeks, but that was about the closest we had come. For liberals and pacifists, this was probably what they would consider "the good years." Then came September 11th. Unfortunately for the pacifists that had made a comfortable home in the media, an attack of *this* magnitude could not go unanswered. Even *they* couldn't "spin" the images of those towers falling to ground in such a way as to prevent a military response. They would have to wait.

After a successful liberation of Afghanistan, and a lightning fast invasion of Iraq, the press knew they had a problem. They knew that *this* particular President wasn't messing around. They saw the writing on the wall. This was a "wartime" president. For a group with a "war in not the answer" mentality, this could not stand. Re-election of a Republican president would mean four more years of conservatism being thrust into the limelight. That might actually give conservatism enough time to become fashionable...and we can't have that. Their biggest problem was the fact that we were into the "war on terror" so deep, that the typical "anti-war" candidate would not do well in the next presidential election. They would need to find a candidate that had enough "street cred" to look tough, but still uphold the pacifist ideals. They needed a liberal war veteran with enough political clout to claim experience. Enter - John Forbes Kerry.

John Kerry was the perfect fit, except for one thing; he came with baggage, lots and lots of baggage. In any other decade this would not be such a problem, but the press forgot one thing...the Internet. As soon as it was apparent that Kerry had won the Democratic nomination, he decided to turn his Vietnam War experience into his campaign platform. In every speech, and public appearance, every other word out of his mouth seemed to revolve around Vietnam. Then the truth about his past started to hemorrhage from the information superhighway. The media countered by questioning President Bush's service during the Vietnam War, all the while trying not to ask questions about Kerry's own service.

George Bush seemed to have little interest in following the media herd back to Vietnam. He answered the questions about his service and moved on. At one point, in an effort to satisfy the press, he even decided to sign form #180, which permitted the release of his military records. Of course this did not appease them. They continued to push the issue. The press dug into

President Bush's past as if they were on a mission from God. At one point, one reporter even wanted to see Bush's paycheck stubs as proof that he had served his full term in the Air National Guard. They tried to track down the people that he had served under, and repeatedly asked where *his* "band of brothers" was.

When it was discovered that Bush actually *had* fulfilled his duties (and then some), the media had to take a new tact. They belittled the fact that Bush had joined the Air National Guard, instead of a full time military branch. I thought this was a little odd, especially after the way they had treated Bill Clinton - a known draft-dodger. I also wondered how I would feel if *I* were serving in the Air National Guard and someone was putting *my* service into the same category as those who ran away to Canada. Besides, Bush was a jet pilot, and there was no way he could have known when or *if* he was going to be sent to Vietnam. Somehow, Dan Rather kept forgetting to mention that.

So the weeks went on and on, and so did the media highlighting of Kerry's four-month tour of Vietnam. Kerry was starting to look the part of a bona fide war hero, until along came a little group of regular guys who called themselves "Swift-boat Veterans for Truth." As it turns out, Kerry was not by himself in Vietnam, he had a few "war buddies."

This is where the left wing media got their "wake-up call." The "Swifties" were a conglomeration of soldiers who had served with or around John Kerry during his tour in Vietnam. All of these guys were telling one story about the events that Kerry had described, but Kerry was telling another. The "nuts and bolts" of this story are not relevant to the topic of this chapter, but the bias coverage of it *is*.

To be credible, the press was obligated to go after Kerry's past with the same zeal that they had Bush's. They did not even try. The "Swifties" were so willing to stand by their accounts of what happened in Vietnam, that they were *begging* to be heard and even wrote a book about it, which later became a best seller. This gave them credibility because if they were lying, then Kerry could easily sue them for defamation of character. In fact, the head "Swifty," Paul O'Neal, was practically *taunting* Kerry into suing him.

In my fantasy world of objectivity, this alone would be enough to warrant a "prime time" exposé by the big media players. After all, eyewitnesses were questioning the character and credibility of a man attempting to become the leader of the free world. Here in the real world though...no chance.

When it became clear to the "Swifties" that no light would be shed on them, they turned to "the new media", AKA talk radio and the Internet. They told their story, and people were listening...lots of people. Then their book went on the best seller's list, and the press almost crapped their pants.

Rather than look into what the "Swifties" were saying, the press decided to attack their credibility. They effectively took the spotlight off the questionable past of a potential President, and put it on a group of veterans. Their claims and assertions went unheard, as their motives, as well as their personal lives, got the "Bush treatment."

As the campaign dragged on, this story branched off into new levels of biased absurdity. More and more copies of the "Swifty" book sold every day, and the press started to panic. They had no authority or power over the Internet, talk radio, or the reading habits of the average Joe. They were going to have to take drastic measures if they were going to get Kerry into the White House.

The election was only weeks away and Bush was gaining in the polls. As the press' anxiety grew, they started getting sloppy. Media scandals started to pop up one after the other. Dan Rather of CBS News led the charge with a story that involved documents intended to embarrass the President, that were later proven to be phony. Then ABC followed when it was discovered that a carefully worded memo was sent throughout the news department from upper management, suggesting that they do what they could to give John Kerry a leg-up in the election through their reporting.

Not to be outdone, NBC followed suit by scheduling a three-day television interview with a gossip writer who had just written a book that was meant to tarnish the image of the Bush family. This would not be so obviously biased, had they given as much (or any for that matter) time to the Swift-boat Veterans.

My personal favorite happened only days before the election. In a television interview, Walter "the most trusted man in America" Cronkite took the prize for "biggest blowhard in town. After Osama Bin Laden released videotape threatening to attack states that voted for President Bush, "the most trusted man in America" asserted that Carl Rove had probably made the tape. To be fair to Walt, he *is* pretty old.

Of course, none of these stories got much airtime because those who would be in charge of *telling* the story actually *were* the story. You can't blame them for not wanting to shoot themselves in the foot.

On the topic of media bias, it's pretty hard to beat the coverage of the presidential debates of 2004 as a classic example. The coverage of these debates demonstrated two things; how *mediocre* our "professional" journalists are, as *well* as how biased they are.

In a presidential debate, "We the People" expect to see exactly where the candidates stand on any given issue. We not only *expect* it, we *demand* it. As voters, we need to see why or why not these people are worthy of our vote. For many people, a debate is their only exposure to the candidate. So, it stands to reason that in a presidential debate, scrutiny of the issues and especially the candidate's *position* on these issues should be first on the list of priorities for those who work in the media. Not any more.

In 2004 (a time of war), the most important issue is what color tie the candidates are wearing. Had I not witnessed it for myself, I would have never believed it. After one vice-presidential and three presidential debates, the most widely covered issue was the *style* of each candidate. Don't get me wrong, I *do* think that how a President composes himself is important, but it's definitely not the main reason to elect him. After all, Ted Bundy was polite and well spoken, and he was a serial killer.

I'm Not Hitler!

I realized, after the first debate, that "style over substance" was going to be the theme of the day. I also realized that there was a good reason for this; style was the only thing the media had to work with if they were going to get John Kerry elected. Let's face it, George Bush is a great guy, but he often looks uncomfortable in front of the camera. He also tends to speak in simple terms, but then again...so do I. Then there is his famous pronunciation of the word "nuclear." It became famous because the press wouldn't let it go. This would not be such a big deal, if they had ridiculed John Kerry the same way for *his* pronunciation of the word "idea." After all, there is no "r" on the end of it.

Much attention was then paid to the facial expressions of each candidate. Even *this* was not treated even-handedly. Bush was criticized for facial expressions that the press considered to be "arrogant," and even "un-presidential." What *I* saw was a look of disbelief and frustration when Kerry would skew the facts. I had the same look on *my* face at the same time.

This too, would not be such a big deal if the same amount of effort were put into criticizing Kerry's expressions. I watched the debates on a channel that was offering split-screen coverage. The first thing that I noticed was Kerry's expressions as President Bush was talking. Every time Bush would make an assertion or a point that made Kerry look bad, Kerry would smile and nod his head as if he were agreeing with Bush. He did this over and over again, always with a wide-eyed look on his face. My wife actually noticed it first. We both thought it was a little creepy. Again, little mention of this in the press.

As all the attention was being paid to issues of style, major issues of *substance* were being ignored. Throughout the debates, Kerry was asked many questions about his plans for dealing with different issues. Again and again, he claimed to have a plan, but was never prodded into actually telling anyone what these plans were. So when it came time to discuss the topic of Iran, I almost fell out of my chair when Kerry *finally* told us what one of his plans were. He basically said that he wanted to employ the same plan for Iran that President Clinton and Madeline Albright had used to deal with North Korea.

Look how well *that* has worked out for us. In my ignorance, I assumed that *that* would be the end of the Kerry campaign. Surely this would be the front-page story across the US the next day...wrong!

Another question that I assumed would have sunk Kerry was about nuclear proliferation. He was asked what he would do to stop the proliferation of nuclear weapons. His answer nearly made my jaw fall to the floor. Rather than tell the American people what he would do to stop rogue, or terrorist-supporting nations, from getting their hands on nuclear weapons, he proclaimed the he would put and end to *our* low-yield nuclear "bunker buster" bomb research and development. Not the enemy's...OURS! Of all the countries in the world that he could have given as an example of being a nuclear threat, Kerry chose *America*. Again, the press gave Kerry a pass and never questioned his judgment.

Better yet was his take on the reasoning behind America going to war. He actually suggested that any rationalization for going to war should have to pass what he called "a global test." I am pretty sure that *no* war would pass a "global test," because no matter why you would go to war, there would be *someone* on that globe who would disagree with it. In the meantime, your enemies would only get stronger. The press' only problem with *this* "Kerry-ism" was the fact that President Bush criticized it during the debate. Never mind the fact that debates are held for exactly *that* purpose.

The icing was put onto the liberal biased cake when Kerry was asked about the issue of "gay" marriage. Rather than answer the question, which was referring to *marriage policy,* Kerry decided to break nearly three hundred years of debate precedent by mentioning the daughter of his opponent's Vice President. Kerry needed a high profile name that would symbolize the "gay community" in his rebuttal to any question related to "gay" issues. He had many options available to him. He could have mentioned any number of prominent openly gay folks from Hollywood or even the political arena. He could have dropped such names as Rosie O'Donnell, Governor Jim McGreevy, or Congressman Barney Franks, all of who were "gay" Kerry supporters. Instead, he took the "low road," and used Vice

President Cheney's daughter (who happens to be gay) as a political pawn. Without ever asking her permission, he asserted in the debate that *she* would probably agree that homosexuality was not a "choice." I have tried to find another instance in history where this has happened, but so far, I have had no luck.

The press (as well as the debate moderator) dropped the ball by not pressing Kerry to answer the question that was *actually asked*, which had nothing to do with the origin of homosexuality. I can only imagine how the press would have reacted if President Bush had used a similar tactic. The reason I can only *imagine* this, is because he wouldn't, and didn't.

Now we fast-forward to *after* the 2004 presidential election. This is where some of the best examples of a liberally biased media can be found. Actually, there were a few examples *during* the election, too. Early on, Election Day was proving to be too much for the press to handle. After months of relying on *polls* to make assumptions about what direction "the people" were planning to take the country, they had lost touch with the concept of *investigative* journalism.

Polls in general are not a bad thing, but they are usually not the most accurate way of finding out what *everyone* is thinking. Besides, there are so many polling companies; they all have different methods, and all end up with slightly different results.

Since I am supposed to believe that the press is equally objective, I can only assume that what happened next was a result of its own incompetence. Late in the afternoon on Election Day, the ballots had *yet* to be counted, but most of the major media outlets were ready to declare Kerry the winner. Relying strictly on "exit polls," they were under the assumption that the entire country had swerved to the left and voted for Kerry...or were they?

I suppose it *is* possible that *all* the exit polls that were being used by the major media outlets were wrong, but that didn't explain why so much stock was being put into them before *any* of the votes were counted. After so much egg had been coating the faces of the media outlets that had "called" the election wrong in 2000, I thought it would take some pretty big cohones to make the same mistake twice. Unless, of course, these same media factions are *all* really, really stupid. On the other hand, there is *one* explanation that was rolling around in my head as a possibility.

Here is where I have to walk the fine line between "probability" and "conspiracy." When I sit back and look at "the big picture," I can only come to one conclusion. In my "common man" mind, it seems pretty obvious that the "anti-Bush" sentiment has become such a regular part of the attitude of the mainstream media, that the goal of swaying the election was less of a widely orchestrated conspiracy, and more of a general philosophy by default. Shedding bad light on the "conservative" and good on the "liberal" seems to have become "business as usual" over the years. I would even go as far as to say that most of the people working in these establishments probably don't even realize that they are doing it anymore.

My theory is that the "anti war" press had to do whatever they could in order to stop what they believe is an unjust war, and threw one last "Hail Mary" pass to try to get an "anti war" candidate elected. The "Hail Mary" pass was just a matter of reporting early in the day that Kerry was looking like the "clear winner," in hopes of discouraging those who might vote for *Bush* later in the day and into the evening. You see, some states allowed their polling places to stay open till 9 pm, but most closed at 7 pm. The exit polls were being reported as early as lunchtime that day. The hope seemed to be that if you were a Bush voter traveling home from work, you might hear that Kerry was the "projected" winner and not bother voting. Whether the exit polls were accurate or not would be nearly impossible to prove at that time. Besides, if they weren't accurate, the blame could be put on the polling companies. It was the perfect crime.

I suppose it *is* possible that there is a massive epidemic of incompetence devastating all of the major media outlets. That seems like such a big pill to swallow though. The irony is in the fact that whether you believe the Election Day coverage was a result of incompetence, or conspiracy...the press is worth about as much to the "average Joe" as a used car salesman in a green plaid leisure suit.

For angry young conservatives like myself, the real fun started after the dust of Election Day had settled. For the next couple of days, the rage we were feeling inside after months and months of watching the press systematically try to destroy the Bush administration seemed to melt away as we watched the press try to figure out what had just happened.

Almost immediately, the press started making excuses for the Kerry campaign.

Some *journalists* who had been closely following the Kerry team even started to tell of the problems they had witnessed during his run for the presidency. The first questions that came to my mind were; "Why didn't you tell us this *DURING* the campaign?! Isn't it your *job* to report the *news*? Why did we hear every insignificant negative detail about the Bush campaign for the past year, and only hear of the riffs in the Kerry campaign *AFTER* the election?"

Then came the finger pointing. Rather than accept the fact that the Democrats had lost because of their "all over the road" attitude toward just about every issue that had come down the pike, the press again took the low road. Admitting a failure to communicate a solid plan to deal with the issues was out of the question. To save the face of the Democratic Party after a decisive election, the press would need to find a "scapegoat" issue that had not already blown up in Kerry's face during the campaign. This left out the war in Iraq, the economy, social security, taxes, health care, education, and national security...you know, the important stuff. The only thing left were those old chestnuts...God, guns, and gays.

According to just about every media outlet in America, as well as some around the world, Kerry had lost the election due to an overwhelming majority of people voting on some sort of a Christian mandate. This may even be true, but the idea that Kerry had lost because most of us just thought he was *wrong*, never entered the minds of the press, or the Democratic Party. It was as if they thought they had *hidden* Kerry's Senate record from us. They completely forgot that the average Joe now has access to such things. They just kept on assuming that it was the *evangelical* vote that brought Kerry down. Using myself as an example, I don't even *go* to church...I just saw Kerry as a threat to our country and voted accordingly. I have to believe that I was not the only one who thought this way, but according to the press, the bulk of the electorate is made up of Bible thumping, gun toting, homophobes. I *am* a "gun toter," so I guess one out of three ain't bad.

Even if it were true that "red states" were mostly comprised of the "religious right," why would the liberal press have a problem with that? Aren't liberals supposed to be the champions of "diversity of thought and expression?" You don't have to look too hard to spot the irony in that...or the hypocrisy.

Until I started this book, I had only a vague understanding of just how far the mainstream media tilts. The examples are wide ranging; from their common refusal to refer to George Bush as "President" Bush instead of "Mr." Bush, to their common refusal to put any of blame for September 11th on former President Bill Clinton. Other examples range from Peter Jennings opening a segment on voter fraud after the 2004 election by saying that the American people have "gotten it wrong again," to the eagerness to report anything and everything that the left wing might dream up. To this day, Jesse Jackson still claims that millions of voters were "disenfranchised" during the 2000 election, but has yet to present *one* person who was illegally kept from voting. For some reason though, he still gets lots of airtime.

Even worse than *slanting* the news, is *creating* it. My understanding of how the press used to be is that they would hear of a story, investigate it, and if anything came of it, *then* they would report it. Today, the press uses a whole new approach to journalism. A good example of this is one I mentioned earlier. Peter Jennings of ABC News introduced a story a few days after the 2004 election. It was a story about *alleged* voter fraud. The thing I thought was most interesting was not the fact that they had decided to run such a story, but *why*.

According to Peter himself, the story came to light because of the massive amount of email that ABC received about the subject. Ironically, the conclusion of their own report was that there was little to no evidence of voter fraud after all...the story still aired though. I was always under the impression that if a story turned out to be a "dud," it wasn't worth reporting. If someone reports a car accident, but it turns out that there was none after all, would the evening news still run a story about that car accident? It sure is nice to know that if I can get a mass email campaign going that says Bill Clinton is actually a "visitor" from the planet Pluto, ABC will produce a report about it.

I mentioned earlier that I do *not* believe that the liberal slant of our most popular media sources is a massive organized conspiracy, and I stand by that. The most logical explanation could probably amount to nothing more than *environment*. This theory can be best demonstrated simply by looking at a map that depicts "red" and "blue" states. The first thing you notice is the fact that the most densely populated areas are "blue/liberal." Yet most of the remaining areas are solidly "red/conservative." New York City, Los Angeles, and Chicago are among the bluest of areas. *Coincidentally*, all of the mainstream media outlets are headquartered in New York City, Los Angeles, and Chicago, as well as the solidly blue Washington, DC.

According to the theory of *assimilation*, how could these news outlets be anything but liberal? If you live in Texas for a few months, your family will notice a southern drawl in your speech when you return home for a visit in Pennsylvania. This is only natural, but imagine living and working for years in an environment where the only socially acceptable ideology is liberalism. Over time, you would probably lean to the left strictly by osmosis. Now compound that over a few generations, and you have a giant Petri dish that grows nothing but liberalism. Unfortunately, our most trusted sources of information have been right in the middle of these Petri dishes for many years.

If I were a betting man, I would be willing to put up a paycheck to say that the typical "blue state" journalist does not purposely make an effort to "liberalize" his/her work. It's just that having little to no exposure to an alternative viewpoint is just bound to show up in any article or report that they might produce. I truly believe that if the major media outlets were based in "red" states, news would be reported exactly opposite of the way it is today. This would suck too, because I wouldn't want the news to be slanted all the way to the *right* either. The sad thing about the way our press handles things today is the fact that objective journalism is no longer even considered to be possible, let alone a goal. I refuse to believe that this is the case. There should be no reason that both sides of an issue couldn't be objectively explained as well as put into proper perspective. And if the media refuses to be objective, then at the very least they have an obligation to be up front about it. If they are going to slant to the left, then that should be put on the screen to let the consumer know. Besides, what's so scary about that? We are living in a time when Britney Spears is making millions of dollars through the miracle of *marketing*...and she has absolutely *no* appreciable talent. So why couldn't a major news network be marketed as "all liberal, all the time?" I would have *so* much more respect for a network that *admits* it's bias, as opposed to one who insults me by trying to *hide* it.

So, who is to blame for media bias? Well, I hate to break it to ya', but *you* are. And so is everyone else who doesn't take the time to *educate* themselves about what is really going on out there. Every day, we make decisions in life. We decide to learn something, or to watch the game. We decide to learn something, or smoke a bowl. We decide to learn something, or accept what a media outlet tells us is the whole story. Basically, it is *our* fault for not asking the right questions, or in most cases, any questions at all. Accepting everything we are fed is not education. After all, the architects of communism knew all to well that if they could control the media, then they could control the people too. Today, there is no excuse for this. We have more access to information *now* than at any other time in history. The six o'clock news no longer holds the monopoly on current events and information.

Thankfully, Al Gore took the initiative to invent the Internet just in time. This technology may have actually made the mainstream media *obsolete*. At the very least, it has raised the bar for journalism standards. Only a couple of questions still remain; What if the Internet hadn't been invented? And how many big news stories were mishandled *before* the age of the Internet?

All logical signs seem to point to liberal bias in the media being less of a *conspiracy*, and more of an institution. I see this as a good thing. Like slavery, segregation, witch burning, and eight track tapes, *institutions* can be exposed and defeated just by getting the word out. A conspiracy can take years to even *identify*. Then you have to get past the network of people conspiring against exposure.

So how can average folks hope to see past a biased media to get to the truth of any given subject? For starters, you need to learn how to spot a "shady" story. If the reporter claims to have gotten his information from "Pentagon sources," "White House insiders," or anything with the word "unnamed" in it, then the story probably has a few holes in it. A credible source will usually allow him/herself to be identified.

Pay attention to *why* a story is being reported in the first place. Is the story being reported because it is actually *news*, or is it a response to an unspecified amount of email that may or may *not* have been sent to the reporter? Does the reporter offer any *proof* of this "massive amount" of email? Does what you hear in a story match what you see in *your* life? For instance, if you are told that the poverty level is at it's highest level in fifty years, do you actually *see* any evidence of that in *your* town?

Probably the best way to avoid bias of any kind is to go straight to the source. Don't listen to what some anchorman tells you about what was said; *hear* the person say it for themselves. That is what the Internet is for. Why listen to a "middle man," when there is probably streaming audio, video, and printed transcripts of what a person *actually* says at your own fingertips. Besides, it's cheaper than a newspaper, and you don't get ink on your fingers.

If you really want to get a better sense of what is actually happening out there in the real world, the most important thing you need to remember is...don't trust anyone!

I close this chapter with one more example of how liberal bias works *against* everyone in this country we call home...liberals *too*, ironically. A few weeks ago, an embedded reporter was traveling with a group of Marines as they attacked terrorist strongholds in Fallujah, Iraq. As the group entered the house that enemy gunmen had been hiding in, a small number of what *appeared* to be dead terrorists were found inside. One young Marine noticed that one of the suspected terrorists was moving and immediately began to shout, "He's faking death!" He then shot the suspect, all while the camera was filming.

Terry Leasure

Of course, relying on the reporter or the cameraman to see the "big picture" and have enough foresight to *not* submit this footage for airing was obviously not a realistic concept. Instead, the "if it bleeds, it leads" agenda took precedent. So, the video hit the U.S. media and was presented in pretty much the same way as the Rodney King video back in the early nineties. The only difference was, *this* time there was *no* controversy.

You see, as someone who actually *does* "support our troops," I understand that it is the job of our military to kill people and break things. *They* are not there to "serve and protect." *They* are not there to direct traffic, or write tickets. *They* are not there to take people into custody to be held over for trial. It is the job of the military to destroy the enemy, *before* the enemy has a chance to destroy *them*. They are not there to administer justice, or practice law.

Unfortunately, liberals do not understand these things. The story quickly became, "U.S. soldier kills unarmed Iraqi." The first problem with this is the fact it had yet to be proven that the enemy fighter was even an *Iraqi*. After all, there are people from all over the Middle East fighting against the coalition forces in Iraq. This individual could have just as easily been Iranian, Syrian, or Jordanian. In any event, that Marine probably didn't have time to check the dude's wallet to see if he was an Eagle Scout, or Al Qaeda.

The second problem is the obvious implication against the U.S. soldier. You see, the people we are fighting in Iraq and Afghanistan have no concept of "rules of engagement" or

"Geneva Convention protocol." All they know is, they want to kill as many of us as possible, and by whatever means necessary. In short, they play dirty, *very* dirty. A common tactic of a terrorist is to booby trap dead bodies. Another is to play dead until a soldier moves in for a closer look, then either fire a hidden gun, or detonate a hidden explosive device, killing that soldier and whoever else may be nearby. This is *exactly* what that Marine in Fallujah was facing when he entered that room. He had an *obligation* to himself, his unit, and even those reporters to shoot first and ask questions later. Any other decision would have been risking the lives of everyone in the room.

Thanks to the anti war press though, the context of this story has quickly become "Should this Marine be court marshaled?" and "Are American forces guilty of war crimes?" Apparently, the left would like to put our soldiers in a position where they need to think that they might be brought up on charges if they kill the enemy. Silly me, I thought that my tax dollars were being spent to *train* soldiers to kill the enemy. A soldier in the middle of a combat zone doesn't have enough on his mind already, let's confuse him by threatening prosecution for doing *exactly* what he was trained *and* ordered to do. Nothing says, "your country supports you" like *pending litigation.*

Though it was just a bit before my time, I can't help but assume that this was not how it was done in World War II. How have we come to a point in time, where the benefit of the doubt is automatically given to the *enemy*, and not our own troops? I can't believe I'm even *thinking* this, but it would almost be worth the destruction of the United States just to watch the power of the media be stripped away by the same enemy that they seem so hell bent on *helping* today. Remember, I did say "almost." But it *would* be ironic if years from now, Katie Couric and Helen Thomas were taken out into the street, beaten with sticks, and forced to wear burkhas by a terrorist-supporting army that *they* had helped to defeat America?

I guess I should just be thankful that the press didn't have this attitude back in the forties...because I *hate* sauerkraut.

Chapter 11
Hey, Norman Rockwell...Paint This!

For the better part of this book, I have been trying to give you some idea of how liberalism affects the security, economy, and even the general landscape of our nation. As I look at how the world around me is changing, I suddenly feel an urge to include a chapter about the *attitude* of our nation as well. It seems that America is in dire need of what Hank Williams Jr. referred to as "an attitude adjustment." Basically, there seems to be a growing divide in the nation today. The press would like you to believe that this divide is more *political* than anything else, making it a matter of just "red" vs. "blue." But from where I sit, the divide goes much deeper. I think that what we have here is a full scale "culture war." I don't know exactly when this war started, or who fired the first shot, and I definitely don't know who's going to win. Nevertheless, I seem to have inadvertently become a foot soldier in this war, and this book is my first salvo.

You see, my motivation for writing about my concerns for the future of American culture showed up about six months ago in the form of our baby daughter. If it were just *me* who had to deal with the way things seem to be going, I probably wouldn't give a crap about culture and morality. But now that I am a father, it's a whole new ball game. The fact that my offspring is *female* only compounds my worries. She's only six months old, but I already feel as if I should be standing guard at my front door with a shotgun in my hands. How *my* genes had anything to do with the creation of something so precious is beyond me. Her mother's genes must have cancelled mine out. All the same, some of the things my daughter will be facing as she gets older scare the crap out of me. Many of these things seem to be coming a more accepted, as well as a *common* part of, our culture.

At first, culture seems like a very subjective thing, especially in a country like America, where the population is made up of people from all over the world. Lately, the same can be said for morality. For all of our sakes, let's hope this is not true.

The good ol' boys at Webster's define *culture* this way; a particular form of civilization, especially the beliefs, customs, arts, and institutions of a society of a given time.

That's all well and good, but it's those last two words in the definition that give me the willies. I worry that the "given time" of American culture might be running out.

The fact that America is such a free and accepting country is actually a double-edged sword. As our nation is made up of people from all over the globe, we get the *bad* as well as the *good* from all over the globe. But we'll get into *that* later. Right now, I think it is worth taking a look at some of the more "home grown" problems our country is facing.

Culture and morality are two separate and different things, but more often than not they go hand in hand with one another. One of the more glaring examples of this can be seen in what we are still, for some reason, calling "professional sports." I put that in quotations because they don't look very *professional* to me.

First let's get something out of the way. I am still a conservative. This means that I am totally incapable of criticizing any athlete for accepting the stomach turning, mind numbing, and embarrassingly shameful amounts of money that they make for playing a *game*. If I thought I could get away with being paid obscene stacks of cash to chase a ball around for a few hours, believe me, I'd do it too. I point my criticism at those of *you* who continue to shovel this seemingly unlimited income into the pockets of these *athletes*. So I thought it would be fun to start this chapter by taking a brief look at some of the "cultural benefits" that sports fans get for their money.

I've never been a sports fan, but I *do* accept the fact that professional sports are a big part of the culture of the United States. After all, "baseball, hot dogs, apple pie, and Chevrolet!" just wouldn't sound right without the "baseball" part. But the problem is not what these sports *were*; it's what they have mutated into. Baseball, football, basketball, and to a lesser extent hockey, used to be games that kids could play in their back yards and have a good time on a Sunday afternoon. They would have *role models* to look up to in the form of the professional team players. These *adult* players would set examples of motivation, perseverance, and sportsmanship, all while making only a *respectable* salary. Today, the game itself is not much different, but the whole "role model" thing has been traded for something called "bling."

Don't get me wrong; I'm sure that the attitude of some professional athletes back in the old days could have used some polishing too. After all, beer and sex have been around for a long time. The difference is, back then there weren't any twenty-four hour sports channels. In fact, player interviews of *any* kind were pretty rare. Today, we get up-close and personal coverage of everything a player does, whether it's an off-the-cuff remark or a murder scandal. Unlike yester-year, when a sports hero's personal problems were more of a footnote in history, scandals seem to have become the whole *point* of having a career in sports. At the very least, a right of passage.

You may think that someone who has little interest in sports has no business criticizing them. After all, what do I really know about sports anyway? Actually, I really don't know a damn thing about sports. In fact, I only have a basic understanding of the games themselves. As for team or player stats...forget about it.

The problem here is not the sports themselves, it's the culture that they seem to be breeding today. *My* beef is the fact that the fallout from the decline of "sports culture" eventually ends up polluting the daily lives of *everyone*, regardless of their interest in sports. Just because I may not be a sports fan, doesn't mean that my child's doctor isn't. If professional sports have taught *him* that cheating is an acceptable way to get ahead in life, will that show up somewhere in his treatment of my daughter? Did he feel that way in medical school? What about one of her teachers? You see, sports fans come from all walks of life. This would not be such a problem if so many people were not as heavily influenced by what they see their favorite athlete doing before, during, and after the game. The fact that some of these people pick up the bad habits of the players that they idolize is *their* problem. The fact that some of these people will have direct contact with my daughter is *my* problem.

So what *are* some of the problems with professional sports today? Well, lately there seems to be no shortage. There are two in particular that seem to be getting the most attention over the past few years though. The first is *steroid use* among athletes. This seems to be most common in baseball, but apparently other sports are having to deal with it too. Even the Olympic games are not immune to the steroid controversy. But I am not going to point fingers and name athletes, because *they* are not the issue here. Their *actions* are what we're talking about right now. Their identities are pretty much irrelevant to the discussion.

Steroid use is one of those rare issues that I have a tough time nailing down. On one hand, I *personally* think of steroids as being just another form of cheating. I think it gives someone an unfair advantage over someone who is unwilling to use an illegal drug. Maybe a competitor has enough respect for their game to stay away from steroids. Or maybe they're just afraid of the health and/or legal consequences of taking them. It's even possible that they just don't want to set a bad example for the kids that might actually consider them to be a role model. Any way you look at it, these are the athletes that have *my* respect.

On the other hand, you *could* argue that steroids are just another way to push the boundaries of science, as well as the limits of the human body. After all, if it's OK to take a drug that can make you healthy when you're *sick*, then what's wrong with taking a drug that makes you more healthy when your not? Of course, "healthy" seems to be a relative term when you're talking about steroids. Taking them might allow you to lift more weight, but it might also give you nut cancer! Then again, there are unlimited types of health risks associated with just about *every* sport.

You could even say that there is not much difference between risking nut cancer, and risking a broken spinal column or a head injury. It's all in the name of competition, and if you're not willing to go that extra mile, then maybe you just don't "want it" bad enough.

Whether you are *for* or *against* using steroids, I think we can all agree that the real issue is *honesty*. If those who want to use steroids were *allowed* to, and didn't feel a need to hide it, then there would be no issue. After all, if there is nothing wrong with using them, why be ashamed of it? Announce it to the world; be proud!

Of course, in fairness to the sporting "purists," there would have to be separate "All Steroid" leagues. There could even be "steroid vs. non-steroid" games in the off-season. That would probably be a ratings bonanza!

The sad part about steroid use is the fact that when a record is broken today, you have to wonder if that athlete had any chemical assistance. What were once sports designed to test man's ability to compete against *man*, have mutated into one giant test to see how medical science can alter or enhance the human body.

In my opinion, this takes the competition from between the athletes and places it between the pharmaceutical companies instead. I feel as if I should be rooting for the *drug company* who can get "their man" to hit the ball farthest, rather than "the man" himself. That's fine if you want to market a new drug, but it doesn't do much for the sport. Even though I have little-to-no interest in sports, I *do* know that I'm a purist. After all, what's so fun about watching someone hit a home run, if you know they couldn't do it without being "on the juice?"

At first, I thought that steroids were just a part of our culture. I assumed that they were something we would just have to get used to over time. I realize now that like a lot of bad things out there, steroids are actually just a *product* of our culture. Liberals would tell you that they are a result of a culture of ultra-competitiveness that is being forced onto our kids today. They would compare *that* to what they would probably call, "a reckless desire to conquer others." Of course they would also have to heap a little of the blame onto the pharmaceutical companies that develop the drugs to begin with. Don't hold your breath waiting for a liberal to apply *that* same standard to people who sell marijuana.

A conservative (that's me) would tell you that steroids are the result of an "anything goes" culture, where whatever you do is OK, as long as no one else gets hurt. Then they would link *that* with the "style over substance" culture that tells us that looks trump brains if you want to be popular (a common liberal concept). Let's face it; a lot of guys are guilty of taking steroids just to take the shortest route to getting laid. It's an easy formula: steroids = "big guns" and women who are attracted to guys with "big guns" = sex.

Realistically, I have a feeling that steroid use has less to do with "right vs. left" and more to do with "right vs. wrong." Either way, I have little-to-no respect for those who use them (except for medical purposes of, course). Even though steroid use may be becoming a socially acceptable way to get ahead of the competition, to me it doesn't pass the "smell test." I know this is not a very scientific way to look at the issue, but I break it down this way. I wouldn't want *my* daughter to use them. It really is just that simple.

Moving on to another popular byproduct of sports culture...*violence*. I'm not talking about *violent sports*. Though I'm not a big sports fan, I *have* been known to watch quite a few boxing matches, and I do love to see a good football tackle. I'm talking about *sports violence*. From bench-clearing brawls at baseball games, to basketball players beating up fans in the stands, and let's not forget those post-game riots. For some reason, there seems to be a lot more violence associated with professional sports lately.

When it comes to sports violence, I think there is plenty of blame to go around. Part of the problem may be in the fact that the "bad boy" image has always been a mainstay of sports culture. Of course, to be the "bad boy" you still need to one-up the "bad boy" who came before *you*. Over time, tattoos and earrings just don't cut it anymore.

Compound the fact that players are getting younger and richer, with the fact that their educations commonly take a back seat to their training, and you have the perfect ingredients to make a ticking time bomb. After all, I'm thirty-four years old and I'm *still* not sure it would be a good idea to give *me* access to fame and fortune. I can't even imagine what kind of damage I would have done to myself at eighteen, having just been handed a ten million dollar signing bonus. At that age, I barely had enough personal discipline to handle the $6.25 an hour that I was making.

More often than not, parents of these young athletes seem to put so much emphasis on how to throw the ball better or how to run faster, that they spend very little time on what to do if they actually *do* succeed at their sport. They are given all the tools to reach their destination, but are totally lost when they get there. Then when they get that first million or so, these kids act as if they couldn't possibly shatter their knee or go to jail.

Blame could also be put on the infiltration of a completely different culture into modern professional sports. "Hip-hop" is probably a harmless enough cultural oddity by itself, but unfortunately it has spun-off a few subcultures that sports (as well as the rest of us) can do without. "Thug" or "gang" culture has been around for a long time, but only recently has the hip-hop culture decided that it was cool to glorify it. It seems to be a little more than coincidence that some of the things you see in the average hip-hop video are showing up in professional sports. The treating of women as little more than prostitutes ("hos") is a mainstay of hip-hop videos. Could there be any connection to *that* and the fact that so many professional athletes are brought up on sexual assault charges?

The perversion of the term "respect" is also a common theme in hip-hop culture. According to hip-hop philosophy, respect is something you automatically acquire just by saying you deserve it. Once you've decided that you deserve it, you need to demand and defend it, often with the use of violence. Something as simple as the scuffing of someone's shoe can even be taken as a "dis" (sign of disrespect) instead of just an accident. Of course when you have suffered the tragedy of a scuffed shoe, you gotta punch someone's teeth out, and if the crowd is big enough, then you better just *shoot* the "scuffer" to maintain your level of "respect." This mentality also shows up on the field, as "sportsmanship" seems to be taking a back seat to "showmanship."

I am really not trying to *blame* the hip-hop culture for the negatives in sports culture, but I do think that it's possible that they tend to feed off each other. After all, some of the same problems seem to plague them both, the idolization of money and fame, and complete lack of self-respect. The sad thing is that as usual, those few bad apples are spoiling the whole bunch. It's not that everyone in the hip-hop scene or professional sports is an uneducated spoiled jerk, but they *are* the ones who get all the "glory."

This brings us back to our old friends "the press." I do think that it is safe to say that the press has a lot to do with the creation of these morons, but in this case their hands *are* sort of tied. Though the press *does* spoon feed your typical misfit with the fame they crave, they *do* have an obligation to report the news. It may not mean much in the grand scheme of things, but if a famous sports figure is accused of shooting someone in a nightclub, it *does* count as news. If a famous hip-hop promoter is accused of a similar act, well...that's news too. It may be a vicious circle, but I still can't blame the press for this one. On this topic, they're just doing their job. It *would* be nice if they wouldn't treat these stories as if they were the biggest news of the day though. No crime committed by any athlete is worthy of the total media blitz that they commonly receive. If Kobe Bryant flies a jet airliner into an office building, I'll accept it as the lead story. Until then, his sexual escapades belong at the *end* of the broadcast. That is not to say that an accusation of rape is trivial, but people are accused of rape everyday without it making the front page.

Just a side note to my opinions on the hip-hop culture. It is true that I may have a personal bias against "rap" and "hip-hop" music. To be honest, they both give me a headache. But my negative feelings about this type of music (I use that term loosely) are pointed only at the music itself. Remember, I'm talking about the *music* now, we've already covered the culture. To take any type of legitimate look at the culture though, you do have to look at one of the driving forces *of* that culture. In this case, the music.

As I have recently turned thirty-four, I am fighting a constant battle between understanding current "pop culture," and becoming an old geezer. So when I criticize any type of currently popular music, I immediately recoil in horror. The idea that I am becoming "that guy who just don't understand today's music" (AKA my father) is just too much for me to bear. But then I think back to what I used to listen to when *I* was in high school. Personally, I was pretty heavily into the "punk rock" scene, with a side order of "speed metal" just to take the edge off. To be honest though, this was a very short phase of my adolescent experience. To be *brutally* honest, I'm pretty sure that I was into *that* particular scene more to look cool and complex, and less because I actually *enjoyed* the music. The difference between the punk rock of my era, and the hip-hop of today is the fact that hip-hop is a major player in the battle for young minds. Punk and speed metal have always been a pretty obscure style of music, whereas rap and hip-hop are all over the place. The irony is that they are equally as annoying to me today.

Putting lyrics aside, I would be willing to bet that if someone did a study, they would find that "punk," "rap," and "hip-hop" music actually make you dumber. I put lyrics aside because there actually *are* some pretty impressive lyrical qualities to these particular styles of music (especially rap). It's that mind numbing, repetitive beat that makes me want to drill a hole in my own head! I truly believe that the lack of instrumentation, harmonic or melodic quality in rap and hip-hop is partially to blame for the lack of imagination and personality in the kids I see today. Now all I have to do is wait for some college professor to prove my point.

For those of you who may be thinking that my opinions on hip-hop culture *or* music have *anything* to do with racism...not true. I offer my B.B. King, Buddy Guy, Jimi Hendrix, Lenny Kravitz, Ray Charles, Muddy Waters, and John Lee Hooker collections as "Exhibit A."

Of course, I do realize that this particular discussion is largely a matter of personal taste, but let's face it, on the scale of musical ability, you have your Stevie Wonders, and you have your "Method

Mans." I know this definitely makes me sound like an old geezer, but I think it's a sad commentary on today's youth when a typical eighteen year old knows the words to at least one *Fifty Cent* song, but has no idea who Miles Davis was. In short, real musicians are the ones that rappers "sample" from when they have no talent of their own. Again, another form of cheating. Again, a socially acceptable part of today's culture...like steroids.

The way I see it, if you really want to learn about a particular culture, you need to look at how they spend their free time. You need to see what they do when they have no obligation to do it. After all, a lot of people take jobs because they pay well or provide good benefits, not because that same job is something they would do for free if they had the time. To study the occupations of a particular culture doesn't say a whole lot about the people themselves. As a very basic example of my point, you can have two cultures from opposite sides of the globe, both with similar infrastructure (cars, trucks, planes, trains, factories, electricity, and running water), but completely different ways of enjoying life after punching out at the end of the day. The truck driver from one country might go home and teach his kid how to build a model airplane, because that's a cultural norm in his homeland. The truck driver from *another* country might go home and teach *his* kid how to properly wire an explosive vest, so it doesn't fail when he blows himself up in front of a busload of other children. This, of course, being a cultural norm in *his* homeland. In both countries though, truck driving is pretty much the same. So to study the trucking industry in these two very different countries wouldn't actually teach you very much about their culture.

It is for this very reason that most of this chapter is focusing on the things that *entertain* us in America. Sports are a big part of just about everyone's culture, so they can tell you a lot about the people from any given country. For instance, in our country, a *ball* is commonly used to play some of our most popular sports. In other countries, a dead goat carcass is used for the same purpose. I'm not exactly sure what that says about *our* country, but still, I think it speaks volumes.

In case you were wondering, I haven't forgotten to go further into the topic of "post game rioting"; I'm just not sure what I could possibly say about it that would be the least bit enlightening. I mean c'mon, talk about morons! How do you get to a point in life where you are *so* passionate about someone else's ability to throw and/or catch a ball, that rolling a police car over, or smashing someone's windows seems like a good idea? Actually, I try not to think about it too much, I'm already too pessimistic about humanity as it is.

Moving on to another driving force in our culture, we are getting into a subject that is very much in my wheelhouse...Hollywood. Specifically, movies and television. *This* topic is right up my alley, not because I have gone to some school to study film or communications, but because I have probably had my face glued to a TV or movie screen for a half of my life. I wish that were an exaggeration, but I'm sure it's pretty close to the truth. As a matter of fact, I even worked in a movie theater during high school. Not because the money was good, or I couldn't find a better job closer to home, but because I wanted to see the newest movies for free. As much of a movie fan as I am though, when Clint Eastwood won the Oscar for *Unforgiven*, I don't remember rolling any police cars over. And as phenomenal as Samuel L. Jackson's performances are (check out *Pulp Fiction*), I don't feel an urge to smash other people's windows after I watch one of his movies. After at least thirty years of consuming just about everything Hollywood has offered me, I consider myself an expert on the subject.

I feel pretty safe in saying that television and movies have had more influence on our culture than anything else since the Bible itself. The jury is still out on whether this is a good thing or not. *That* probably depends on how you look at it. After all, there has always been the question of art imitating life, or vice versa.

As I mentioned in an earlier chapter, the power that Hollywood has to shape popular opinion is beyond comprehension. Political power pales in comparison. Television and movies tend to dictate how we think, talk, and interact with each other. Sometimes examples of this can be seen in something as innocent as a popular catch phrase that eventually modifies someone's attitude. In the early eighties, how many employers regretted the hit TV show "Alice" after telling the boss to "kiss my grits" became fashionable? Another more serious example could be seen as recently as this past year, when "Fahrenheit 9/11" taught us that it was fashionable to be fooled into believing the worst about our country by using slick editing and liberal innuendo.

Then there are the extreme situations. These are those ever popular cases where a certain movie or song is linked to someone's death. Sometimes it's a murder, sometimes it's a suicide; other times, it's just some moron trying to mimic something he/she saw in a movie. Either way, it has been popular for some time to blame Hollywood.

I personally remember an example of this back in the early nineties when an obscure football movie was said to have caused the deaths of some kids who were trying to recreate one of the movie's scenes. The scene involved the characters lying down in the middle of a busy highway as an act of bravery. I don't remember the exact details, but apparently when some kids tried to do this in real life, there was no happy ending to *their* story. Of course, this became a national news story, and everyone was pointing their fingers at Hollywood. As if these kids wouldn't have eventually found some other spectacularly stupid way to "off" themselves. Not that I'm trying to insult the *parents* of these geniuses, but c'mon! If your teenager for any reason thinks that laying in traffic is a good idea, then you have dropped the ball as a parent.

Don't get me wrong; eventually Hollywood *is* probably going to be the downfall of our society, but not for the reasons you may think. Immediately, you might be assuming that the ultra-violent, over-produced, turbo-sexed crap that passes for entertainment today will turn our children into soul-less murdering criminals. My answer to that is "Texas Chainsaw Massacre." Here was a film that came out when I was still in diapers, and even by today's standards is still one of the bloodiest movies to ever hit the screen (loosely based on a true story, *ironically*). In fact, this was just one of many films that represented an entire genre of movies dedicated to one-upping each other in the categories of "blood and gore." The point being; an entire generation of kids grew up watching these flicks, yet never got around to severing anyone's arm or eating someone's eyeball. So when someone points out how violent movies are these days, I always ask them if they ever heard of a guy named "Leather-face." The only difference *now* is that the quality of the special effects used to portray the violence is far more realistic.

As someone who grew up on "Tom and Jerry," I can tell you that I have always known that if a hammer hits you on the head, it *will* hurt. The great thing about violence is that it's pretty easy to figure out. It's fairly cut and dried. That's why "make believe" violence is so entertaining. It's pure escapism. When Bugs drops an anvil on Yosemite Sam's head...it's funny. When Moe hits Larry with a pipe wrench...it's funny. When Neo hits Agent Smith...it's not funny, but it is dramatic. Whether it's Vincent Vega or Rooster Cogburn doing the shooting, everyone is pretty clear on the whole "bullet vs. flesh" thing. Beyond that, people were getting shot and/or brutalized way before Hollywood got into the business.

As I just mentioned, violence is one of those things that is pretty easy to understand, even at a very early age. It's basically a "cause and effect" thing. This brings us to the next most commonly cited cultural scourge coming from "Tinsel town"...SEX. Unlike violence, *sex* is probably one of the most confusing, complex, and personally influential things that most of us will ever deal with in our lifetime (especially if you're a guy). After all, I'm thirty-four and I still have a million questions on the topic. When I was being thrown headlong into the uncharted waters of puberty, the single-most monolithic part of my psyche was *sex*. Like most teenage boys, little else was capable of holding my attention, but at the same time, there was nothing more intimidating. It seemed like every passing day brought a new question. I soon realized that the answers I got from my parents were vague at best, and *asking* the questions was no day at the beach either. So in order to satisfy my curiosity, I did as most young men in my situation had been doing for years, I consulted the experts...Hollywood.

As hard as it may be to believe, this was not such a bright idea. Actually, I would probably have been better off having had no sex education at all, as opposed to what I was learning from movies and television. The entertainment industry taught me that the primary function of a woman was to provide a place to hang a pair of breasts. Don't get me wrong; I *am* a heterosexual male. I love to look at breasts as much as the next guy, but it took me a lot longer than it should have to realize that there is more to women than what's in their shirts. There's also what's in their pants! Just a joke.

To understand where I'm going with this, you need to know that I grew up in the late seventies and early eighties. The common theme of the day was that women were only as powerful as their men allowed them to be. The "chesty dimwit" was a very popular stereotype in both movies and TV. Characters like Chrissy on *Three's Company* stole the show in prime time. Daisy Duke was always able to help foil Boss Hogg's plans with the use of her "T&A" as opposed to her "IQ."

Then, as the eighties got up to speed, a new paradigm started to emerge. The power hungry, upwardly mobile, glass ceiling smashing, professional career woman was quickly becoming the new "in" stereotype. Again, right out of Hollywood, as if decreed from above. The pendulum had swung from one extreme to the other. Hollywood saw to it that women would no longer be seen as a weaker, dimmer species good for only one thing. Now they would be seen as some sort of multitasking super heroines, able to easily climb the corporate ladder while still finding the time to juggle a husband, boyfriend, two kids and a cat. All while wielding their sexuality in much the same way that "Dirty Harry" wielded his .44 Magnum. Of course this is paralleled with the male stereotype being that of *boys* trapped inside the bodies of men, always needing the help and or comfort of a "mother figure."

These stereotypes can be seen even today in some of the most popular TV shows around, such as "Sex and the City" and "The Sopranos."

One stereotype that seems to have remained a constant (at least in my lifetime) is that of the parent. Examples of parents being portrayed in a positive light are few and far between. Parenthood is usually written into a script as something to avoid altogether. Mothers are usually shown as being overwhelmed, overworked, or overbearing. Fathers don't get off any easier either. They are usually portrayed as being out of touch, distant, uncaring, and even abusive. In most family-oriented sitcoms, the *children* are almost always portrayed as the only ones who know what's going on at any given time. Looking back at the most popular shows or movies from my era, I'm sure that there are plenty of exceptions to this rule, but the only one that comes to mind at the moment is "The Cosby Show."

If you were to accept the typical Hollywood version of the *typical* American family, you would probably assume that you would be better off dead, than to be *sentenced* to parenthood. This might explain why I didn't even *try* to start a family until I was in my thirties. In fact, I can remember being asked by one of my friends, if I were given the choice between contracting the AIDS virus, and getting a girl pregnant, which would I choose? I told him I would take the virus because the *agony* of children would last longer. Looking back now, I realize that I was a dumb ass.

This begs the question "Why bash the American family?" When it comes to sex and violence, I can understand the logic behind lacing a movie or TV show with guns and boobs. After all, a large segment of the population enjoys watching explosions, car chases, gun fights, and of course beautiful women. It only makes sense to put things like this in a movie in order to make box office dollars. Besides, sex and violence are nearly impossible to conceal, so you know pretty quickly if you're going to be offended by them, giving you the opportunity to turn off the tube, or leave the theater.

On the other hand, concepts like "family bashing" make me scratch my head. As big of a movie fan as I am, and with as diverse a taste in cinema as I have, I don't recall ever getting up in the morning and saying to myself "Man, I'm in the mood to see a movie that makes American family life look like an exercise in futility!" Is there *really* a market for this? Or is there some other motive? Could there be some sort of agenda coming from Hollywood?

Before we get too involved in trying to answer such lofty questions, maybe we should check out some of the other *less* noticeable themes coming from the coincidentally "blue" state of California.

There is the popular theme of women being just as capable of being just as good a soldier on the battlefield as a man. How many times have we seen this in the movies? Sometimes as a supporting sub-plot such as in *An Officer and a Gentleman*, or even the main plot of movies such as *G.I. Jane* or *Courage Under Fire*. Through movies like these, we have learned that women under five foot tall and less than one hundred twenty pounds can kill the enemy just as effectively as a six foot one, two hundred pound man. In addition, they can also take a punch or a bullet just as well too.

In a movie, this is all well and good, but as we are seeing in "real life" Iraq and Afghanistan, this is just not the case. If you show me a woman who thinks she should be allowed on the battlefield, I'll show you a woman who has never been punched in the face or raped by a man twice her size. Back in chapter two, I mentioned my friend Scott's petite female co-worker. Whenever I think of her, I realize how easy it would be for an average sized man to physically *destroy* her tiny frame and reduce her to a bloody mass on the battlefield. Conversely, when I think of my friend Scott, or any of his *male* co-workers, I realize how easy it would be for any one of *them* to turn *me* into a broken, bloody mass. Unfortunately, our government didn't figure this out before they allowed women into the ranks. Now sisters, wives, daughters and mothers are coming home in boxes, but we *still* consider ourselves to be a *civilized* society. Are we so blinded by political correctness, that this is now the new face of "respect for women?" Chivalry is dead... liberal politicians murdered it.

Just for the record, as of today's writing, it is February 2005 and we *still* have not heard a word from Jessica Lynch about her ordeal at the hands of the enemy. Ironically, I have absolutely no interest in basketball or Kobe Bryant, but I know more about *him* than I ever wanted to. It's almost as if someone is trying to keep the results of the great "women in the military" social experiment a secret. I'm sure there will be a movie about *that*, coming to a theater near you.

Not likely, that would mean admitting the failure of yet another liberal concept.

As you may have already guessed, my theory is that the idea of sex and violence being the scariest thing coming out of Hollywood is probably way off. The way I see it, *liberalism* is the real "monster in the closet" waiting to attack our children.

One of the more subtle liberalisms to hit the silver screen is the ever-popular idea that having money is synonymous with being evil. This concept goes way back. In fact, this theme can be found in some of Shakespeare's greatest works. People have been ripping him off ever since. From the early days of cinema where "the evil land baron" was always out to steal the poor farmer's land, to "the evil corporate mogul" of today, the "rich" are almost always written as the bad guys. Then there is the Hollywood mainstay of portraying anyone in a management position as being an overbearing, power-hungry, back-stabber, or just a complete moron. OK, *that* particular portrayal may be pretty realistic, but still, it's not nice to stereotype.

But seriously folks, Hollywood teaches us at a young age that being wealthy is a bad thing. This is not to say that the Enron scandal was just a fluke, but for anyone to assume that most of those who became "rich" did so by ripping people off, seems to be a pretty big leap of cynicism. Besides, as I explained before, it is the affluent's spending habits that keep the poor employed. After all, someone has to *build* the yacht before someone can *sail* the yacht. Unfortunately, supply side economics is not a very popular theme at the box office. So most of us who were educated by the silver screen grew up having a built-in prejudice against anyone better off than ourselves. Looking back now, I wonder if this attitude had anything to do with some of the less-than-stellar working relationships I've had with former employers.

The flip side of the "evil rich" stereotype is that the "poor" are almost always portrayed as the "good guy." Countless movies have been made where the lead character is written as a "drifter" who comes into town only to be hassled by some sort of authority figure, usually a sheriff or a local "rich guy," sometimes even a rich local sheriff. Then the "drifter" reluctantly becomes the savior of the oppressed townspeople by taking down the sheriff. Some of my favorite movies have this very plot summary. Though this theme makes a pretty good Saturday afternoon movie, I wonder if it's repeated use by Hollywood has anything to do with some people's dislike of lawmen?

To go even further, Hollywood has made some pretty good coin by changing the definition of "good" and "bad" guys altogether. More and more movies are made today where you are asked to sympathize and even root *for* the criminal, and consequently root *against* the lawman trying to stop him. The criminal then becomes the hero of the movie, and the lawman of course becomes the villain. As in the movie *Heat* with Robert DeNiro and Al Pacino, the lawman is more often portrayed as a tragic figure whose life is in shambles and whose judgment is questionable.Conversely, the criminal is portrayed as being very smart, charming and levelheaded. The fact that the character on the *opposite* side of the law may be a thief or a killer becomes a rarely spotlighted footnote to the plot of a lot of movies these days. This is not exactly a new paradigm, after all *Les Miserables* and *Robin Hood* have been around for quite a while, but today, it's becoming the rule as opposed to the exception.

Other popular Hollywood stereotypes include that of the drug addict who is almost always supposed to be sympathized with. After all, it was the fault of society (the rich) that led him/her to such a helpless position in life.

Then right behind the drug addict comes the homeless person, or some variation of both. Filmmakers have always been able to belly up to the sympathy trough with *this* character. This of course is because most of us think of the homeless as some type of victim, ironically because of Hollywood stereotyping. Hopefully, you can see the vicious circle there, if not, please consider the following.

The Hollywood stereotype of the homeless, is much like the Hollywood stereotype of pretty much everything else...slightly skewed. Here is where I am going to make an assertion that will probably make you think I have lost my mind, or am just incredibly insensitive. The reason Hollywood cashes in on the "homeless victim" thing is because it's an easy sell, partially because of guilt, and partially because of gullibility. When it comes to a silver screen representation of the homeless, as humans we tend to have a "there but for the grace of God go I" mentality. But think about that for a minute. What would it take for *you* to actually be living on the street?

I'm Not Hitler!

If you lost your job, would it be *impossible* to find another? It may not be your dream job, but could you not work *somewhere*, doing *something*? Would you not even be able to afford a bus ticket to an area where there *is* a job? Even if you couldn't find any job anywhere, could you not draw unemployment, or welfare? If you lost your house, would it be *impossible* for you to find a cheap apartment somewhere? Would you not have one family member or friend to help you until you got back on your feet? If not, why? What did you do to *so* alienate yourself from everyone else, that not *one* person cares if you end up eating trash in an alley? If things are so bad out there, why are *you* the only one in that alley? Why isn't every alley in town overflowing with homeless people?

Keep in mind that I am only applying the following theory to American citizens. Citizens of some other nations have legitimate reasons for being homeless, but not Americans. It is my belief that there are two basic types of homeless people, the mentally ill who have fallen through the cracks of society, and those who on some level of their psyche actually *want* to be homeless for one reason or another. I give the mentally ill a pass on this, because it's not always *their* fault that they ended up on the street. After all, they *are* sick and probably do depend on someone else's help to get by.

I give no such pass to anyone else. I contend that if you are an American citizen in the twenty first century, and you are homeless...it's because you want to be. So what are some reasons that a person would want to be homeless? I *suppose* that there are a handful of people who decide to just chuck it all, and ride the rails, or bum around just for the adventure of it. I've read stories and seen documentaries about folks like this, and to be honest I actually *admire* their sense of adventure and even *envy* them on some level. But these are not the homeless people I am used to seeing in the dumpsters behind the shopping centers where I deliver. The homeless people *I* see are not carrying a backpack, a guitar, or a notebook full of interesting stories from the road.

Realistically, if you see a homeless person rummaging through a dumpster, he/she is probably running from the law, an alcoholic, a drug addict, or is just plain lazy. Actually, lazy may be a bit of a stretch, because it takes a lot of work to be homeless. Besides, most of the laziest people *I've* ever met can usually be found sponging off someone else, either by glomming onto someone more successful than they are, living off of a relative's money, living off the government, or winning frivolous court settlements.

Those first two methods of living the "lazy" lifestyle don't really bother me too much. I figure if someone is willing to support a freeloader, then who am I to argue? As sad and pathetic as it may be, it really doesn't affect *me*. It's those last *two* that really chap my ass.

You see, living off of the government is actually code for "living off of you and me." The same can be said for frivolous lawsuit settlements. The money going to support people who live off the government comes out of *our* pocket in the form of taxes. Remember, the government does not *make* money; it *uses our* money to operate. Then as consumers, *we* pay for the settlements that companies pay out due to frivolous lawsuits by way of higher prices. We pay *again* by way of higher insurance premiums. And of course, we pay one last time because higher prices mean a higher tax rate.

So if you know someone who recently sued a company without having a *valid* reason, don't forget to thank him/her when you go to purchase a product or service from that same company, because a small percentage of that lawsuit will be paid by you.

Yet again, you will be waiting a long time for Hollywood to make a movie about the drag that excessive litigation puts on our society. For some reason they seem to think that making movie after movie about how the "little guy" wins a court battle against the "evil corporation" never gets old. In reality, this theme was played out a long time ago. Besides, some of us actually think that a movie about the mentality it requires to become totally dependent on someone else would be a lot more interesting, as well as realistic.

The list of cultural influences that Hollywood has produced is probably impossible to calculate. Some are more benign than others, but some are pretty serious. Movies like *Philadelphia* taught us that the real tragedy of AIDS is the bigotry that the gay community faces. Strangely, no movies come to mind that depict the fact that if you live a monogamous, non-promiscuous, heterosexual lifestyle, you'll have very little chance of contracting the virus to begin with.

Countless movies have taught us that a "black" man can't get a fair trial, yet O.J. Simpson walks around a free man to this day. Movies have also taught us that the Vietnam War was a waste of time, as well as an imposition of American values on an otherwise peaceful communist government. Thanks to movies like *Platoon, Apocalypse Now, Hamburger Hill, Full Metal Jacket,* and *Born on the Fourth of July,* we now know that the average soldier in the Vietnam War was a pot smoking hippie who did not know why trying to stop the spread of communism was a good thing.

Then there are those "pet" projects that seem to seep out of Hollywood in a slightly less aggressive way. They usually pop up as small subplots that lend little to a movie or TV show. Other times they become talking points for the Hollywood elite when they make appearances on talk shows. You have to keep a sharper eye out for *these* particular themes, but after a while you see them pretty clearly. The easiest way to spot them is to realize that there is little difference between a stereotype, and a Hollywood liberal "pet project."

Typical examples include the ILLEGAL immigrant character that is always written as a hard working family man who is only here in America to give his family a better life. He never breaks the law, never has a communicable disease, and never requests help from the government. But since this is a chapter about influences on our culture, allow me to inject a little reality into the script. There are different cultures all over the world. Are we to assume that everything coming in from another country is an *asset* to our culture? If playing the bongo drums is a common part of your culture, then there is probably nothing wrong with you coming to our country and sharing *that* part of your culture with your new neighbors. But what if it's a normal part of your culture to train dogs or chickens to fight to the death for sport? What if it's a normal part of your culture to make your wife walk behind you in public? What if it's a normal part of your culture to mutilate your daughter's genitals, or stone your wife for disrespecting you in public? When conservatives are portrayed in movies or accused on talk shows of being disrespectful to the cultures of others, is *this* what they are talking about? Is our concern for traditional American culture really just a "knee jerk" reaction?

Then there is the "gay" character that is always written to have the highest qualifications for parenthood. We'll get into *that* whole discussion in an upcoming chapter, but the most questionable part of the "gay" character stereotype is not the *quality* of the character, it's the *quantity*. Over the past few years, homosexuality has gone from being *accepted* to being downright *cool*. Could the fact that Hollywood has been bombarding us with not only gay supporting characters, but also *entire shows* about being gay have anything to do with that? From "Queer Eye for the Straight Guy" to "Will and Grace," apparently I am to assume that being gay is no less common than being *short*. I have no real statistics on this, but I work with about one hundred and fifty other men, and they *all* have wives and girlfriends. Maybe it would be different if I were working in California or New York.

So at the end of the day, who is actually to blame for any downfall of American culture? Since we do live in a free society where the government has very little control over what we see and hear, I have to conclude that *we* are responsible for what direction our country travels. Who else's fault would it be anyway? If your teenage boy can't find a job, is it the government's fault? Or is it yours for letting him talk and dress like a "gangsta' rapper?" Whose fault is it that you don't understand most of what's going on in the world, but you can tell me how many home runs some guy hit last year? Whose fault is it that the only thing your kids know about history is what Oliver Stone taught them?

You see, the phrase "We the people..." was written for a reason. We the people are responsible for *ourselves*. I know that whole concept escapes most liberals, but that's just the way it is. Ironically, we actually *do* have the power to change the things that we claim worry us. For instance, the only way Hollywood can corrupt the mind of a child is if there is a parent that let's them do it. Ask yourself some questions. How often do I let my kid watch TV? How often do I pay attention to what he/she is watching? Do I myself understand what he/she is watching? How much money did I give to Hollywood this week? If I don't like the message a certain show is sending to my kid, did I buy any products from the companies advertising during that show? Am I raising my kid to be able to handle and understand the things he might see or hear unexpectedly? Do I discuss what he/she sees on the screen, or am I too busy or too scared to bring it up? Do I allow my kid to mimic the things he/she sees or hears on TV? Do I actually know what CDs, movies, or video games my kid has access to? Do I know the ratings symbols on the packages?

The reason that I'm focusing on the "kid" aspect of this discussion is because today's kids are going to be in charge of tomorrow's culture. *We* are the ones who are in charge of directing this nation, via our children. Besides, Hollywood only makes crap because there is always someone out there willing to buy it. Every time I see some kid walking down the street with his pants falling down below his ass, I realize two things...how gullible some people are and how brilliant some people are. For that to happen, certain things have to fall into place. First, a marketing genius need to come up with the idea, sell it to a production company and market it through a movie or a rap video. Second, a parent needs to be completely oblivious to what's going on in their kid's life. Third, the kid needs to be so starved for attention that he is willing to look like a complete moron to get it. It also helps if both the parent and the kid have the IQ of a mushroom.

The pants-falling-down look is just one of many marketing ploys used to distract people long enough to sell them a big steaming pile of excrement. Britney Spears passes for entertainment because her boobs distract us. Rappers pass for entertainment because gold teeth, gold chains, and bad attitudes distract us. These are not new concepts, but people still fall for them every time. If you were to strip most of today's entertainers of their images, and force them to get by on talent alone, they would starve to death. Meanwhile, B.B. King is still packing the house with a guitar, a smile, and a butt-load of talent, well into his golden years. He's never had to drop his pants or pretend to be a *thug* to sell a record. Norah Jones has not yet had to show us *her* boobs to become a success either. But I see very few kids wearing nice suits or playing jazz piano.

If I were a conspiracy theorist, I might assume that the

entertainment industry as a whole is trying to dumb-down the population in order to make it easier to make a profit, or to further some leftist agenda. I just don't think this is the case. Instead I think it is more plausible that entertainment is no different than anything else we consume. We are too busy to care about quality. Today, we are more into convenience. We are willing to accept mass produced music and movies, so that's what we're given. The entertainment industry knows this, and they're just giving us what we want. They will always be willing to crank out the McDonald's version of entertainment as long as we are *not* willing to demand a steak dinner. My plan is to raise my daughter to understand that true talent needs no gimmick.

On the bright side, there may be some light at the end of our entertainment tunnel. Over the past few years "reality television" has become more and more popular. I think of this as a good thing. Though the term "reality" may be stretched from time to time depending on the show you're watching, TV stars are no longer the sole arbiters of what's entertaining. As a TV addict myself, I didn't even realize until recently just how much *my own* viewing habits have changed. With the exception of *The Simpsons* and the occasional *Seinfeld* re-run, I almost never watch sitcoms anymore. They just don't grab my attention. Today, I am more likely to be watching something on "The Discovery Channel." I would rather watch a show about people who build cars or motorcycles and the personal dramas that come with them, than any make-believe, predictable, agenda based crap that usually comes out of Hollywood. Besides, I can identify with *real people* much easier than characters that were manufactured in some focus group. Apparently, I'm not alone. The most popular shows on TV today are reality based. Shows like *The Apprentice, Fear Factor, Survivor, American Chopper,* and *American Idol* are pulling in big ratings now.

Much to the dismay of Hollywood actors and writers, *real* people are decidedly more entertaining, and more interesting as well. And if the viewer actually *learns* something from watching the lives of *other* real people...all the better. After all, watching a real person struggle with other real people can actually make you feel better about your own situation in life. That's because life, unlike a script, is not predictable, and does not always have a happy ending.

As I sit back and try to write about things I notice about culture in America today, I can't help but notice a few other things that make me shake my head.

Most of my life, I have been slow to adapt to new technologies. I didn't buy my first CD until 1992. Two years ago, when I purchased my first computer, I was totally computer illiterate. For the most part, I still am. Most of my experiences in front of our computer are just a series of trials and errors. Nevertheless, I "git-r-done" one way or the other. So when it came time for me to write my first email, I was working strictly on assumption. I sent emails to everyone I knew to let them know that I was now "on line." Over the next few days people started to make comments about my email writing style. I was told that most people don't bother writing full sentences, let alone paragraphs. Then they would follow that up by commenting on how good my spelling and punctuation are. Now that I have been sending and receiving email for a few years, I see that they were right all along.

Apparently, it is now a cultural norm to just pound on the keyboard like a baboon on Valium, and hope that some sort of message gets typed. It was only recently that I learned that I own the only computer on the planet with "spell check." It was around that same time that I realized that people have enough time to put those little smiley/frowny faces at the end of sentences, but not quite enough to capitalize or punctuate. This may not be the most extreme example of how we seem to be letting our culture slip away from us, but I do consider it to be a clue.

The way I see it, being sent a poorly spelled email is just one of many things we are willing to accept "as is." On the other side of the coin, we are also willing to put little effort into writing them. In a world where it is getting harder and harder to communicate with people you haven't known for half your life, you would think we would make more of an effort to keep our most common means of communication intact. Language is one of the most important parts of any culture. When a culture allows their language to be destroyed, it is the beginning of the end of that culture. If emails were the only part of our language that was falling into mediocrity, I probably would have never brought it up. Unfortunately, a whole list of things is chiseling away at the language of our culture.

ILLEGAL immigration, sliding educational standards, political correctness, and poor parenting are all working together to eventually kick our collective cultural ass. After all, does the average person have the time or motivation to learn English, Spanish, and "hip-hop," as well as all of those stupid email abbreviations? My guess is, no. That's not even to mention any of the other couple-hundred languages that are competing for dominance in America. Wouldn't it be nice if we could all speak one common language? Wouldn't it be nice if we were all able to communicate and get to know each other better?

At this point, the typical liberal response would probably be to accuse me of putting down other people's cultures. Commonly used terms for this are *imperialism, isolationism*, and the old lefty favorite, *fascism*. The truth of the matter is, I have never heard anyone on my side of the aisle say that people need to forget everything (or *anything* for that matter) they know about their homeland. We just want people who come here from other cultures to respect the fact that America has a culture of its own. And if you come to someone else's home and plan to call it your own, you have a moral obligation to adapt to *their* culture, not assume that they should adapt to yours. Besides, it would be impossible for an American to adapt to the hundreds of other cultures that set up shop here.

Common decency and self-respect demand that if you want to become an American, you need to learn our language, customs and history. Beyond that, if the culture in someone's homeland is so great, then why did they leave there in the first place?

Another popular response from the liberal elite is to ask why English is assumed to be the official language of the United States. I've always considered that to be a bit of a reach, but just for the sake of argument, I'll bite. When you go to the Smithsonian Institution to see the original documents of the founding of our nation, are they written in Spanish, German, French, Pig Latin, Esperanto, "hip-hop," or English? I rest my case.

America's culture has always been pretty loosely defined. That is because we are a "melting pot." We are a conglomeration of many cultures. But if this nation is going to survive, we all need to be on the same page. Our history has not changed because of the amount of any one foreign culture moving to America. The future is a different story. As the principles and traditions of *others* become more common in America, the original principles and traditions of this nation will become more and more vulnerable.

Contrary to popular belief, conservatives are a very welcoming bunch. Most of us are descended from immigrants ourselves. Speaking for myself though, if you'll take notice, *my* immigrant ancestors had enough respect for *their* new country to learn the language and teach it to their own children.

If you're still thinking that American culture has nothing to fear, then keep a few things in mind. In America, we are *still* debating the whole abortion issue. That means that even in the year 2005, there are *still* people out there who don't get the fact that a baby does not magically appear on the date of it's birth. It takes nine months of growing. These people are known as the "pro choice" lobby. Apparently, the *choice* is between killing an unborn baby or letting it live, not between keeping one's legs open or shut. Abortions are provided by doctors who ironically take an oath to *protect* life, and are often funded by taxpayers. I was going to let Hollywood off the hook on this one until I watched a re-run of *Lethal Weapon III* recently. The actress playing the role of the *teenaged* daughter of Danny Glover's character was wearing a "pro choice" T-shirt in a prominent scene. Of the endless slogans to put on a T-shirt in a major motion picture, I wonder why *that* particular one was chosen? It had absolutely nothing to do with the plot, and was every bit as obvious as a typical *product* placement.

A lot of men are afraid to even *think* about the abortion issue, let alone *talk* about it. Not me; I gained credibility on the issue on the day I discovered my testicles. You see, you can't make a baby without those (at least not yet). I gained even further credibility on the day I saw the sonogram images of our daughter. At twelve and a half weeks, she already looked like a tiny little baby. She had arms, legs, ribs, and you could even see her face! When I saw my daughter's image on the screen, I thought back to my liberal years. I remembered how one of the more popular ways to rationalize abortion was to tell people that a baby is just a "blob of tissue" for the first half of a pregnancy. I bought into that mentality hook, line and sinker. I knew that would be the rationalization I would use if I ever accidentally got a girl pregnant. I was truly a moron. What I saw on that screen was no "blob"...it was my daughter. It was then that I realized that a law needs to be passed that requires a pregnant woman to get a sonogram using the new 4-D technology, before she can kill her child.

As with many liberal concepts, the language is changed to sanitize the issue. That is why the term "abort" is used instead of "kill." When "right wingers" like myself point this out to liberals, we are called "demagogues." To tell the truth, I don't even know what that term means. Not because I am incapable of picking up a dictionary, but because I know that whatever a liberal calls me is either dead-on and should be taken as a compliment, or is off by a mile and should be ignored. Both scenarios tell us more about *them* than me.

I have always thought that sanitizing the language to promote your cause was a pretty good way to tell if you might be wrong about something. After all, if you're *for* something, be proud of it. Commit to your position. If you are "pro choice", don't half-ass it. Stand up and shout it from the rooftops that a woman has the right to kill her baby. Put a sign in your yard that says "One American citizen has the right to kill another on the basis of convenience, or financial burden!" Make another one that says, "Penises accidentally fall into vaginas!" Don't forget the sign that says, "Consequences are for babies!" The only thing worse than a liberal is a liberal that can't embrace his/her own liberalism.

Am I a "no exception" pro-life conservative? No. It is my personal belief that an exception should be made in cases of rape. After all, this is the only way that a woman can become pregnant against *her* will. No man has the right to force a woman into pregnancy. Statements like those will usually send a liberal into a convulsive fit, but they're true nonetheless. Popular opinion equates pregnancy from failed contraception to pregnancy against one's will. That makes no sense to me. It was the woman's *will* that allowed her pants to come off. Is it not true that "no" means "no?" Did "no" disappear from the English language when I wasn't paying attention? Rest assured that *my* daughter will be learning the meaning of "no."

Personally, my favorite liberal rationality for keeping abortion legal is what I call "the coat hanger defense." This is the idea that abortion should be kept legal to prevent women from resorting to so-called "back alley abortions," which are apparently sometimes performed with a coat hanger. According to popular opinion, I am supposed to feel *bad* for a woman who is injured or killed while attempting to kill her baby. I guess I'm also supposed to shed a tear for an armed robber who gets killed by police while holding up an old lady. Since the Sept. 11th terrorists died in the process of killing *those* people, should we be feeling sorry for *them* too? Let's say, for the sake of argument, that abortion was illegal, and a woman's only option to have one was the "back alley" method. Who is *forcing* her to? Did someone put a gun to her head? If so, we have laws against that. Did the government step in and demand her to do it? Maybe in other countries, but not *this* one. The answer to these questions is NO. Women who kill their babies in "back alleys" make the conscious decision to do so. If they die or get injured in the process, you will have to remind me as to why I should lose any sleep over it. How these women ever adopted the role of "victim" is beyond me. Hey, there's an interesting word...*adopted*. That word is used in our culture almost as rarely as the word *abstinence*. How's *that* for irony?

Do men have any responsibility when a woman gets pregnant? Yes. But it is the *woman* who actually holds the power to destroy the baby. It is for that very reason that I'm not dwelling on the man's role in this discussion. He *does* have rights and responsibilities, but at the end of the day, he has very little power over what the woman actually decides to do with the person growing inside her.

It is at this point that liberals will usually respond with some sort of assertion that people should be able to have sex if they want to, because after all, it's a natural thing. Actually, *natural* doesn't enter into it. Poisoned berries are *natural*, but we don't eat *them*. As for being able to do what we want...c'mon. How many things can a person do without consequence? Oh yeah... *consequence*. Without that little word, we would *all* be able to jump out of an airplane a thousand times without parachute failure. It's that little word that reminds us that people actually *do* get killed by drunk drivers, no matter how *fun* drunk driving may be. Like skydiving and drunk driving, *sex* is something that we *choose* to do. Like skydiving and drunk driving, if you can't handle the *consequences*, you probably shouldn't do it.

Does the fact that I lost my virginity at an early age make me a hypocrite? Maybe.

Or, it could make me a person who wants to keep someone else from making the same mistake I did. Trust me, if I had access to a time machine, I would have kept it in my pants. After all, I have nothing to show for any of my sexual conquests but a list of women that I'm uncomfortable bumping into today.

Abortion on demand might *never* become illegal in America, but maybe someday we can make it obsolete. Then again, a whole generation of kids was taught by a sitting President that *oral* sex is not sex. Compound *that* with the persistent push to teach children more and more about sex in public schools, and we may have to wait a little longer.

Liberalism's fascination with killing the defenseless has now seen to it that unborn babies are not the only ones who need to worry about being killed for the sake of convenience. Apparently, anyone who does not have a "living will" is now on the hit list. As of today's writing, a woman in Florida is being starved to death BY COURT ORDER. I repeat, BY COURT ORDER! No, she was not a convicted murderer who chose this as her method of execution. She was just a regular person who in her early twenties committed the crime of not writing a "living will." As a result, after she came down with a medical condition that left her in a near-vegetative state for about fifteen years, there was a dispute over what her wishes actually were.

Despite the fact that only one person (her husband) said she wanted to die, but many people (friends, family, and nurses) said she didn't, a judge ruled to err on the side of <u>death</u>. Despite the fact that there was enough evidence, as well as witnesses, to call into question the husband's motives, the judge refused to reopen the case and opted to order her to be killed. Despite the fact that for every doctor who claimed she was a lost cause, there was another who said she could be rehabilitated; the judge ordered her to be put to death. Terri Schiavo was sentenced to death by a judge who was acting on the hearsay of another unsigned document. She committed no crime. This decision set a legal precedent, as well as sent a message that is loud and clear; "If you don't get a living will, we're gonna kill ya!"

Going back to the Hollywood theme, as I watched the mainstream media repeat over and over how Terri Schiavo would die "peacefully," "with dignity," and "suffer no pain" even though she would be without food or water for weeks until she died, I couldn't help but think of the movie *Soylent Green*. Is Terri Schiavo a test case for a future culture of euthanasia for the sake of convenience? Will we eventually get to the point where it is socially acceptable for the elderly or handicapped to be put to death? Think about it, we already do it to the unborn. Needless to say, if I ever hear of the government issuing rations of little green wafers for the masses to eat, I'll be running through the streets just like Charlton Heston.

I also couldn't help but wonder why the judge didn't free up the bed space earlier by ordering a bullet to be put in her head just to get it over with.

Apparently, this is just another cultural phenomena that will eventually be considered "normal." As long as we continue to take our marching orders from Hollywood, and hail people as heroes for being able to throw a ball, our culture will continue to be (as we say in the trucking business) "bent over the fuel tank."

So, how do we fix the things we see as threats to our culture? This is yet another fork in the ideological road. A liberal is likely to take one of two popular positions on culture and morality. The "government dependent" liberal (AKA socialist, communist, or Democrat) will tell you that culture is something that can be controlled and regulated by either throwing money at it, or regulating it through excessive legislation.

The "if it feels good, do it" liberal (AKA anarchist, hippie, or Democrat) will tell you that since all cultures are morally relative, there should be no standards or oversight whatsoever.

As for me (whatever label you want to give me), I believe that American culture is something that should be *protected*, not regulated. This is based more on practicality than anything else. You see, the fact that we are accepting of other cultures (that's part of *our* culture) means that *regulating* our culture would be impossible. I believe that a modern culture such as ours will always be a fluid, evolving, and ever-changing thing. The question then becomes; how do we keep it from evolving into something *bad*?

The answers are pretty simple: education, education, education. You see, you can't protect *anything* unless you understand *what* you're protecting, *why* you're protecting it, and what you're protecting it *from*. This was the whole point behind writing this book. This nation will not survive unless certain discussions are had. Those discussions will never happen if people never realize there is a problem to begin with.

Being a realist allows me to understand that Norman Rockwell's America is a thing of the past. That does not mean that our *future* can't be just as pleasant as a scene from one of his paintings. America can always be a singular culture that others try like hell to become a *part* of, or we can let this nation become a "multi-cultural" clearing house for third world rejects.

Since liberals tend to think with their "feelings" instead of their brains, they don't see how stupid "multi-culturalism" actually is. If they did, they would understand that "multi" means "more than one." Then they might understand that "more than one" implies *separation*. That means that person "A" would belong to *one* culture, and person "B" would belong to another different, but still *separate* culture. My tiny truck driving intellect does not allow me to see the big difference between "multi-culturalism" and "segregation." When you break it all down, they are both just different terms for the separation of people.

I wonder what would happen if "*uni*-culturalism" would ever become politically correct? Maybe people from all over the world would come to a place to share in *one* common culture, assimilating to *one* common group of people, speaking *one* common language...*united*. We could call such a place..."The *United* States of America".

As I come to the end of this chapter, I realize that the topic of American culture is something way too massive to be squeezed into just one chapter of any one book. Actually, it's probably too big to be squeezed into *volumes* of books. Then again, the purpose of this book is to spark interest, or whet your appetite, not cover any one topic from front to back. Besides, to be honest with you (as well as myself), I'm no expert on any of the topics that I'm writing about, I'm just a guy who is pretty confident about his way of looking at things.

Some of you may be wondering how anyone can write about culture without mentioning religion. This was done by design. One of the most common misconceptions about "the right wing" is that we are all just a bunch of religious zealots, or "Jesus freaks." One of the other reasons I am writing this book is to *dispel* that myth. It is my belief that even though religion is a major factor in the evolution of most cultures, there is no law that requires someone to belong to one in order to have conservative principles. Where is it written that an atheist has to be liberal? Do people really need the Bible to tell them that cheating, stealing, and killing the unborn is wrong? I firmly believe that I would write this same book word for word, no matter what faith I belonged to, if any. Religions are a *source* for philosophies and principles, they are *not* the philosophies and principles themselves. I am writing about the philosophies and principles behind conservatism. Where they may or may not have originated from is really not that important to the point of this book. Besides, the only people I am trying to alienate in this book are liberals.

Chapter 12
Parental Guidance Suggested

Way back when I was a liberal (the dark ages), I had opinions on a wide range of subjects. Today, I still have a big ol' pile of opinions, but many of them have changed. One such opinion is my view of parenting. When I was younger, I assumed that unless you actually had a kid of your own, you had no business criticizing the parenting skills (or lack thereof) of others. Now that I've spent some quality time in the "real world," I see that yet again, I was wrong.

Some people may think that it takes a lot of balls to have opinions about parenting, let alone write a chapter in a book about it, especially when I am a *rookie* at best. These people, much like my younger and dumber self, are wrong.

Truth be told, I have pretty good "street cred'" on the subject for a few reasons. One, I *am* a parent (that's a given). Two, I *had* parents. Three, I *know* parents. Four, I live and work among the products of other people's parenting. For those of you who aren't keeping score, numbers two through four give pretty much *everyone* the ability to have opinions on parenting. I know that this concept is a about as socially acceptable as eating potato chips in the theater, but I think it's something we need to get over. You see, we *all* have to live with the results of what other people bring into this world. When you bring a person into the world, they are not *isolated*. They cause a ripple effect that touches everything and *everyone* it meets. It is up to the parent to decide if this will be a *good* ripple, or a bad one. Someone once said "no man is an island unto himself." That is why we *all* have the right, as well as the *duty,* to discuss what makes a "good parent."

Even though criticizing someone else's parenting skills is politically incorrect, I believe that it is a step in the right direction if we want to save our culture, as well as help the next generations of children. After all, the left's whole purpose in life seems to be criticizing conservatives. Why should *they* have all the fun? It was no accident that I wrote a chapter on parenting right after a chapter on American culture. Without one, you can't have the other.

Looking back now as an adult, I am pretty comfortable with the mistakes my own parents made in raising my brother and me. They were not bad parents by any stretch of the imagination, but they *were* humans. That means that they were prone to imperfection.

Thankfully, one ball that my parents *didn't* drop was pounding into my head at a very early age just how hard it is to raise a child. If I were a little more insecure at the time, I could have mistaken this concept for expressions of regret, but they were slick enough to not let that happen. They always made a point to <u>stress the stress</u>. Being realists themselves, they had no illusions about what was foremost on my mind as a teenage boy. This motivated them to remind me on a daily (sometimes hourly) basis how much financial and psychological stress a baby would cause in my life. My dad was a master at this. After all, he was a guy too. He knew how important things like cars, girls, and hanging out at the mall were to me, so he knew how to use those things as tools to scare the living daylights out of me.

Just the *thought* of not being able to afford chrome rims for my Vega because I would have to pay for diapers made me wake up in cold sweats some nights. To me, getting a girl pregnant was a fate worse than death. At age fifteen, I actually believed that having a baby was the most stressful and expensive thing that could ever happen to someone. I could never think of anything scarier. The idea of being thrown into that kind of responsibility was terrifying. As it turns out, now that I'm thirty-four and have a baby of my own...I WAS RIGHT!

I was right, not because I was born with the knowledge that parenting was a lifetime commitment, but because my parents *taught* me that. Parenting has turned out to be every bit as demanding as I had always imagined...and then some. If it were not for my mom and dad's constant reinforcement, I could have ruined my life as well as the life of my child and her mother by having a baby at too early an age. As a grown man with a good job, I can't even begin to imagine how I would have done this twenty years ago.

The liberal in you may be thinking that these statements are a good argument for abortion. If you were paying attention in the previous chapter, you would know that these statements are actually a good argument for keeping it in your pants.

This throws us headlong into one of my favorite topics...discipline. Having the ability to discipline yourself is not always easy. In fact, it's a pain in the ass most of the time, and it's rarely fun. As boring or unentertaining as personal discipline may be though, it is usually what keeps us out of jail, debt, and the emergency room. Personal discipline has served me well every time I have applied it in my own life. Like most of us though, I have not applied it as often as I should have over the years. Luckily, it never resulted in any serious dilemmas in my life.

Discipline can take many forms. It can be what gets you out of bed and into the gym when you're fifty pounds overweight, or it can be what keeps you from trying that first hit of weed when all of your buddies are trying to talk you into it (something I know all about). It can also be what keeps you from buying that new 190 mph sport bike when you have a responsibility to put food on your family's table (also something I know all about).

The left likes to remind us that no one has cornered the market on personal discipline, and they're right. Very few of us walk around without a skeleton or two in our closet. The problem is that "the left" tends to use this as a justification for the "if it feels good, do it" mentality. They commonly point to the personal shortcomings of anyone who has ever dared to criticize their lifestyle. A liberal will focus so intently on the hypocrisy of the messenger that the substance of the message is totally lost on them. It's almost as if the fact that conservatives are no less human than anyone else, means that it's OK to do whatever you want. Personally, when someone is doing something wrong, that's all I need to know. Whether they are a hypocrite or not is really *not* that important to me; that's *their* problem. It's how they deal with it that tells me how credible they are as a human being. Besides, when you peel enough layers away, we're *all* hypocritical about *something*, but wrong is still wrong. So this leaves you with the choice of promoting the concept of doing the right thing, or promoting the concept of doing the wrong thing. If you rob banks for a living, is it really so bad as long as you go around telling people that robbing banks is a bad thing? Or should we tell people that you have no business telling anyone not to rob banks, because you're a hypocrite? Rather than use it as a teaching example of what can happen to you when you don't discipline yourself, liberals will always distract themselves with the hypocrisy issue.

So what does hypocrisy and personal discipline have to do with parenting? Pretty much everything! Very few (if any) people are *born* with personal discipline. In most cases, personal discipline is something that is only achieved as an adult. This makes sense because of the fact that once you become an adult, you are on your own. Your parents are no longer responsible for your actions. In short, you are your own person. That's why it's called *personal* discipline.

Personal discipline is usually only acquired after some kind of structured upbringing. That's where *parenting* comes in. There are many different styles and methods of raising kids in a *structured* environment. Parents who are can afford to do so may send their child to some sort of boarding school. These are usually people who are too busy or too lazy to raise a child on their own. In my opinion, this makes them benefactors, not parents. On the other hand, at least a boarding school is *some* type of structured environment. It's just sad to see people hand their kid off for someone else to raise.

Fortunately for those of us who do not make six figures, there is no law that says a structured environment requires tuition, or scholarships. In fact, raising a child right does not cost as much money as a lot of people think. Besides, you can be filthy rich and have no parenting skills at all. There are three prerequisites for being a good parent, and none of them cost a dime. You need courage, will, and you guessed it...personal discipline.

As a parent, you are going to need the *courage* to face the many scary situations that having a child in the twenty-first century is going to throw at you. You are going to need the *will* to do the things that will teach your kid right from wrong. Finally, you are going to need *personal discipline* to set the example. That means that no matter how pissed you are at your spouse, you still need to control your temper. Your kids will *see* and *remember* what you show them. You will need to have enough personal discipline to not blow the kid's college fund at the blackjack table. You will need the personal discipline to realize that your kids need you to be around for as long as possible. That means you need to get the skydiving and bungee jumping out of your system *before* you have children.

No matter how you slice it, an undisciplined child will be an undisciplined adult, so it is up to the adult to break that cycle. This brings us back to the hypocrisy issue.

What if you are a parent who has a "checkered past?" Maybe you used to drink too much, gamble too much, or did drugs when you were younger. Does that mean that you are disqualified from being a parent? Does that mean that you have no right to criticize or discipline your kid for doing the same things you did as a younger person?

Well, that depends on what school of thought you subscribe to *now*. To be a consistent *liberal*, if you catch your kid smoking a joint, you should probably look the other way. After all, *you* used to smoke weed too, and heaven forbid if you were a hypocrite. To be a *good parent*, you would play the "do as I say, not as I did" card, and discipline him/her into the next century. If there were such a thing as a parenting handbook, the first rule would have to be "Get over yourself!" Don't forget that there is no law that says your kid needs to know *every* intimate detail of your past to begin with. After all, the goal is to break the cycle and raise your kid to *not* make the same mistakes you did.

Don't get me wrong, being a hypocrite is still a bad thing, but when it comes to things that you've done in the past, unless you have access to a time machine, you're wasting your time dwelling on it. Just look at them as learning experiences not to be repeated by your kids.

Now that we've got some of the personal issues out of the way, let's get into some of the nuts and bolts of parenting. If you've been paying attention so far, you will already realize that I don't lose a lot of sleep worrying about being politically correct. So if you are a person who is easily offended, you might as well close this book and go back to the safety of your P.C. utopia, because I'm going to hit you with both barrels.

Let's start with "stereotyping." This is something that we conservatives are accused of that we actually do! Then again, so does everyone else. Just try to tell me that liberals don't stereotype those of us who don't hug trees and eat tofu. The truth is, we all do it, but only a few of us admit it, and even fewer do it right. I, on the other hand, embrace the practice and have elevated it to an art form.

First of all, you need to forget everything you think you know about stereotyping. Then you need to open your mind (I love saying that to liberals). Right out of the gate, you need to completely forget the idea of stereotyping people on the basis of physical characteristics that they are born with. These things include: skin, hair, eye color, height, or handicap. Ironically, these are usually the most common characteristics for stereotyping. I would throw *weight* into the list too, but technically you *can* control how much you weigh after you reach a certain age.

So what's left? Since stereotypes are most commonly *visual*, we'll stick with what we notice about a person when we first see them. And since this is a chapter about *parenting*, we'll stick with parents and children as our subjects. Right about now, the liberal in you is telling you that you can't tell anything about someone just by looking at him or her...wrong. Once more, your inner liberal is telling you that it is wrong to even try...wrong again. So just what is it that we are looking at? I'm glad you asked.

When I expose myself or my family to someone, I think it's a good idea to know if that person is likely to be a plus or a minus in our lives. Unfortunately, people don't walk around wearing signs that describe what kind of person they are...or do they? Well, lucky for us, a lot of them actually do. In fact, some people are wearing giant flashing neon signs that tell you just what kind of person they are. You just have to know what to look for.

Topping the list of neon character trait signs is the cigarette. If you are over sixty, I am willing to give you a pass on this because you probably got addicted to nicotine before most people had even heard of the word. As for everyone else, this rant's for you. First I would like to deal with all of you parents who smoke. You *are* stupid; let's just get that out of the way. Now let me tell you why. You don't even have enough respect for your kids to stop a habit that will in all likelihood cause them harm. That makes you selfish *and* stupid. Top that with the fact that you have been bombarded with information telling you how and why smoking is stupid since you were a child, so you can't even claim ignorance on this one. Yet, you still light up. So now you can add *arrogant* to the list.

According to liberals, you're probably poor because there is a Republican in the White House, but you still find the money to buy cigarettes. That's the money that is supposed to be going toward buying shoes and coats for your children. OK, people will smoke no matter who's in office, but even if you're rich, you should be putting that cigarette money toward something for your kids. But if you're a smoker, and not making lots of money, you *are* neglecting your children. Then there is the whole "courtesy" issue.

Only a smoker would set the example for his/her child of having no respect for others, and assume that it is their *right*. Case in point: A smoker will sit down in a public restaurant, light up, and see nothing wrong with it. The fact that your taste buds are directly connected to your sense of smell means nothing to him. The fact that he/she just ruined my meal means even less. Did they pay for my meal? Did they even buy dessert? No! To make matters worse, they're doing it in front of their kids. That means that I have to sit there with a hoagie that tastes like an ashtray, knowing that eventually, that kid is going to grow up and ruin my hoagie in the future too! Using their logic, I should be able to walk over to a smoker's table, and fart on their meal, and no one should say anything about it. At least farting is a necessary function, not a common cause of lung disease.

It is also the smoker that assumes that everyone is supposed to bend over backwards for them. Case in point: A smoker assumes that in a "smoke free" environment such as the workplace, a special "smoking area" needs to be constructed just for them. OK, fine. Right after that, we can build a bar for the alcoholics, a crack house for the druggies, a casino for the gamblers, and a motel room for the sex addicts. Only a smoker would assume that their employer is obligated to make a special area designated for the sole purpose of supporting a bad habit.

As low as a parent who smokes is, there is one level lower that you can sink. That is the level of "pregnant smoker." If you are a woman who is pregnant, and you're still smoking, you are a *complete* moron. It's times like this that I am reminded of just how little writing skill I have, because I have no way to accurately describe just how stupid you are. In fact, that statement is really all I can come up with. Yet, you're going to be what passes for that baby's *parent*.

Hopefully now you're starting to see why my brand of stereotyping is a little more legitimate than others. Where you might only see a person who happens to be smoking a cigarette, I see a person who would put a bad habit over the well being of his/her own child. To me, that says a lot about someone.

Then there is the smoking teenager. Where there is a smoking teenager, there is a parent who is either not paying attention, or they just don't care. I consider this to be a sign that tells us about the "parent" of that kid. After all, if they dropped the ball on the "smoking thing," then you have to wonder what else they forgot to teach their kid about.

No matter how you slice it, smoking is one of those things that you have no legitimate reason for starting. Therefore, if you do, it's probably for one of two reasons. You either believed that it would make you look cool, or you just wanted to go along with the crowd. In both cases, it was a move that only served to show the rest of us that you *were* a person with poor judgment, and *are* a person of weak will. The fact that you do it in front of children (especially your own) shows us that you are an idiot.

Fortunately for me, when I was about four years old, my father accidentally burned my hand with his cigarette while counting out money in the checkout line at the grocery store. After that day, he never smoked again, and I have had a personal problem with cigarettes.

Moving on to a stereotype that liberals consider to be a "family value," we open the door to the wild world of "freedom of expression." Don't get me wrong, expression *is* a freedom, and as a conservative, you will never hear me call for government regulation of it, but that does not mean that everyone has to accept or tolerate everyone else's form of expression. It also does not mean that all forms of expression are a good thing.

"Expression" is one of those words that I think can be a pretty good indicator that a parent is a moron and should probably be avoided. The word is commonly found in the phrase "He/she's just expressing him/herself." Whenever you hear that phrase, do yourself a favor and walk in the other direction.

A few months ago, as I was making my deliveries, I was listening to a talk show on National Public Radio. They were discussing various reasons why people may or may not be moving to the Midwest. A caller asserted that she would not be moving there because she wanted to move to an area where other kids wouldn't beat up her son for dyeing his hair pink and wearing a dress to school, because that was how he chose to *express* himself.

The first questions that came to my mind were "Just what is this kid expressing? A desire to get beat up? A mental imbalance? The fact that he has no social skills? Or the fact that his parents have absolutely no idea what they're doing?"

You see, the last time I checked, children do *everything* to express themselves. This can be anything from writing on the living room walls, to jumping off the porch roof. Should we let them do *those* things too? After all, they're just trying to *express* themselves.

From everything I've seen in my lifetime, I am pretty sure that kids will always express themselves one way or another; it's up to the *parent* to teach them how to do it in a way that won't bite them in the ass later in life.

As the liberalism continued to ooze from the speakers in my truck, I found myself screaming at the faceless lady who called in from the Northwest. "Express himself?! If you want him to *express* himself, teach him how to draw, teach him how to play music, teach him how to build something, teach him how to write! How can you not see that your kid is begging you for attention?! Teach him how to do something *other* than alienate himself from the rest of his community!"

When I finally realized that I was probably scaring the people who were passing me with my angry shouting gestures, I decided to put in a B.B. King tape and cool off for a while. I think the thing that bothered me most about what I was hearing in this discussion was the fact that no one had questioned this woman's premise, let alone her judgment. Everyone continued on as if she had said something as normal as a comment on the weather. Then I reminded myself that I was listening to NPR, and it all made sense.

When I think of all the people throughout history who became famous for expressing themselves, I think of musicians, architects, artists, playwrights, comedians, poets, spokesmen, authors, and athletes. I don't recall too many famous people whose expressions were limited to wearing a dress and dyeing their hair.

On a personal note, when I was in high school, I was heavily into skateboarding. This activity was a major part of a larger subculture that most of my friends were into at the time. This meant that on any given day, I could be hanging out with any number of social rejects. From the "punk rock" scene, to the "goth" scene, most of my friends had hair and clothes that would, well...curl your hair. Being a part of this crowd required a certain amount of effort in the game of fashion one-ups-man ship. At the time, like most teenagers throughout history, my biggest fear was being thought of as a social outcast, or less than cool. I was *willing* to do anything to maintain my social relevance. I was fully prepared to cut my hair into a Mohawk, because I was convinced that would solidify my position as "coolest dude in school."

There was only one thing standing in the way...my father. When it came time to actually put the razor to my head, I had a moment of clarity. This was a bad idea, no matter how I went about it. I had never even brought the concept to Dad's attention because I knew it would take him about two seconds to crush my dream of social superiority. Thankfully, I was smart enough to realize that *surprising* him would result in something even more socially stifling than not having the coolest hair in school...and that was not having wheels. I had visions of riding the bus to school with no car, no skateboard, and no hair (*keeping* the Mohawk would not be an option). I decided it would be best to just put the razor down and concentrate on keeping my car. At the time, I didn't understand what his problem was. After all, it was just a haircut; it would grow back.

I had always assumed that my father was just an out-of-touch parent who didn't understand how important it was to be cool. Now that I am in my mid-thirties, I realize that he not only understood how *important* it was to be cool, but he also understood how *irrelevant* it was too. The difference is the fact that back then, I thought *I* was the one who had wisdom, when in reality, I was clueless.

There could be any number of reasons that my dad wouldn't let me get that Mohawk. Maybe he didn't want to be embarrassed; maybe he didn't want the family photos to look ridiculous, maybe he just thought I would look like an idiot. Or, maybe he understood what I now refer to as the "look at me" complex.

He probably knew then, as I know now, that people who go to extreme lengths to be noticed for their appearance, probably have insecurity issues. The phrase "put your best foot forward" always sticks in my mind when I see one of these people. I usually end up with questions about them bouncing around in my head. "Let me get this straight, your 'best foot' is purple hair?" Am I to understand that you woke up one morning and thought that paying someone to poke a hole in your nose would make you more interesting, attractive, or...intelligent? Did you actually believe that a tattoo on your neck would make you more of an individual? Did the twenty seven other guys at the mall with tattoos on *their* necks think the same thing?"

While we're on the subject of tattoos, I would like to clarify something. There is a world of difference between the tattoo a U.S. Marine wears to signify his brotherhood in arms, and the one that "Timmy the fry cook" wears to signify that he wants to piss off his dad, or the one "Jeff in Accounting" wears to signify that he has trouble getting laid. Of the three examples I've given, one commands respect, the other two command me to make fun of you. I'll let it up to you the reader to decide which is which.

The bottom line on people with a "look at me" complex is their need for attention. That itself says a lot about them. I'm no psychiatrist, but if you are *so* starved for attention that you are willing to stain, or punch holes in your skin...I think it's safe to say that you have issues. It probably doesn't mean that you're a serial killer, but it might be a sign that you're insecure. Then you have to wonder *how* and *when* you became insecure. Did it happen last week, or gradually over time? This brings us right back to the prime suspects...the parents. Who else is more responsible for the personality traits we have as an adult?

This supports my theory that if a parent does not force you to find more practical and creative ways to *express* yourself, then you're probably going to end up going through life asking people to look at your *body*, instead of your body of work. I think this might also explain why I run into so many kids today that have tattoos and lip piercings, but can't seem to speak in complete sentences.

It seems to me that if you believe that your self worth is something *visual*, you might eventually develop a "what's the point?" attitude about the rest of you. After all, if everyone already thinks you're "cool" because you have a bone through your nose, why put so much effort into your education? Since the bone in your nose has elevated your social status, now you can claim superiority over those nerds who study all the time and use big words.

This eventually becomes the message that a kid receives when a parent doesn't bother to teach them that being a slave to whatever is considered to be cool at the time is the surest way to fall flat on your ass. Ultimately, *cool* comes and goes, but there are some things that remain constant. A nose ring will not help you learn algebra, pink hair will not win you a scholarship, and tattoos on your neck will not get you a mortgage loan. Besides, tattoos and piercings used to be about standing out in the crowd; now the only ones who stand out in the crowd are the ones that have neither.

If "being cool" were limited to the fashion debate, I probably would have never brought it up. After all, it's not *my* kid we're talking about (and it's not going to be). But a kid's eternal quest to fit in with the rest of the crowd is now a gamble with life and death. Not just his/her own, but also anyone they might come in contact with.

This brings us to a subject that could have just as easily been handled in the last chapter...that's right, the "drug" thing. Illegal drugs may actually be more of a cultural issue, but I believe that it's a bit more fitting to bring it up under the context of parenting. After all, it's usually a parenting issue that drives people to illegal drugs in the first place.

Before we get too deeply involved here, let's get something straight. I am no longer interested in hearing from people (usually liberals) about how there should be no distinction between alcohol and illegal drugs. This theory is old and tired at best. In reality, there *is* a difference. The difference is in the practical effect, as well as the practical purpose. I break it down this way; alcohol is an addictive substance, as are illegal drugs. The similarities pretty much end there. Unless you weigh about ten pounds, a beer or a glass of wine has little to no effect on you when drinking them as intended by the one who produced them. They do nothing more than add another tasty flavor to a meal. The same could even be said for a shot of hard liquor. These products do not become a problem until they are *abused*. This is *not* the case for illegal drugs.

Whether it's just one joint, one line of cocaine, one acid tab, or one hit of heroin (when used as intended by the one who produced them), the effects are *immediate*. They are also immediately addictive. As for the "tasty flavor" thing...let's be realistic. I doubt that anyone has ever cared what type of "crack" goes best with filet mignons. All this is pretty moot though, because the principles I am about to mention apply to drugs *and* alcohol abuse. I just wanted to dispel the myth that there is a moral equivalent to using heroin and drinking a can of beer.

Drug use is one of those things that are pretty cut-and-dried to most people...unless they're a liberal. I think it's a safe bet to say that given the risks involved (and do I *really* need to list them?), the typical parent would try to steer his/ her child away from doing drugs. For them, finding a *joint* in their son/daughter's room is probably going to be a "capital offense." In most cases this is probably going to be followed by some type of serious punishment.

Liberals, on the other hand, tend to have a different perspective on the subject. Much like the woman I mentioned earlier who wanted her kid to *express* himself, a liberal might look at the *joint* as a form of expression, or better yet, *experimentation*. Experiment with what? Their mind? Apparently, these parents believe that their pot smoking teen is going to be the next Nobel Prize winner for pharmaceutical experimentation. As if he/she is down in the laboratory studying the effects of marijuana on lab mice with an electron microscope. Add to that the idea that most liberals look at marijuana as a harmless, natural herb, instead of a first test of personal willpower, and they see little reason to make a big deal over it. Besides, they don't want to *alienate* their child; that might hurt his/her self-esteem. Don't forget the whole hypocrisy thing that I mentioned earlier in this chapter.

Don't get me wrong. I'm not completely naive when it comes to smoking pot. When I was in high school, weed was easier to get than beer. As a result, most of my friends smoked it. Though I never tried it myself, I had my share of "contact highs." As common as weed was in my teenage years, I never once witnessed, or heard of anyone in my social circles "freaking out" as a result of smoking a bowl. I never heard of anyone jumping out of a window because they thought they could fly after toking a joint either. Truth be told, the effects from smoking weed that I witnessed in my youth were less scary and dangerous, and more sad and pathetic.

What I saw happen to *my* friends eventually became the evidence I needed to convince myself that not giving in to peer pressure was not such a lame/corny concept after all. You see, most of my pot-smoking friends went either one of two directions. They either moved on to bigger, badder drugs, or they stuck with the leafy green standard. The ones that "moved on" eventually got caught up in the usual pitfalls that accompany heavy drug use. Occasionally I'll read about them in the paper after they get busted for this, that, or the other thing. Essentially, they have become evidence for my theory that marijuana actually *is* a "gateway drug" after all.

Those that had found enough personal discipline to not stray from what Ozzy referred to as "Sweet Leaf" suffered a different fate. I guess the best way to describe what happened to them is - a perpetual state of apathy. I still talk to some of these folks today, and I always get the same vibe from them. Not too many highs, not too many lows. Just a consistent lack of motivation and interest. It's as if they made it to age nineteen and just stopped right there. A lot of them are still working the same job they were back then, usually delivering pizza, or squirting U-joints down at the "Quiky-Lube." Some of them still live in their parent's house.

I don't bring this up to sound judgmental. I just wanted to demonstrate the irrelevance of the whole "gateway drug" debate. Whether you end up snatching purses to support a heroin addiction, or delivering pizza at age thirty-five because weed sapped your ambition, you have definitely made a wrong turn somewhere along the line. For those of you who are paying attention, that means that marijuana is bad as a *first* drug, or an *only* drug. If marijuana was the only drug out there, I wouldn't have even mentioned it, but that's just not the case. So as for the "gateway" thing, it is my belief that given all the information we have about drugs today, if you are *still* dumb enough to try a *first* one, you are very likely to try a *next* one...hence the term "gateway."

The following story applies to the current topic, so please bear with me. I consider myself to have been very lucky. Life issued me a pretty good set of parents, but like all others, they weren't perfect. Most of the time, their imperfections had an expected negative effect. In one particular situation though, their ball dropping had an unexpected *positive* effect.

My grandfather on my mom's side of the family was a career

alcoholic, as was his son (my uncle). This had never been any type of secret in our family; it was just accepted and worked around. He wasn't the jolly/fun type of alcoholic either; he was actually a mean old bastard when he was drunk. My mom usually dealt with this by keeping my brother and me in the car until she made sure he hadn't been drinking when we would go to visit him and Grandma. As this had always been standard practice, my brother and I never thought much about it as we were growing up. Until Willie Nelson came to town.

I was probably about seven years old at the time, which meant my brother was about four. My parents had gotten tickets to see Willie Nelson at the fairgrounds and needed a babysitter for the night. Apparently, babysitters were hard to come by, so they recruited my mom's parents. Rather than wake my grandparents up at a late hour, they opted to stay out all night. I think the *theory* was also to let us have a sleepover with our grandparents, which we *should* have enjoyed.

The night went as we had expected it to. My brother and I had some snacks, watched some TV, and went to bed. We slept on the couch in the living room as my grandfather watched TV. I hadn't realized that he was totally drunk at the time. Then came the tirades. Fortunately, my brother had been out like a light for a while due to the medicine he had to take for the cold he had. I on the other hand was only pretending to sleep.

By the light of the TV, I listened as my own grandfather cursed my mother for ever having us "snot-nosed bastards." He went on to call my grandmother names that I had never even heard of at the time. Eventually, he turned off the TV and continued to insult and curse the people that I knew and cared about. At this point, the only light in the room was the glow of his cigarette, and what little leaked in through the window from the street outside.

Thankfully, my grandma woke up and heard what was going on. She came out to the living room, and very quietly took my brother and I back to sleep in her bed. I remember being terrified that my grandfather might fall asleep and burn down the house with his cigarette. Grandma did her best to make us feel better, and we eventually fell asleep.

To this day, nearly thirty years later, I can still see that cigarette glowing in the dark, as well as recall that overpowering smell of booze. It wasn't until recently that it dawned on me that my parents had left my brother and me in the care of a known alcoholic. As I look at my own daughter today, I can't even imagine doing that to her.

The upshot is that that one episode became a defining moment in my life. I could never stand the sight or smell of cigarettes after that. They always reminded me of that night from then on, and still do to this day. Between my grandfather's verbal abuse, and my father's clumsiness in the checkout line, my aversion to cigarettes was pretty well etched in stone. As for alcohol, I never had a *visual* connection with that night and booze. You see, my grandfather always drank out in the garage where no one could see him. We only saw (and heard) the after effects. That lack of visualization probably kept me from having a total hatred of alcohol, but seeing my grandfather drunk *did* force me to keep a tight reign on myself, as most of my friends were getting too drunk to walk in high school.

This brings me to the point of this story. The only thing that kept *me* from losing *my* self-discipline as a teenager was *fear*. Though I *did* drink beer and even hard liqueur on a pretty regular basis when I was in high school, I almost never got drunk. I would have just enough to make me feel relaxed, then stop. Truth be told, most of the time, I would often pretend to drink more than I actually did. Sometimes, I would even dump the beer and refill the can with water. That way I could maintain my social status and still be in control of myself. After all, that was my biggest fear...not having control of myself. I was pretty sure that I was never going to be a mean/nasty drunk like my grandfather, but I never wanted to take a chance. Then there was the "driving" factor, and the "moron friends" factor. Could I *really* trust these guys to not shave my eyebrows if I passed out? I didn't want to have to find out the hard way...like my friend Kevin did. The point of this story is that not everyone is blessed with an alcoholic grandfather who will scar them for life in such a way as to repel them from temptations like drugs and alcohol. *Those* people need to rely on other sources to guide them. Such sources are called <u>parents</u>.

It's probably a lot more difficult to keep your kids off drugs today as opposed to when my parents raised my brother and me. Let's face it, there's a whole new buffet of illegal drugs out there that never even existed thirty years ago. Hollywood is no help, with their constant glamorization of the drug culture. Then there is that ever-popular mentality out there that tells people that all their personal woes can be treated with *prescription* drugs. It's a little hard to convince "Junior" that smoking a joint is a big deal when he knows damn well that *you* can't get through a day at the office without your bottle of Prozac. Leading by example (which is a staple of good parenting) pretty much goes out the window at that point.

As tough as raising kids today may be, I still consider using that as an excuse to be a cop-out. Think about it. Since the dawn of man, raising children has never been easy. Cavemen had to protect their children from dinosaurs, as well as hunt for their food. The early American settlers had to raise children while battling the elements, Indians, and coyotes, all while exploring a new unfamiliar land. The fact of the matter is, no one has ever said that raising children is easy, nor is it supposed to be. But if you do it right, it should all work out in the end.

The difficulty level of raising children may also explain why the recent phenomenon of being a child's "buddy" instead of his/her parent is now a part of our culture. Realistically, this practice wouldn't have lasted too long out on the frontier. Since everything from fixing breakfast to wiping your butt was a major endeavor, being a parent was probably not thought of as being such a chore. Today however, we have gotten too used to everything being simplified for us. We live in the age of microwaveable meals, and "broadband connections." Is it any wonder that we automatically expect raising children to be simplified too? Sure, there are a lot of advances in the technology used by parents today. Nowadays, we have disposable diapers, baby monitors, and educational DVDs. All of these things make the day-to-day work load a little lighter, but they have little to do with the actual <u>duty</u> of parenting.

You see, there is a mile-wide gap between being a "buddy", and being a parent. The first difference that comes to mind is the fact that most of the people who helped me get *into* trouble in life were "buddies." It was always my parents that put me back on track when I was going off course. Then there is the fact that I have never feared, and have rarely respected, any of my "buddies." As for them respecting me...not a chance. Though I have no scientific evidence to back me up, it seems to me that if you want to be a "buddy," you should get a dog, or join a bowling league. If you want to be a parent, then you better be ready to be a loving, caring, son of a bitch. Because being a parent means that you are going to have to be one step ahead of your child every waking moment of your life, and more often than not, you're going to have to get in your kid's face when he/she screws up. When it comes time to get in his face, if you're his "buddy," don't be surprised when he doesn't take you seriously. On the other hand, if your aim is to be his *parent*, he/she will have every reason to expect some type of consequence when he/she does something stupid. I underlined the word *consequence*, because I believe it to be the most important word in the parental handbook. As a matter of fact, it's probably the only one that matters in life. After all, life is basically just a *series* of consequences, some good, and some bad. For example, if I am continuously late for work, the consequence is that I will be fired. The consequence of being fired is that I will be out of cash. The consequence of being out of cash is that I will not be able to put food on my family's plate...and so on, and so on. Wouldn't it be nice if there was some method of explaining the concept of consequences to children so they don't have to learn about them the hard way as an adult, by which time it is usually too late anyway. This brings us to my favorite parenting topic...discipline. Not *personal* discipline as I discussed earlier in this chapter, but *parental* discipline. You know, the type that teaches children not to play in traffic, before they experiment with it on their own.

Don't get me wrong; one of the harder things about being a parent is disciplining your child. In fact, it's so hard that in recent years there has been a growing movement to do away with most traditional forms of discipline. This movement is commonly led by people who like to refer to themselves as *progressive*. A "progressive" parent is usually not too hard to spot in a crowd of people. They can commonly be found at the security office of your local shopping mall, trying to explain to the security staff how "little Johnny" was just trying to *express* himself when he pushed the popcorn stand into the water fountain. But hey, it's easier to give the security guard some line of "BS" than it is to teach a kid right from wrong.

Before we get too involved in the whole discipline thing, we need to get something out of the way. That *something* is the liberal concept of "moral relativism." This is a common philosophy (and tactic) of a typical liberal, and is applied to most (if not all) issues that affect our lives. For example, I recently heard a caller to a radio talk show claim that America could be considered a "terrorist nation" just like Iran, because *we* have a nuclear weapons program too. Therefore, we have no right to tell *Iran* that they can't have nuclear weapons of their own. The fact that the United States doesn't usually go around publicly proclaiming a hatred of Iran and calling them "the Great Satan", all while sponsoring people who will purposely target innocent citizens that don't follow their particular brand of religion, was somehow lost on this caller. He also forgot about the fact that our leaders are <u>elected</u>, and there is a long list of checks and balances that keep American leaders from becoming too powerful. But in Iran, it is common practice for religious wackos to *kill* their way to power. The logical person might see the difference between America having nuclear weapons to make a potential enemy think twice before attacking us, and a dictator who believes it is their duty to "destroy the infidels" owning nuclear missiles. The liberal on the other hand, sees no difference at all...just another moral relativity.

When applied to parenting, moral relativism makes just as little sense. Unless of course you are fishing for reasons to not discipline your child. After all, that would be hard work. The moral relativity of discipline is that to a liberal there is no difference between spanking a child on the butt with an open hand, and knocking a child's teeth out with your fist. Telling your child that what he/she just did was really stupid is no different than burning him/her with a lit cigarette...it's *all* abuse!

If this same logic were applied to the legal system, there would be a lot more people getting "the chair." After all, jaywalking and first-degree murder are both crimes, right?

Thankfully, I learned about moral relativity long before I brought my daughter into this world. Otherwise, I probably would have bought into the same politically correct hogwash that a lot of today's parents seem to have fallen for. In the end, the only one who would have really suffered would be my daughter. You might think that it is pretty ballsy of me to assume that *my* brand of parenting is not going to blow up in my face. After all, as of the writing of this book, my first and only child is not even two years old yet. That equates to a rookie pilot predicting a successful flight before flying an untested aircraft. Then again, my confidence is rooted in a lifetime of observing what does and does not work. I have simply opted to reject the methods that I have seen fail, and adopt the ones that succeed. For example, I know that pacifying a disrespectful child will ultimately cause him to be a self-centered jerk as an adult. I didn't read that in a book, or learn it in some college course. I *experienced* it first hand with some of the kids I grew up with, and the parents that let them get away with murder. So, as an adult myself, I now know that my child will occasionally need to be reminded that her mother and I are in charge at all times. If nothing else, this book will be a constant source of motivation for me to be a better parent. Because, after all the things I've written in this book, if my daughter ends up selling herself to support a crack addiction, my face sure will be red.

So, if you're not supposed to spank a child in order to discipline them, then just how do you get the point across to a child who only has a few years under their belt? That's just it; I truly believe that you <u>are</u> supposed to spank a child. Not because of any religious doctrine or cultural norm, but because of the basic mechanics of it. Consider this. Whether you believe in a Supreme Being or not is irrelevant. One thing is for sure though, *who* or *what*ever designed the human body, seems to have purposely constructed the human butt to do two things very well- provide a place to sit, and absorb the impact of a father's hand after it's owner had been told repeatedly not to play in the street. Think about it, there are no major organs in that area to be damaged, and lots of nerve endings for memory retention. The butt is also placed at the rear of the body, so as to minimize the odds of a poorly aimed daddy hand accidentally hitting a vital organ or the face. The placement of the butt also makes *blocking* more difficult for the child, because his/her legs will not bend in that direction. The soft, fleshy construction is also much easier on the hand of the spanker. Then there is the added psychological effect of something terrible coming up behind you, which reinforces the notion that you *don't* want to repeat the action that warranted the spanking in the first place, but on a more cerebral level.

I don't defend spanking because I believe it is the *only* effective form of discipline, but it definitely is *one* effective form of discipline. In recent years, the "time out" has become very fashionable. This is when a child is told to sit in a chair for a given amount of time when he/she misbehaves. This method is socially acceptable due to the fact that there is no *abuse* involved. The problem is that this method teaches the child about *patience,* but not about consequences, respect, or shame. Basically, the kid will know that as soon as his time is up, he can go right back to doing the same thing he was given the "time out" for, and the worst that will happen is a few more minutes of "time out." Where's the consequence in that? How does a "time out" reinforce the fact that what the child just did was really stupid? Where does the *shame* come in? Why *wouldn't* the kid continue being bad? What's the downside?

This is why I always considered myself to be lucky to have the parents I was given. These two were masters at creative discipline. One of my earlier memories was the time I had said a bad word and my mother put a bar of soap in my mouth. It was very cliché, but very effective. It had all the necessary elements of a good punishment: consequence, shame, and a lasting impression. It was later followed by the old "pepper on the tongue" trick for *lying* to my mother. Her version of "time out" was to sit facing the corner as my little brother made faces at me when she wasn't looking. On occasion, she was even known to apply the old elementary school tactic of making me write something a hundred times. Though I didn't know it at the time, that method had the added element of bolstering my writing skills.

The "big guns" of her disciplinary arsenal was "the paddle," a 3/4 inch thick piece of nature's wrath that never failed to make an impression. You see, my mom is not a large woman, so the bare hand method never had quite the same effect. The paddle was just the thing to remedy that problem. If all else failed, she always had the option of playing the "wait till your father gets home" card. It was always hard to top that one. But one day she did.

It was a beautiful summer day and I was out in the front yard innocently throwing stones at cars as they passed by. When an old Mustang came down the street, I thought it would be a good idea to whip another one; I was wrong. As it turned out, the neighbor lady caught me and told my mother. This resulted in the be-all and end-all of paddlings, but *that* was just the warm up pitch. The home run came when she marched me down the street to the owner of the old Mustang, and made me knock on his door and apologize to him in person. The short path to his front door was probably about fifteen feet, but to me it seemed to go on for miles. The combination of fear and shame was practically choking me. I can still feel the heat radiating from around my neck to this day. In the end, the Mustang owner was very understanding and accepted my apology, but that never really made me feel any better about what I had done. Though there was no actual damage to the car, my reckless behavior had taken a major blow. In this case, the lesson learned came not from the paddle, but from a knock on a stranger's door.

In our house, spankings were generally used as the "attention getter." In most cases, they were the first of a two-pronged effort to teach my brother and I that acting like a complete moron is no way to go through life. Prong number two was usually some sort of punishment that was designed to make us think of what we had done, long after our butts had returned to their normal color. The most common way to accomplish this was to know ahead of time what our favorite thing in the world at the time was, and take it away for a pre-determined time. Notice that I did not say, "until we learned our lesson." That's because my parents were smart enough to know that any kid worth his/her salt can (and probably will) fake sincerity at the drop of a hat. Time off for good behavior (or good acting) was not an option. Whether it be Legos, bicycles, or video games, two weeks meant two weeks.

This method was used well into my teenage years, and very effectively I might add. For example, I had decided to skip school one day. This ill-fated plot taught me two lessons. First, if your father owns his own tow truck, don't spend the day running around in your *friend's* car. Otherwise you will find *your* car missing when you get back. Second, when you're seventeen, riding the bus to school when everyone knows you have a car is one of the lamest things that can happen to you.

Along with discipline, one of the most important ingredients to being a good parent is respect. Without this, discipline will not work. This lesson was taught to me at our kitchen table one night when I was feeling a little too ballsy. I don't remember what my father and I were arguing about, but it must have been a pretty big deal. For some strange reason, I thought I was old enough, big enough, or smart enough to intimidate my dad. I was wrong.

At some point in the conversation, I said to my father, "Go ahead and punch me if that's what gets you off, and I'll just call the cops." I knew I had made a mistake before I had even finished the sentence, but that didn't stop the words from coming. As if on cue, he calmly reached into his pocket and pulled out his money clip. He set it on the table in front of me. It was packed tight with at least three or four hundred dollars. I asked him what *that* was for. Without blinking, he looked me in the eye and said, "That's to pay the fine, now let's go outside." If back-pedaling were an Olympic sport, I would have brought home the gold after that. Bluff or no bluff, as I reached into my pocket to feel *my* money clip, I knew I was beat...it was empty. It was a fitting reminder that I could not beat my dad on any level, physically, mentally, or financially.Because the idea of *fearing* his son was such a foreign concept to him, my respect for my father was solidified on that night, and without one punch ever being thrown. Ironically, I probably *could* have gotten my dad thrown in jail just for even a *threat* of violence, but at the end of the day, I would have lost a father, a source of allowance, and a handful of teeth.

The point of that story is to demonstrate that being an authority figure is probably the most important part of being a parent. You see, if your child has no reason to fear any consequences from you, then it stands to reason that he/she will have no reason to *respect* you either. Once that happens, you might as well start a savings account marked "bail money," because you're gonna need it. Besides, maintaining authority over your child is not as difficult as you might think. The only thing you need to remember is that what you are *actually* prepared to do is really not that important. It's what your kid *believes* you are prepared to do that will make all the difference whenever he/she decides to challenge you. Since life is full of authority figures (bosses, police, referees, wives), the sooner your kid learns to respect them the better.

As for spanking, there are a few rules that need to be followed - always use an open hand, or a <u>thin</u> wooden or plastic paddle, because as the paddle gets thicker, it becomes less of a paddle and more of a *club*. Don't spank exclusively, save it for the really important points. Spanking is only one form of discipline and should be used sparingly. Otherwise, your child will think that hitting is how you're supposed to solve *every* problem. At the very least, *routine* spanking becomes ineffective over time. Finally, you need to know that spanking should take place in the home, not in public places. Not because they are not effective in public, but because there are a lot of weirdoes out there who equate a spanking with child abuse and might call the cops. Usually, these people are either liberals who never had kids, or liberals whose kids are running around like pint sized wrecking crews on speed.

Speaking of "speed." Another popular way to deal with kids today is to put them on prescription drugs. The arguments against this could fill more pages than I am willing to write at this point. I will say this, though. Aside from being akin to playing Russian roulette with your kid's physical and mental well being, the *message* it sends them should be reason enough to "Just say NO." Why would I want my child to assume that taking some sort of drug can solve all of their emotional problems? Why would I want them to think that life is too hard to handle without some type of pill? I thought a parent was supposed to teach the exact *opposite* lesson. Besides, being a child is nowhere near as tough as being an adult. What do we assume will happen to these kids as adults after they have been medicated through their childhood? I am sure that the results would vary from kid to kid, but I would be willing to bet that no good could come of it. Basically, if your child is so hyper, depressed, or emotional that they need to be drugged just to keep them from destroying your house...then you're not doing your job as a parent. Those kids need paddlin', not Ritalin.

Moving on from the topic of discipline, another common mistake that parents are making today is what I call "the substitute parent." You probably know this better by its original name...*television*. Obviously the *quantity* of TV that a kid watches is a big problem today. I don't think there are many people who would disagree with that. The other part of the pie that most people seem to overlook is the *quality*. You're probably waiting for me to go off on a tirade about sex and violence in television today. Yes, those *are* problems, but there's more to it than that. I can't prove it, but if I didn't know better, I'd say that children's television shows today are designed to make a kid dumber. Before I explain my theory, keep this in mind. I'm no moron. My tastes in TV and movies are wide ranging. Subtext is rarely lost on me. I understand the underlying messages in movies like *Doctor Strangelove* and *Citizen Kane*. I understand esoteric humor, and I have even been known to watch a few Fellini flicks. I had no trouble following *Twin Peaks*, and I believe it or not, I get most of Dennis Miller's sub-reference oriented jokes. But I would be willing to pay big money if someone could please explain "Pokemon" to me!!! Every time I try to watch this seizure inducing, mind numbing, waste of airtime, I feel as if IQ points are falling out of my head. I have actually gone as far as asking the children in my wife's family what "Pokemon" is about. I've gotten various answers, each of which seemed to trail off into oblivion just before justifying the purchase of some "Pokemon" trinket. I may not understand the premise of this particular cartoon, but I know a commercial when I see one.

Cartoons used to be based on simple concepts. After all, they were aimed at children. Some such concepts might include a cat chasing a mouse, a dog chasing a cat, or a hunter chasing a rabbit.

Not only were these concepts easy to understand, but they were realistic too. As it turns out, cats actually *do* chase mice - etc. Then as you got older, you would graduate to more sophisticated cartoons such as "Speed Racer" or "Johnny Quest," both also based on *plausible* (although unlikely) premises. Cartoons like "The Flintstones" or "The Jetsons" used unrealistic backdrops to poke fun at real life scenarios like blue-collar families trying to get through the day. Let's face it, we've all had to deal with a "Mr. Slate" at some point in our lives...some of us still do.

The point is that these cartoons made sense then, and they make sense now. So why would a parent expose their child to something that they can't make any sense of themselves? If you don't understand something, are you really *sure* that it's not harmful? Just what *are* the long-term effects of having your child repeatedly watch a cartoon whose premises and plot lines are so convoluted that even an adult can't explain it? By the way, I'm really not trying to single out "Pokemon." In fact, it seems that *most* of today's cartoons are going this route. If you don't believe me, just turn on the TV any Saturday morning and see for yourself. Children's programming sure has gone a long way since I was a kid...in reverse. Then again, maybe it's just me. After all, I don't get "SpongeBob SquarePants" either. Why is he square? Why is his name "SpongeBob" as opposed to "Bob the sponge?"

Here's some food for thought about the *quantity* of television that children are watching today. When I was a kid, and our parents took my brother and me for long car ride, we had no choice but to use our imaginations for entertainment. This could mean anything from naming the brands of cars and trucks as they went by to a simple game of checkers. If nothing else, we would ask our parents questions about things we saw out the window. This taught us conversational skills and helped us in learning about the world around us. Today though, we have headrest-mounted flat-screens with DVD players to keep the kids occupied. The constantly changing scenery with every educational opportunity you can imagine is totally lost on these kids. Questions are neither asked, nor answered. The world passes them by as they stare blankly at the screen...probably "Pokemon."

Recently, I realized just how easy it is to fall for the idea that children are meant to be raised by television screens. For our daughter's first Christmas, my father bought her some DVDs from a popular series designed for infants and toddlers. His heart was in the right place, but I think he forgot to factor in my limited attention span, and poor short-term memory. These are both very likely to be the result of too much "Tom and Jerry" and not enough "Tom and Huck." If I had spent a little more time reading, studying, and paying attention to the teacher, I might not have to drive trucks for a living. Don't get me wrong, I do love driving trucks, but I'll never see a six-figure salary doing it. Meanwhile, my daughter will still need shoes and college tuition.

As for the DVDs my dad had purchased, they were innocent enough, but I still saw a problem. Though the images presented on the screens were educational, I think it's a bad idea to set a precedent of learning by television screen. It seems to me that when it comes time to learn by *teacher*, there's going to be a problem. You see, no matter how talented a teacher is, he/she will not be able to compete with the production value and flashy graphics on a TV screen. Once a child becomes used to seeing flashy images with musical backgrounds, a teacher is going to have no luck holding their interest. I have no reservations about presenting this as a <u>fact</u> rather than theory, because I myself am a classic example of what happens when you watch too much TV as a child, and that was *before* the age of educational DVDs and headrest flat-screens.

In the end, I decided to put the DVDs away and not allow my daughter to watch them. My dad has always been pretty understanding and respectful of our wishes, so when the time is right, I'll tell him all about it...but not today.

I wish we lived in a world where lame cartoons and excessive television viewing were the only things that parents had to worry about, but that's just not the case. Truth be told, there are lots of bad things out there that can ruin, if not *end,* your child's life. Some of these things come in the form of subtle influences and have a more gradual but equally negative effect. Most of these things are not easily recognized until it's too late. Worse yet, they can be found in some of the most unlikely places. I realized this one Saturday morning a few weeks before our daughter was born.

Every year since as far back as I can remember, my hometown middle school has sponsored an annual pancake breakfast to benefit local charities. I thought it might be interesting to see how the school had changed since I was there last, so we went. And change it had. Not structurally, or even cosmetically, but there were a few very big differences nonetheless. As we walked into the cafeteria, the first thing that jumped out at me was a giant electronic sign mounted on the facing wall that was scrolling the upcoming events schedules. This would have been fine except for the two *advertisements* that were part of the sign. First of all, when I was in school, if there were any commercial advertisements at all, they were too subtle to notice. The real problem I had, though, had to do with *what* was being advertised. To the right of the scroll was a four-foot by four-foot backlighted advertisement for the latest "Mario Brothers" video game. To the left was a matching sign that was advertising a popular action-adventure television series, complete with a picture of one of the teenage female characters wearing a *very* low-cut shirt that left little to the imagination.

Seeing this brought to mind a few questions. Do television, video games, and boobs no longer distract kids from their schoolwork? Do kids need to be *reminded* to watch TV, play video games, and look at boobs? How many of my tax dollars went to this idiocy?

After we finished our pancakes, I took my wife for a tour of my old school. This was a depressing mistake. As we walked the halls, we were both noticing the hundreds of student-drawn posters that lined the walls. As I took notice to the *themes* of these posters, my wife pointed out the poor grammar and bad spelling that peppered them. There were such themes as "Everyone's a winner" and "We're all equals." I found this to be a little disturbing, because life has taught me repeatedly that we are *not* all winners. In reality, only those that *win* are winners. Life has also taught me that we are *not* all equals either. In reality, there are big people, and small people; there are smart people and dumb people. There are go-getters and there are slackers. There are nice people, and there are complete jerks. Yet, as disturbing as some of the poster themes were, I have to admit, it was the grammar and spelling errors that really got under my skin. There were actually kids that had been allowed to substitute "da" for the word "the." There were words with too letters, and others with too *few*. I was trying to imagine *my* teachers letting *me* get away with that...it just wouldn't have happened. I would have been told to re-do the poster or take an "F." As we walked out of the school, I felt as if I had just visited "Bizarro World." Then I realized that the baby we were about to have was probably going to be at that very school someday. On that day, it became painfully obvious that trusting a public school to educate my kid was no longer an option.

That pancake breakfast demonstrated to me in living color why parenting should be considered a more noble <u>duty</u> than it seems to be today. Not only does a parent need to be a *teacher*, so that their kid doesn't go through life thinking that "da" is actually a word, but they have to be a whole list of other things too. When you have children, it is your duty to be a teacher, nurse, therapist, linguist, judge, jury, jailer, policeman, handyman/woman, quality control specialist, supervisor, motivational speaker, chef, personal trainer and disciplinarian.

Parenting is a job, duty, obligation, and privilege. Unfortunately though, nowadays it's considered to be more of a *situation*. In fact, it's usually considered to be a situation that you get into *accidentally*. But however you *end up* in that situation, you need to realize that there's <u>no</u> turning back. It's the parent's job to make sure that their kid does not cause problems for themselves or the rest of us. It's rarely easy, it's not always fun, and it's a 24/7 occupation with no vacations or weekends off. But if you do it right, it'll be the most rewarding thing you ever do.

Chapter 13
When it's left to the Left –
My Katrina Rant

OK, let's be honest. Being a conservative has yet to win me any popularity contests, and this chapter is definitely not going to help. Not because conservatives are the mean-hearted souls that we're commonly painted to be, but because our ideology is based on common sense, self-reliance, and practicality...not feelings. In short, liberals tend to handle issues based on how they feel about them. Fixing the problem usually takes a back seat to making sure everyone *feels* good based on *intentions* rather than actual *results*. On the other hand, conservatives tend to *think* about the issue, weigh the options and try to find a solution that actually fixes the problem. Of course, to the left, this means that conservatives *have* no feelings. Quite the contrary. In fact, the irony of the whole liberal/conservative debate is that when applied, conservative principles almost always result in good feelings. After all, what feels better - *intending* to win the race, or *actually* winning the race?

On it's own, this basic philosophy in harmless enough. It's when I apply it to certain issues or events that I get dirty looks. This (as well as a few other things) became painfully obvious to me during the days and weeks following Hurricane Katrina.

First, I would like to preface all of my assertions by telling you up front that I have never been in a hurricane. This means that anything I know about hurricanes is based on what I have seen on TV, read in books, or just plain old-fashioned deductive reasoning. Taking these things into account, I imagine a hurricane to be like all of the worst storms I have ever experienced...times ten. This leads me to believe that I would want to have <u>no</u> part of one. Don't forget, I'm just a truck driver who barely made it through high school, but even *I* know that hurricanes are bad news. Keep this in mind as I explain my position.

My interest in hurricanes is mostly casual, but I *do* have friends that live in Florida, so when one approaches the South, I pay a bit more attention. I also have relatives in Biloxi, Mississippi, so when Katrina was projected to head that way, I paid a *lot* more attention. As it turned out, I was not the only one paying attention. My brother-in-law, his wife, their five children and a couple of hundred thousand other people were able to put two and two together, and drive in the opposite direction of the storm. Remember, hurricanes are not like earthquakes, you *do* know when they're coming. The *magnitude* can sometimes be a guessing game, but c'mon...a hurricane is a hurricane. I don't want to be in a "category two" or a "category *twenty-two*" storm, and I sure as hell wouldn't force my family to ride one out.

Here is something else I know, *despite* my limited education. New Orleans was built well <u>below</u> sea level. This is a handy little bit of information to have when the hurricane that is approaching your BELOW-sea-level town is projected to *at the very least* be bringing record-breaking amounts of rainfall. Breaking it down in mathematical terms, it looks like this; record amounts of rain + possible gale force winds + house BELOW sea level = leave town. It's actually a pretty simple equation. So, why did a dumb truck driver like myself understand this, but thousands of people in New Orleans not?

As you can imagine, my wife was very worried about her brother and his family in the days leading up to the hurricane. I reminded her that her brother was no dummy and would do the right thing. After

Katrina had passed, and the first videos of the destruction began to dominate the television, my wife asked me what I thought about all those people in New Orleans. I told her that that's what happens when you don't pay attention to what's going on in the world around you. She looked at me as if I had three heads. I elaborated a bit. I reminded her that those people had the same warning that her brother did, but ignored it. She asked me if I felt at least a little bad for them, I said "No, not really". By her tone of voice, I could tell that any further comments from me had better get a mental "test run" before I actually said them. It was a good thing I decided to do that, because my next comment was going to be, "I think Katrina was God's way of thinning the herd." In my mind, the comment made sense, but for her to actually hear it would have meant days of torture. So I opted to take a different route. I told her that I felt bad for the children, because after all, you can't pick your parents. And I also felt bad for those who depended on others to get to safety, but were abandoned. The elderly and handicapped came to mind.

After our conversation, I thought about for a while, and almost started to think I might have been wrong for feeling the way I did. That lasted until the next morning when I woke up and turned on the news. The most disturbing footage I saw was not of houses or landscapes that had been destroyed by a hurricane. It was the human garbage that was plaguing the ruins. By "human garbage," I don't mean the dead bodies floating in the water. And I don't mean the man-made debris that was just everywhere as far as the eye could see. When I say "human garbage," I'm talking about the <u>looters</u>. In a disaster of this magnitude, I can understand going into an abandoned grocery store and taking some drinking water or food for your kids. This was not what I was seeing on my TV screen. I watched as people were leaving Wal*Marts with shopping carts full of purses and jewelry. I saw people going out the door with entire racks of watches and plasma televisions. What I saw made me ashamed of my race...you know, the *human* race. It was then that I realized that I was right to begin with. I *don't* care about these people.

Assuming for the sake of discussion that there is a God, my "thinning the herd" theory may have been a bit presumptuous. But I *do* believe that this hurricane was his way of bringing a few things out into the open for *everyone* to see. In fact, I would say that hurricane Katrina not only caught a lot of people by surprise, but it also caught a lot of people "red handed." Another silver lining to the cloud of Hurricane Katrina is the fact that this storm demonstrated the pitfall of liberalism better than this or any other book ever could.

What does a hurricane have to do with liberalism, you ask? Plenty. OK, to be technical, the hurricane itself didn't have much to do with liberalism, but the aftermath did. The first example I noticed even surprised *me*, and I know to expect *anything* from the left. It wasn't even one day after the storm when the finger pointing started. Of course, everything bad comes directly from George W. Bush...but we knew that already. So I guess I shouldn't have been too shocked when popular lefties tried to blame the President's refusal to sign the Kyoto Accord for Hurricane Katrina. That's too loony to even respond to, so I won't. Then there were the assertions that the military wasn't able to rescue everyone on the first day because they were too busy fighting "Bush's illegal war" in Iraq. Personally though, my favorite crackpot assertion came almost as if on cue. It took about three and a half seconds for the left to realize that people with dark skin mostly populate the city of New Orleans; you may know them as "blacks." So it stands to reason that when a natural disaster hits a city mostly populated by "blacks," most of the people affected will probably be "black." Consequently, if you see video coverage of hurricane victims, there is a very good chance that they will be "black." These images were like Christmas presents to the race-baiting crowd.

As bodies were still floating down the streets of "the Crescent City," some on the left took the opportunity to make claims of racism. There were actually people asserting that the reason rescue efforts were taking so long was because President Bush doesn't care about "black" people. According to them, the size and scope of the disaster had nothing to do with it. The fact that fuel and water supplies, as well as all forms of communication, had been damaged or destroyed had nothing to do with it. The fact that roads were submerged and/or choked with debris, and bridges were destroyed making it nearly impossible for military convoys to get to the most affected areas, had nothing to do with it. The fact that there just aren't enough helicopters in existence to rescue *so many* people in an acceptable amount of time had nothing to with it. The fact that gangs were actually *shooting* at rescue helicopters had nothing to do with it. That's right, George W. Bush ordered the United States government to take their time simply because he doesn't like "black" people. General Colin Powell, Condoleezza Rice, and Justice Janet Rogers Brown would probably be interested to know that the guy who hired them is a racist...and blind too, apparently.

My favorite wacky racism theory came from Louis Farrakhan, when he asserted that President Bush probably blew up the levies to flood-out the "blacks" in New Orleans. Had I not actually heard the audiotape of this with my own ears, I would have probably thought that someone was making a parody of him. I don't even know how you would properly respond to something like that...so I'm not even going to try.

In the surge to blame the Bush administration, others kept asking why he didn't send in the troops before the hurricane hit so they would be there immediately afterward to help. Let me get this straight, you want to *put* people and equipment in the path of a category five hurricane? What good is a helicopter if it's wrapped around a tree? A dead soldier isn't going to be of much help either. Beyond that, can you imagine the political outrage from the left if President Bush would have *invaded* and then *occupied* New Orleans? The truth of the matter is, Presidents go to great lengths to not usurp the authority of Governors. Even though it is perfectly legal to do so, overriding a Governor's authority in a case of natural disaster is usually just not done. That's because there is an assumption that the Governor of a state *can* and *will* handle their own problems until they request help from the Federal Government. All of this is pretty moot though, when you consider that if the people weren't there to begin with, they wouldn't have needed rescued in the first place.

Just why *were* there so many people still in New Orleans during the hurricane and after the levy break? When you start to peel away the layers of *that* particular onion, you find that there are quite a few plausible theories. But since this is *my* book, we're going to stick with *my* theories.

To understand the problems that plagued the evacuation and rescue efforts in New Orleans, you need to be aware of a few things for the issues to be put into proper context. First, you need to know that New Orleans has a large population of poor and unemployed people. This is important, but not for the reasons you might think. The press has been trying to convince us that so many people were stranded in the city because they were too poor to leave. This almost makes sense until you think about it rationally. The term "poor" is a very relative term in the United States. Then when you modify it by saying "too poor," you are forced to ask a few questions, such as "Too poor to do *what*? Too poor to own a radio? To poor to *listen* to that radio when it's telling you to evacuate due to an approaching hurricane, or a broken levy? Too poor to own a TV? Too poor to watch someone else's TV to get the same message? Too poor to buy or borrow a newspaper? Too poor to own a phone? Too poor to *borrow* a phone? Too poor to hear through "the grapevine" that you might be in the path of a category five hurricane? Too poor to own a car? To poor to get a ride out of town from someone who does? Too poor to buy a bus ticket? Too poor to buy a train ticket? Too poor to have relatives in another state?"

If there is any validity to the "too poor" theory, then when all the water is drained from the city, there should be no cars, trucks, motorcycles, televisions, telephones, radios, newspapers, buses, trains, bicycles, cigarettes, name brand clothes, "X-boxes," "Nike's," CD players, or twenty-inch rims found *under* that water in the "poor" sections of New Orleans. I'm sure there is nothing but tattered rags, worn-out shoes, and empty bean cans under that water.

I just don't buy the whole concept of being "too poor" to move. Even hobos can get from "Point A" to "Point B" one way or another. I am willing to accept too sick, too handicapped, too young, or too old, but not too <u>poor</u>.

Just for the sake of argument though, and the fact that so many of our old buddies in the press keep offering it as a probability, let's go with the "too poor" theory. But wait a minute, then you have to ask *more* questions. Why are so many of the citizens of New Orleans so poor? Where are their jobs? Isn't New Orleans a port city, as well as a tourism and trade icon? Where do all those "Mardi Gras" dollars go? Who's in charge down there?

There must be some mistake. You see, Democrats and liberals have been running the show in New Orleans for over half a century. They have held positions of power from one level of government to the next. Everyone from the dogcatcher to the Governor of Louisiana is a proud Democrat. But this can't be. Something doesn't add up. I keep seeing and hearing about how poor the people in New Orleans are, but Democrats and liberals control the city. It was my understanding that if liberals and Democrats were in charge, there would be no poverty, crime, or unemployment. What happened?

I'll be glad to tell you what happened. Liberalism happened! The whole philosophy of liberalism is based on letting the government hold your hand and meet your every need as you go through life (all at tax payer expense of course). If you have a health problem, Uncle Sam will get you a doctor as well as medicine. If you need transportation, Uncle Sam will give you a ride. If you need a place to live, Uncle Sam will give you an apartment. If you're hungry, Uncle Sam will feed you. On the surface, this all sounds pretty good. But what happens when Uncle Sam can't or won't help you? Who do you turn to then?

That's the failure of liberalism. When a person becomes conditioned to look at the government every time he/she needs something, eventually that person will become totally dependent on that government. So when the government fails, the people are helpless. It's the same theory as taking a lion out of the jungle. If you put a lion in the zoo, eventually it will depend on a human to be fed. It will be used to having its meal pushed through a trap door at a given time every day. It will no longer need to hunt, so the lion's hunting instincts and skills fall away to nothing. But what happens when the zoo closes and the lion is released back into the wild? Simple, he either starves or gets eaten.

Hurricane Katrina effectively demonstrated the human equivalent of tamed lions being released back into the wild jungle after the zoo closes. In this case, it was liberal (tamed) humans being forced into the real world after their government fails them in an emergency. Don't get me wrong, I wouldn't expect the government to be able to act swiftly and competently in the aftermath of such a huge disaster. But then again, that's the point. I don't *expect* the government to do anything. That's what being a conservative is all about. We *hope* the government does what we pay them to do, but we know not to *depend* on it. As a result, we learn to take care of ourselves, because we know that we can end up in the jungle at any time.

The long and the short of it is that the people they continually elected for over fifty years have promised the residents of New Orleans the moon and stars. Instead, all they got was food stamps, unemployment, welfare, weak levies, and total government dependency. New Orleans has been a liberal proving ground for decades, and the only thing anyone has to show for it is a few billion gallons of dirty water. Do I really need to point out the irony of that to you environmentalists out there?

Even though I despise liberalism, I have never thought of liberals themselves as being corrupt or incompetent. After all, corruption and incompetence knows no bounds and can be found on both sides of the aisle. Unfortunately, when liberalism is applied to issues that involve security or money, it tends to leave the door wide open to corruption and incompetence. That's because liberalism is usually based on how people *should* react to things and not how they actually do. The "human" factor commonly takes a back seat to "good intentions." So it was for this reason that I was not surprised to hear about some of the things that went on in Louisiana before and after Hurricane Katrina.

For starters, the decision to have a mandatory evacuation of New Orleans came way too late. This was the fault of the Mayor of New Orleans as well as the Governor of Louisiana. No matter how upsetting it may be to mainstream media, it's not the President's job to evacuate specific towns. After all, isn't that the whole point of having Mayors and Governors to begin with? The same scenario played out after the hurricane when the levies gave way in New Orleans...too late with the warning yet again. Then, to top things off, the people who were able to escape the flood were sent to the New Orleans Super Dome, which was already full of people who hadn't fled the hurricane soon enough.

Unfortunately for the Mayor and Governor, as they were falling over each other trying to blame President Bush for their mistakes, a few pictures were circulating around the internet that told a different tale. That's right, the infamous "bus pictures" were getting out for the whole world to see. These were pictures of hundreds of school and city buses that were left to be flooded rather than be used for evacuation purposes. This meant that not only were taxpayer funded resources not used to help those same taxpayers, but now those same resources were going to have to be replaced at taxpayer expense! If they were going to let the buses sit, they could have at least moved them to higher ground so they wouldn't be ruined in the flood. There is some bitter irony in the fact that these were the same buses that were used to get voters to the polls in previous elections.

Then came Hurricane Rita. As if someone were playing a cruel joke on the people of the Gulf Coast, yet another disaster was looming on the horizon...literally. To most reasonably intelligent people, *this alone* would be reason enough to not allow the citizens of New Orleans to return home...but not the Mayor. Against the warning of the President, as well as a whole list of government agencies, the Mayor of New Orleans told his citizens to come back to town. Yeah, that's right. You know, the town that was still under water in many places. The town that had no electricity, emergency services, telephone services, sewage services, hospitals or even drinkable water. As bodies were still floating in the water, the Mayor of New Orleans was urging his people to return to a land that was soaked in toxic water and sludge. It was as if he had never heard of the term "waterborne disease". According to the press though, this was not what they consider to be "incompetence." So little was mentioned in the mainstream media about the Mayor's mistakes.

Then again...his name isn't "Bush." I often wonder what would have happened to all those people who were told to come home, if Rita had maintained category five status and directly hit New Orleans.

Another lesson in liberalism came with the crash course in "supply and demand" that Katrina provided us. As it turns out, a pretty big chunk of our nation's oil supply comes from the Gulf of Mexico. Not only that, but a pretty big chunk of our gasoline supply is refined in the Gulf Coast region as well. This was not a secret, but it was also not exactly common knowledge among the people of the United States. Let's face it; most of us don't stay up all night thinking about how our gasoline is supplied to us. As long as it comes out of the pump when we squeeze the handle...it's all good. That is, until we hit about three dollars a gallon. When that happened, about half of the country suddenly became interested in where our gasoline comes from.

The temporary shutdown of oil platforms and refineries by Hurricanes Katrina and Rita taught us quite a few things. We learned that there is a difference between crude oil and gasoline. That means that no matter where the oil comes from, it needs to take a trip through a *refinery* before it becomes gasoline. We learned that over the past thirty years, the demand for gasoline has grown by leaps and bounds...but the number of refineries has stayed the same. That's right, we haven't built a new oil refinery in this country for about thirty years. At the same time, the population of people and automobiles grows more every day (keep that in mind the next time you see an ILLEGAL alien at the gas pump, or on the highway). "Why haven't we built any new refineries"? you ask. As it turns out, the gift of high gas prices comes directly from our old pals "the environmentalists." It was the environmental lobby that saw to it that building refineries in the United States would become a crime.

Back in chapter nine, I explained how environmentalists had put a stop to any additional oil drilling in the United States. I wrote chapter nine months before these hurricanes ever showed up. There is probably a little irony to the fact that even though I was well aware of the fact that unquestioned environmentalism was going to hurt our country, I had no idea that it would happen so soon. I pictured a more gradual decline in our ability to sustain our own demands. I imagined a slow increase of the price per-gallon until people would finally get angry enough to start asking the right questions. Who would have thought that only a few months later, we would be paying over three dollars, and in some cases over four dollars a gallon for gas? It also never dawned on me that one natural disaster could make us so vulnerable. I had never even thought of that.

Thanks to Katrina and Rita, we also learned what a President does and does not have the power to do when it comes to fuel prices. When the prices at the pump skyrocketed after the first hurricane, people began to demand that the President do something about it. Do what?

Wave a magic wand?

Apparently, some Americans were under the impression that a President has the power to turn water into wine, or gasoline as the case may be. You see, gasoline is a product, like jellybeans, or CD players. It is also a commodity, like orange juice, or lumber. That means that the free market, not the President, controls the price of gasoline. Presidents can no more raise or lower the price of fuel, than they can the price of "Pop Tarts." When it comes to controlling the price of fuel in America, the President has only a handful of options, all of which need to go through Congress. He can tap into the nation's strategic oil reserve, which is not part of the free market; it belongs to the government. But since there is only so much oil in the reserve, it wouldn't ease the daily price of fuel for very long anyway. He can add or raise taxes on the production of fuel as President Carter did back in the seventies, but that becomes the exact opposite of lowering the price of fuel, because as we all know from chapter eight, taxes are part of overhead, which is part of the purchase price. You younger readers may want to ask your parents about "odd and even days." Consider that a homework assignment.

Another thing that a President can do to ease the price of fuel is something that I only recently learned about, courtesy of Katrina and Rita. The following is something that I learned as a result of being in the trucking industry. As I was going down the interstate one night, I started talking to a driver who was hauling gasoline to mini-marts in Washington, D.C. He gave me quite an education. As it turns out, one reason for the high price of fuel is the many blends of petroleum. At first, you are probably like me and assumed that he was talking about the three or four different octanes that you can choose from at the pump...not quite. Actually, octane has nothing to do with it, because *all* gas stations get three or four octane choices. When was the last time you saw a gas station that only offered 93 octane? What the truck driver was talking about was fuel <u>blends</u>. These are fuels that have varying degrees of chemicals that allow them to evaporate slower. The amount of these chemicals is dependent upon *where* the fuel is going to be delivered. That means that a load of fuel that will be delivered to a rural area, will have a different *blend* than a load going to an urban area. Believe it or not, there are about *fifty* different blends of petroleum that need to be specifically refined for specifically designated areas of the country. Oh yeah, did I mention that this process is not cheap, and comes right out of your pocket at the pump. Did I also mention that these blends mean absolutely nothing to the engine in your car? Guess who it does matter to. You guessed it...the environmental lobby. That's right, these different blends are supposed to lessen the effects of air pollution, as if that's the biggest problem I have when it comes time to pay the mortgage or buy diapers. Thanks to years of over-regulation, the tree hugger lobby has succeeded in putting a few less gallons in your twenty dollars worth of gas. But don't forget, they couldn't have done it without the help of your friendly neighborhood elected representatives. Remember that when you have to break open your kid's piggy bank to drive to the polls next time.

Unfortunately, this revelation was brought to my attention over a CB radio at about 1:30 in the morning late one night. It's not exactly the lead story on CNN. On the bright side, it did make news after President Bush temporarily waived the blend restrictions on fuel in the aftermath of Hurricane Katrina. Of course, it was only a temporary fix, but it did throw some light on the issue. Now we can only hope that enough curiosity was sparked to start some interest and debate on the subject. I think that if enough people realize how costly *we ourselves* have made the oil refining process, they *might* reconsider their priorities. Don't get me wrong, I don't want to pollute the air, but three dollars a gallon...PLEASE! Besides, has anyone actually *proven* beyond a shadow of a doubt that gasoline sitting in underground tanks actually does that much damage to the environment? I'm willing to bet that they haven't.

Another tactic a President can use to affect change in the price of fuel is simply to get the word out, otherwise known as using the "bully pulpit." The theory being that the people will put enough pressure on their elected officials to create new legislation that would solve the problem...like a bill to allow more drilling and refining. That is pretty much what the Founding Fathers had in mind when they set this little country up in the first place. You know...the whole "by the people, for the people" thing. Unfortunately, for this method to work well, you need to have a willing press to help you get the word out. That tends to be a problem if you're a President that has a little "R" after your name.

This brings us to what the hurricanes have taught us about media coverage. They taught us that rushing to judgment could be an Olympic event. When rumors of gang rapes, murder, and mob rule at the New Orleans Super Dome began to circulate, our ever-competent media decided that the most responsible thing to do would be assume the rumors were true, and run stories that claimed exactly that. Apparently, they never considered the idea that this might hamper the rescue efforts being attempted by unarmed, non-military agencies and organizations. After all, if you were in charge of a group of unarmed, unprotected rescue workers, would you send them into a zone full of armed rapists, bandits, and gang members? As it turns out, most of the rumors about lawlessness and mayhem turned out to be just that...rumors. I guess we'll never know if scaring away rescue workers with stories of mob rule actually cost people's lives, but who cares...as long as the ratings were good.

I couldn't help but wonder why so many of my questions about the events before and after Hurricane Katrina weren't answered until I took the time and effort to research them for myself. Then again, if you have been paying attention, that's nothing new. Why did I have to learn about fuel production from a truck driver on the CB radio? Why weren't the pictures of the flooded buses given more airtime? Why were so many of the Mayor of New Orleans' *comments* given air time, but no hard *questions* about his response to the disaster were asked? Why were so many of *his* comments accepted at face value, but the President's warranted more grilling? Why did so many people from everywhere else have so much *less* difficulty evacuating?

Another lesson in liberalism came during the evacuation of areas in the path of Hurricane Rita. In fact, you might call it a "combo-lesson." That's because with one single

Hurricane-related issue, we learned about human nature vs. liberal theory, economics, as well as yet another lesson on supply and demand. That issue was "price gouging." To be honest, I have to admit that even I learned a thing or two about this one.

After watching days and days of massive media coverage of Hurricane Katrina, when word came that Rita was going to make landfall, the people in her path decided not to wait around for some type of government assistance. They somehow managed to leave on their own. All things considered, the evacuation was going pretty well, until traffic started to back up. Even this wasn't too big of a problem, until cars started running out of gas. "Why", you ask? Good question, and I happen to have an answer.

The people evacuating Rita's path were running out of gas because the gas stations were running out of gas. Everyone was running out of gas because of a number of factors; one being the disruptions in the fuel-supply chain after Katrina, another being the logistical problems of getting fuel trucks into towns where all traffic is being routed in the opposite direction for evacuation purposes. But one of the biggest reasons for a shortage of fuel during the Rita evacuation is the not-so-well understood issue of "price gouging." Better yet, *lack* of price gauging.

Like most people, even a free market conservative like myself frowns at the mention of price gauging. So when I read an article that was defending the practice of price gouging, I realized that there actually *are* two sides to every story. I'm paraphrasing, not plagiarizing the article, because I don't remember who wrote it, but I do remember the premise. The writer theorized that price gouging is just another part of the free market system, and has a legitimate place in society. I thought he was a little dense, until I read the rest of the article. The gist of his theory went something like this. When the state and local governments decided to take action against price gouging, they were actually doing more harm than good. This is because the price of fuel was not allowed to adjust for changes in the market; in this case, a mass evacuation due to an approaching hurricane. This meant that there was little-to-no incentive for people to plan their trips accordingly. Everyone immediately decided that it would be best to top-off their fuel tanks before they evacuated. And why not? After all, the price of gas hadn't raised enough to matter. The end result was a flood of people lining up at the gas stations, and being sucked dry...whether they needed the extra fuel or not. That left the many motorists who really needed the extra gallons stranded. This is the exact point where price gouging starts to make a little more sense.

You see, the free market at that time called for an unusually high demand for fuel in a short period of time. A higher price at the pump in the affected area would have forced the people of that area to prioritize more. Let's say the price of gas is capped by the government at

$2.80 a gallon. A driver will see no reason not to stuff in that last three gallons to fill his tank. If the same driver goes to the same station and finds the price has gone up to $4.50 a gallon, he will take his mostly full tank and keep driving until he finds cheaper gas later in his trip. The high price will also force others to prioritize. They might opt to carpool, take a bus, or even ride a bike. This will leave that original three gallons plus a whole lot more for someone willing to pay the $4.50 a gallon...someone who really *needs* it. The end result is shorter lines at the pump, longer-lasting fuel supplies, and fewer cars stranded at the side of the road.

Then, after the hurricane has come and gone, the market adjusts itself back to normal prices for fuel. After all, if there is no emergency, or disruption in supply and demand, it would be pretty hard to sell gas at $4.50 a gallon, when it's going for $2.80 a gallon in the next town over. Basically, gas stations will go right back to competing with each other on an even playing field, as opposed to one station having business as usual, and another dealing with a mass evacuation and price caps.

Before you liberals start thinking that I have laid out a good case for raising the price of fuel just to force people to conserve energy, consider this. We're Americans. We are a free people, and we are very used to taking advantage of that fact. We like to drive, and we like to *enjoy* driving. We like to also like to boat, fly, ride motorcycles and race cars. Come to think of it, we'll race just about anything. Being a free people also means that we do not have an appreciation for other people telling us what we can and can't do, especially when it comes to driving. Besides, the government could only raise the price of energy by implementing more taxes, and taxes tend to be a bit unpopular. Do you actually think people would live like that for any substantial period of time unless they absolutely had to? Not in this lifetime. You have to consider the "human factor." Humans (especially *American* humans) will only sacrifice so much for so long.

Speaking of taxes and sacrifice, the recent hurricanes taught us a little bit about both. Just when you thought Katrina had nothing more to offer, she exposed even more liberalism, this time on Capitol Hill. As if all-important issues of the day had miraculously been addressed, certain members of Congress had time to take care of one more pressing dilemma. How to distract the public from bad legislative decisions that cause high oil prices, while placing the blame elsewhere at the same time? The answer came in the form of publicized Congressional hearings that questioned the role of oil companies in the high price of fuel. It turned out to be less of a questioning and more of a mass editorial by Congress, but hey...it's just "Big Oil." I'm not sure what they were hoping to accomplish with these hearings, but it seems to me that Congress had really stepped in it by having them. You see, in the age of live "C-span" coverage, these clowns were put on record with whatever came out of their mouths. So when "Big Oil" explained to them exactly why prices were so high, it fell on the deaf ears of Congress, and was rebuffed with liberal platitudes. All on live TV.

One common theme was that oil companies are obligated to give money back to the American people, or lower fuel prices because their profits are so high. Really? Obligated? Says who? The last time I checked, people went into business to make money...as much of it as possible. Of course, liberals think of this as a crime, and there are a lot of liberals in Congress. It never even dawned on them that oil companies might have such a high profit margin because they're not allowed to grow their businesses any further. After all, that would mean more oil exploration, drilling, and refining...we can't have that. Some of Washington's best and brightest suggested that "Big Oil's" profits should be taxed more, ensuring that money would go to the less fortunate (the government) and not the evil oil companies. The question then becomes, "Why produce more oil, or even stay in the business at all, if your profits are going to taxed away?" It's as if our elected officials have no idea how businesses operate. As I mentioned in an earlier chapter, businesses DO NOT pay taxes. Taxes are factored in as part of company overhead and passed on to the customer as part of the price of a particular product. Gasoline is no different. To raise taxes on the oil companies would only mean higher prices at the pump for you and me.

You would think our elected officials on both sides of the aisle would have a different perspective on the oil industry as a whole. Or maybe I'm nuts after all. But in my wacky, mixed-up mind, biting the hand that feeds you is usually a bad idea. For some reason, these geniuses that keep getting elected to positions of power keep forgetting that without oil, everything stops. Yes, *everything*. The United States, as we know it, would come to a stop.

If anything, the government should be doing everything in its power to SUPPORT the oil industry. In a perfect world, they would recognize the importance of a strong and profitable oil supply, and get out of the way of the people supplying it. Instead, the oil industry has become a political "whipping boy."

I don't mean to venture too far from the topic at hand with my screed about the oil industry, but it did become a pretty big factor after the hurricanes blew the lid off of our energy problems. It seems a shame that a tragedy of such a devastating magnitude had to teach us what a little common sense could not. Or maybe it's just wishful thinking that we've learned anything at all.

On the bright side, even if we have yet to actually *learn* the lessons of Hurricanes Katrina and Rita...the discussions have begun. As the media seems to become more and more flooded (no pun intended) with scandals and controversies concerning the aftermath of the hurricanes, they appear to be losing their ability to control the flow of information to support any agendas they might have had. One such controversy emerged when the Mayor of New Orleans vowed to rebuild it as a "chocolate city." Immediately afterwards, there was footage of him trying to spin his way out of it...unsuccessfully.

This brings us to the discussion of what direction New Orleans will go in now that so much has changed there. Now that so many people have left the city, there are fears that it will change the balance of political power there. Others seem to be wondering who will fill the gaps left by those who will not be returning. This brings us to the topic of rebuilding the city. As you can imagine, there are lots of jobs that are being created because of such a massive rebuilding effort. Would anyone like to take a guess as to who is going to be showing up to fill those jobs? If you said "ILLEGAL immigrants"...give yourself a prize! Rather than go into a ranting prediction of what would happen to any given city if it's original inhabitants were suddenly replaced by thousands of ILLEGAL aliens, I think I'd rather just sit back and watch the fireworks from a distance. I'm sure it wouldn't be a big deal anyway. After all, look at how *modern* and *cosmopolitan* Mexico is.

At the end of the day, ILLEGAL immigration has turned out to be only one slice of the educational pie that Mother Nature has put on our table. After all of the death, destruction, and tragedy, she has provided us with a chance to learn something, and rebuild for the better. You could even say that she has given us a chance to really examine our priorities and perspectives on life in general. But above all, she has provided us with the ultimate lesson in personal philosophy. You can be the type of person who overcomes an obstacle, or the type that waits around until someone else moves it for you. You can be self reliant, or completely dependent on your government. You can think for yourself, using logic and common sense, or you can fall for every hook, line, and sinker that the media throws in your direction. You can learn from history, or assume there will be a different outcome...next time.

Chapter 14
Judge Not, Lest Ye Be Liberal

As a newcomer to the world of politics, I find myself learning something new just about every day. This has been both a blessing and a curse. On the one hand, I might learn something that can give me new insight on a particular issue that I don't know much about. On the other hand, what I learn might scare the crap out of me. Apparently, that is why they say, "ignorance is bliss." I'm occasionally reminded of the character "Neo" from *The Matrix*. You see, at some point, I swallowed "the red pill." Now that it has been revealed to me just how things work, I often wonder if I would be happier if I was still in my comfortable little world of liberal ignorance.

Admittedly, this chapter has been the one I have dreaded writing the most, if for no other reason than its relevance to all of the chapters that came before it. In fact, I believe so strongly that the topic we are about to explore is so important that it's actually intimidating to write about. Only because I fear that my lack of writing skill might not do it justice, and I want you to understand its importance to your way of life. Another intimidating factor of this topic is the immediate glaze of boredom that you can see in people's eyes whenever it is brought up in a discussion. Trying to keep a reader interested in such a topic is going to be a real test for me, but then again...so has the rest of this book.

Of course, the topic at hand is the Supreme Court. Before you start skipping pages, you need to consider the following. You actually *do* care about the Supreme Court...you just might not know it yet. In fact, if I am even moderately successful at writing this chapter, you will put the Supreme Court at the top of your list of things America should worry about. You might even kick yourself for not paying more attention in civics class.

To understand the importance of the Supreme Court, we need to get a few incidentals out of the way first, starting with a little bit of background about our government, and the Supreme Court's role in it. I'll make this as painless as possible.

If you think of our government as a never-ending football game, then you can equate our elected officials with the coaching staff. You can then consider America to be a massive Super Dome. As it turns out, "We the People" are actually the team owners, and everyone plays by the same rulebook...the United States Constitution. As you might imagine, there are two dominating teams (The Liberals and The Conservatives) both hoping that the referees (Supreme Court justices) will interpret the rulebook to make calls in their favor.

This is not a *perfect* analogy of our system of government, but it's pretty close. It is ironic though, how so many people have such a vast knowledge about the game of football as well as it's players, but so *few* know the first thing about the people making *important* decisions in their lives. They can tell you all about "first downs", but have no clue about the "First Amendment." This attitude demonstrates the biggest flaw in my football analogy. In the world of football, regardless of a team owner's knowledge of the game, he has a vested interest that motivates him to pay attention to the success of his team. As a result, the owner will do what he can to find and hire the people he believes will get him to the Super Bowl.

Unfortunately, this is not the same thinking that many Americans bring to the table. In fact, if we were to accept the football analogy, it would be a much different scene in the "owner's box" on game day.

First of all, the owner's box would be empty because the owner didn't even care enough about his team to find out when or where the game was. He would just assume that it was someone else's problem, and then go home and watch "American Idol." The idea of his team winning, losing, or going broke wouldn't interest him in the least because he was too busy playing "X-Bo." And when the game officials continued to make bad calls that go against the rule book, or just make rules up as they go, he wouldn't even bat an eye.

The sad irony of this is that in *football*, the stakes usually involve two things, money and/or pride, not much more. As for American democracy, the stakes are a hell-of-a-lot higher...*including* money and/or pride.

For starters, some of our most basic rights are now up for grabs. From freedom of speech, to the basic human right to live, our liberties are on very shaky ground. This was not how it was meant to be.

When our nation was founded, it seemed pretty obvious that we were going to need every American citizen to be on the same page when it comes to government. So it was decided that there would need to be a document written that would explain, in plain English, the rules and regulations of our government. This document was known as "the Constitution of the United States." The guys who wrote it were known as "the Framers." Much like a group of carpenters frame a house, these men had metaphorically *framed* our system of government.

This was no easy job when you consider the following. How long does it take a typical group of people to agree on *anything*? Having worked in the pizza industry, I can tell you from personal experience how long it can take for five guys to decide what kind of pizza to get for lunch. Imagine trying to get a group of guys to hammer out an entire system of government! Just the fact that they pulled it off is amazing enough, but *what* they came up with is nothing short of a miracle. *These* guys planned a system of government that would apply in the future, define and protect basic human rights, and be adaptable if necessary. Sometimes, it takes all I can do just to plan an afternoon with my family.

It's too bad that I never appreciated what our forefathers were able to accomplish until now. Until September 11th, 2001, the founding of our nation was just another lame subject that I had to know about in high school. Now that I can see how the framer's work is being slowly dismantled, I realize that the only thing *lame* was my apathy.

The long and the short of what our founding fathers designed was a system of government that is ultimately controlled by the people. It was also created with the understanding that human beings can abuse unchecked powers...and often do. They dealt with this by inserting a system of checks and balances on the government. Basically, if one man gets a little too big for his britches, there are one or two others that will pull him back into line. Everyone has to answer to someone else. This is why our federal government is divided into three branches - judicial, executive, and legislative. According to the "rule book" (the Constitution), this system is supposed to work pretty well. And for well over two hundred years it has.

Here is where things start to fall apart. You see, our whole system of government is predicated on the notion that our elected officials actually pay attention to what the rulebook says. Until recently, this has never been much of an issue. My, how things change.

Like professional athletes, we might find ourselves in a position where we *wish* the rulebook says something that it doesn't, or that it didn't say something that it does. This is natural, and people on both sides of the political spectrum experience this all the time. A conservative might *wish* that the constitution prohibited "gay marriage," and a liberal might *wish* that the constitution prohibited people from owning firearms. On both topics someone is going to be disappointed. This proves the theory that you'll never make everyone happy. Then again, the Constitution of the United States was never meant to make people happy. It was meant to protect our rights, and not much more.

With this comes good news and bad news. The good news is, there is a process for changing the things in the Constitution that we disagree with. The bad news is, there are also a few loopholes that can allow people to make an "end run" around the Constitution. This makes it possible for the whims of a few to affect the freedom of many.

The legitimate way of changing the Constitution is by passing a constitutional amendment. This is a long and tedious legislative process, and it was designed to be exactly that. After all, it wouldn't be a good idea to have a system where destroying liberty is a piece of cake for whoever might happen to be in power at any particular time. If you want to make a change in the Constitution, you are really going to have to work for it, and you will have to get the support of a lot of people. The *people* have a role in the process by voting for the representatives that have views that are similar to their own. They also have the ability to lobby, petition, or meet with their representatives in hopes of educating or changing their minds on a given issue. The people also have a role in the process by being able to run for elected office themselves.

Or, you can change the Constitution by having the Supreme Court distort what it says, right before they make a ruling that will then become the law of the land. That's right...the "loophole." Actually, *this* method of changing the Constitution is less of a loophole, and more of a blatant disregard for the legislative process. It's also a total abuse of power, and only results in making the Constitution irrelevant. As if that's what the founding fathers had in mind.

Unfortunately for us, if you are a liberal Supreme Court Justice, the opinions of our founding fathers don't carry much water. To understand why this is a problem, you first need to understand what the job of a Supreme Court Justice is. It is their job to *interpret* and *apply* the Constitution to cases that come across their desk, and not much else. *Changing* the Constitution is supposed to be left to the legislative process that I mentioned a few lines ago. For Justices who respect the law, putting aside their personal ideology is probably not that difficult. After all, they realize that their primary reference point is supposed to be the Constitution of the United States, not personal or popular opinion. Changing the constitution to suit a personal agenda or bias would be considered a sin to an ethical Supreme Court Justice.

In a perfect world, all Supreme Court Justices would possess such personal discipline. But here in the real world, there are those who just can't resist the temptation to wield the power of their position like a battle-ax. This is not to say that they are evil, or trying to harm anyone. In fact, in most cases, I would assume that they are acting in what they *believe* to be the best interest of the people. But benefit of the doubt aside, this does not justify fixing what isn't broken, or perverting what our founding fathers worked so hard to create. As my mom said at least a million times, "That goes for both of you!" Conservative Justices are no more entitled to abuse their position than liberal ones. Even though I truly believe that conservative principles can only *help* people, forcing them by judicial abuse is no way to institute them. Besides, that would fly in the face of two primary conservative principals...freedom, and small government.

Justices who have this philosophy are called "originalists." This means that they believe in the original text of the Constitution, and make their judgments according to what it actually says...not what they *wish* it said. Justices who believe that the Constitution is a "living, breathing document" that should be changed or interpreted according to what's popular or socially acceptable that week are called "activist judges." They seem to believe it is their purpose in life to "change the world," and some even admit to it. Don't get me wrong, there's nothing wrong with wanting to change the world. Heck, writing this book is *my* little attempt at doing just that. Then again, I'm not a Supreme Court Justice.

Granted, I am about as far from being an historical scholar as you can get, but that doesn't mean that I fell off the turnip truck just yesterday morning. In fact, I am willing to bet that you could scour every historical archive known to man from now until hell freezes over, and never find one official document that includes the phrase "change the world" in the job description of Supreme Court Justice. The sad truth of the matter is that some people have a tough time dealing with positions of power and authority. So when such power is appointed to someone with an ax to grind or personal agenda, the results can be a real kick in the nuts.

This is why there is more than one Justice on the Supreme Court.

Unfortunately, it's not a foolproof system. But realistically, there probably is no system that can sufficiently deal with the ignorance, arrogance, or deception of human beings.

Ignorance in the sense that there are Justices on the bench that seem to be completely clueless about what our founding documents say. The same ignorance can also be found in people who elect officials who appoint such Justices, without taking the time to find out what their judicial philosophies are...or if they even have any to begin with. I would venture to say that a large percentage of voters don't even know what a judicial philosophy is.

Arrogance in the sense that there are Justices on the bench who seem to believe they have been anointed the saviors of America. They have no problem with eroding the relevance of our founding documents, so long as it makes them feel accomplished, or furthers their agenda. This goes for the Justice, the one who appoints the Justice, and those who vote for the one who appoints the Justice.

Finally, *deception* in the sense that there are Justices on the bench who seem to have conveniently, or coincidentally, changed the judicial philosophies that they professed to have when they were originally being considered for the job. Then there are the skilled politicians who use distraction to slip a *cooperative* Justice under the radar to further their agendas. Or they use the art of *implication* to destroy the reputation of a political opponent's judicial appointee. You see, the power held by the Supreme Court is not lost on our elected officials on either side of the aisle. For one party in particular, this fact can actually mean the difference between returning to power, or becoming obsolete and irrelevant. Well, maybe not the party specifically, but the liberal philosophy that currently controls it could become the next "dinosaur" of political ideologies. Unfortunately, liberalism has found a pretty solid "toe hold" by way of the Supreme Court.

Liberals in particular see the courts as a last-ditch effort to implement and impose their agenda on people who would otherwise reject it. If the people go to the ballot box and shoot down a liberal initiative, that should be the end of the matter until the people can be convinced to change their mind. But since the left looks at the people as being intellectual lightweights, they refuse to go back to the drawing board when one of their proposals are given the bum's rush. Rather than take the hint, they try to *force* their "brilliance" onto the people by opposing Justices who might interfere with their agenda, and appointing Justices who don't. This means that an idea that the people voted *against* can be declared "constitutional" through the judiciary and get a green light anyway. And vice versa.

One glaring example of the liberal elite's desperation to impose their agenda is the fiasco that routinely follows the announcement of President Bush's judicial nominations. Being a total rookie in the world of politics, I think it's safe to say that the judicial nomination process during the Bush administration has probably taught me more about politics than I could have ever learned in some college course. Don't get me wrong, what I was learning about the nomination *process* was interesting enough, but it paled in comparison to the crash course I was getting in political strategy.

One such political strategy amounted to nothing more than simple wordplay. Take the word "mainstream" for example. This has become a favorite word of politicians lately. The funny thing is, the wrong people keep claiming to have a lock on the *mainstream* ideals of the American people. If your party truly did see eye-to-eye with the "mainstream" of society, then doesn't it stand to reason that it would be the one that *won* elections? This oversight in logic did not stop the *minority* party from trying to convince us that *they* were actually the ones who understood mainstream America. They did this by voting and speaking out against the Bush judicial nominees, claiming that they were "out of the mainstream." OK, just for the sake of argument, let's say that this was Bizarro World, and somehow the *minority* party was the "mainstream" party. What does the mainstream have to do with judicial nominations? What does it have to do with the Constitution of the United States? Is there an amendment that says a Supreme Court Justice is supposed to adhere to whatever philosophy happens to be the trend of the week? Is there even one sentence in the Constitution that orders a Supreme Court Justice to follow the whims of the ruling political party? Can someone tell me where it is written that being "mainstream" is a requirement for nomination to the Supreme Court?

Election results aside, you would be hard pressed to accurately conclude <u>anything</u> about mainstream opinions or ideologies in the "melting pot" that is our nation. How would you even attempt to research such a thing? Polls? Questionnaires? Focus groups? This is why our founding fathers didn't mention "mainstream" *anything* when they laid out our system of government. It seems to me that if your elected representative is concerned about the "mainstream of society," then that's a giant flashing neon sign that he is a complete moron with no understanding of our Constitution.

Another tactic being used by liberals to hold up or stop judicial nominees is known as the "filibuster." This is when members of Congress make excessively long speeches for no other purpose than to delay legislation, effectively buying time to affect or stop a vote. And I'm not kidding when I say "excessively long" speeches. The late Strom Thurmond filibustered the Civil Rights Act of 1957 for over twenty-four hours. As childish as it may seem, the filibuster does have a place in our process of government. In fact, not only did Jimmy Stewart immortalize the filibuster in the 1939 movie *Mr. Smith Goes to Washington,* but its use is protected by the Constitution of the United States. The problem is that the Constitution allows for the use of the filibuster in seven instances...and the nomination of Supreme Court Justices is NOT one of them. So to use, or *threaten* to use, the filibuster during a judicial nomination is, by definition, unconstitutional. The Senate gets around this little *technicality* by way of a change in the rules of Senate procedures. Even though the change had been agreed to years earlier, this too was unconstitutional because it amounts to the Senate agreeing to simply ignore the rulebook.

The long and the short of the change in rules is basically the decision to allow a filibuster to delay or derail a vote on the confirmation of a judicial nominee. A 60% majority Senate vote, as opposed to the standard 51% ("simple majority"), is needed to end such a filibuster. To complicate things even further, any vote to change the rules back to the way they were originally would most likely be filibustered, too. *This* filibuster would require a 67%

majority to be broken. Not an easy sell to the power-hungry.

On the bright side, when it comes to fixing the judicial nomination process, there is an option...go "nuclear." Actually, the "nuclear option" is a term being used to describe a vote to abolish the use of filibusters altogether in the judicial nomination process. It is being called the "nuclear option" because some politicians think it will destroy some Senate traditions. Those of us on "the right" have taken to calling it the "Constitutional option" because it returns the judicial nomination process to the way or founding fathers spelled it out in the Constitution. Admittedly though, *nuclear* option" makes a better headline.

I suppose, at the end of the day, it doesn't really matter what you call it because it's probably not going to happen anytime soon anyway. That's because some of our elected officials have decided to put political expediency ahead of protecting the rights of the people. Rather than take a stand for what's right (as they were elected to do), some have decided "play it safe" and shy away from the constitutional option for fear of losing future votes. Others have sunk even lower, opting to vote against it because they don't want to lose the ability to filibuster *liberal* justices in the future. To me, that's like saying that two wrongs could somehow make a right. I can understand this coming from liberals today because they are the minority party and are probably feeling a little desperate. The shame of it all is the fact that today, this mentality is coming from people who have the nerve to call themselves Republicans. This makes me wonder what the point of winning an election is, if you're not going to act like a winner.

Probably the meanest tactic used to sink judicial nominations (or any other type of nomination) is to simply imply and/or insinuate things about the nominee that will make them look like something they're not. Basically, the opposing side digs and digs until something from a nominee's past is found that can be used to make them look like Adolph Hitler's little brother, or worse. It can be something as trivial as one line from a nominee's college term paper that is taken out of context and spoon-fed to an eagerly awaiting media boob. Or it can be a total mischaracterization of a judge's ruling from years earlier, delivered by the media to a population that might not understand the subtle nuance of legalese. It wouldn't be so bad if this idiocy was limited to the nominee, but it isn't. The pasts of the nominee's family members are scoured for anything that can be spun into a scandal too. Even a nominee's children are considered "fair game." Some prospective justices have actually declined nominations because they knew the process would be too hard on their families.

There is a part of me that believes in the old saying, "If you can't take the heat, get out of the kitchen." But then again, who says there needs to be "heat" when it comes to nominating a Supreme Court Justice? Find out if he understands what the constitution says and move on! Do I really need to know why his adopted son's skin isn't a particular color, or why he dresses his children a particular way? Do I need to see his wife cry during a confirmation hearing in order to get a handle on his judicial philosophy? Don't get me wrong, I do understand the need to find out what kind of person is going to be putting on the black robe, but there is such a thing as too much information. At a certain point, you go from interviewer to interrogator. It would be nice if the people we elect to represent us would learn the difference.

Now that we have a basic (and I mean *very* basic) understanding of how a Supreme Court Justice ends up on the bench, you might be wondering what the big deal is. Why do those of us on the right get so bent out of shape over the Supreme Court? After all, they're all reading from the same Constitution to make their rulings...right? Well, not exactly.

As a matter of fact, as of the writing of this chapter, there are actually Supreme Court justices on the bench who believe that it's OK to look *elsewhere* for guidance in making their rulings. In their opinion, looking at the legal practices of other nations for precedents is just fine and dandy. But here in the real world, it's nothing more than an open invitation to corrupt our entire system of government, as well as our way of life.If it is decided that looking to the rest of the world for legal justification or precedent is OK, or even intellectually preferable, then where does that leave our Constitution? What's the point of it? What's to stop a judge or Supreme Court Justice from shopping around the globe until he/she finds a ruling that suits their agenda...whatever it may be?

Let's say the Supreme Court received a case where someone claimed it was unconstitutional to wear blue T-shirts on Thursdays. After searching and searching, the court could not find anything in the constitution about the right to wear blue T-shirts on Thursdays. According to the law, that would mean the case is supposed to be sent to the legislative branch for a vote and possibly an amendment to the constitution. Little did the public know that some of the Supreme Court Justices personally despised the practice of wearing blue T-shirts on Thursdays. Their "change the world" mentality led them to scour the globe until they finally found a tiny Third World dictatorship that had outlawed the wearing of blue T-shirts on Thursdays...under penalty of death. Using this tiny nation's law as their legal precedent, these few justices were able to convince a majority to rule in favor of deeming the wearing of blue T-shirts on Thursdays to be unconstitutional. The fact that the wearing of blue T-shirts on Thursdays was not only *legal* in most countries, but also *mandatory* in others was completely ignored by the same justices.

It's all fun and games if we're talking about wearing blue T-shirts on Thursdays, but what if we were talking about the right to not be taken off life support? What about the right to protect your family? What about the right to own property? Should a Supreme Court Justice have the power to examine Middle Eastern law to justify a ruling on women's rights here in America? Should they be allowed to look at Thailand for legal precedent involving children's rights? Beyond all of this though, I think it speaks volumes when a Supreme Court Justice can't seem to figure out what our own Constitution is saying about any given issue. It seems to me that looking to another country's legal decisions for the purpose of making a decision here is akin to a referee looking at the local basketball team's rulebook to make a call at a local football game. What does this say to the countless people who have fought and died for our country? Imagine making such a sacrifice only to be told, "Oh yeah, that document that defines the country you died for is now worthless because we have decided to ignore it."

This brings me to yet another irony. When it comes to the American people, the left sees no problem with labeling the United States Constitution "optional," unless it happens to comply with their agenda. But when a civilian-beheading, child-exploding terrorist who has never set foot on American soil allegedly gets mistreated by U.S. forces, then we can't pile on the constitutional rights fast enough. For some wacky reason, I was under the impression that it was called the *United States* Constitution. Apparently, it's actually called the "Every Third World S@#%-Hole in the World Constitution". It's also ironic that when we attempt to bring freedom to other nations, it's called "imperialism" or "forcing our values on other cultures." But when the left tries to apply American constitutional rights to people in other nations (even our enemies), it's called "protecting their rights." The only problem is the fact that the United States Constitution does not apply to citizens in other countries. Besides, if our law applies in other countries, that would mean that other country's laws apply here...right? Does that mean that I can have three wives and ride a camel down Main Street on the way to my opium field? After all, those things are legal in other countries. Could I go to China and speak out against communism in a public square without being arrested... or executed? After all, that's legal in America. If everyone's laws applied in every country, the only logical outcome would be total anarchy. That's probably why it doesn't work that way.

This is just another example of why liberals seem to be all over the road when it comes to the power of government. On one hand, they complain about the abuse of government power, but they regard Supreme Court Justices who are guilty of that very thing as being intellectual icons. They forget that under that black robe is a real person who is just as corruptible and prone to mistakes as anyone else. They forget that at one time in our history, the Supreme Court gave the green light to slavery. They forget that to this day, the "right" to kill an unborn baby is still being upheld. They forget that it is not the job of a Supreme Court Justice to "get creative," or save the world. My theory is that the left is less interested in what the

Constitution actually says, and more interested in getting someone on the bench who will legalize their bad behavior...all while claiming the intellectual high ground.

A good example of liberals using the courts to institute something that would otherwise be rejected by the public is the fight to legalize "gay marriage." On the list of issues that give conservatives a bad rap, this has got to be among the top five. As usual, it's not because of our *actual* opinions, but because of media and pop-cultural *perception* of our opinions.

The popular perception of the conservative view of gay marriage is that we hate gay people. This is usually followed by the notion that our opinion is motivated solely by religious doctrine. It is true that you could say the Bible considers homosexuality to be a sin, but then again, the Bible says a lot about a lot of things. My point is that if the media *allowed* you to hear the *real* arguments against gay marriage, you would know that it has nothing to do with hate, or the Bible. You might not *agree* with the arguments, but you would know that we are not "hate-mongers" after all.

Liberals see gay marriage as a constitutional issue. This is ironic because there is no mention of homosexuality in the Constitution. By law, that makes it a legislative issue. Apparently, when the left reads the Bill of Rights, they see it as a license to do whatever you want, so long as the person next to you can do the same thing, and no one is harmed in the process. When those of us on the right read it, we see it as a declaration of the right to equality in the eyes of the law. According to liberals, since it's legal for a male to marry any *female* who will have him, that means that it is OK for him to marry any *male* who will have him too. I would argue that a gay man has the same exact right to marry any woman he wants...just like a straight man does. By definition, that is "equal rights." If you want to marry someone of the same gender, that is a *"special* right."

Then there is what I call the "law of logical conclusion." Simply stated, if the definition of marriage is changed to include those of the same gender, then the next logical conclusion is that "others" will use the exact same rationales to be married too. After all, if I have the right to marry a man, then I should also have the right to marry *two* men. Maybe a man and a woman. If I have the right to marry a man, then I should also have the right to marry my brother. If I have the right to marry a man, then I should have the right to marry my mom, dad, sister, son, daughter, aunt, uncle, grandma, and/or grandpa. What would *that* family tree look like? What would *that* divorce settlement look like? Better yet, what would *that* offspring look like? Nothing strengthens the institutions of marriage and family like incest and polygamy.

I hate to sound like a broken record as I write this book, but the same mentality keeps popping up. Liberals spend so much time *feeling* about the issue of gay marriage, that they forget to *think* about the casualties that get left in its wake. Rarely will you ever hear the nuts and bolts of raising a child discussed with the topic. Occasionally, you might read a statistic that supports or denounces gays raising children, but almost never any detailed analyses. Some questions that I have yet to see answered involve role models and practical examples. If two gay men raise a boy as their own, who teaches the boy about relationships with women? What do they use as a reference? If they raise a girl, which *male* will be able to commiserate and identify with her during her first period? If two women raise a boy as their own, which *female* will be able to commiserate and identify with him after his first erection or nocturnal emission? Which *female* will be able to relate to the boy through personal example how embarrassing it was to have a "boner" in gym class? Of the two "dads," which one will teach their daughter to use a tampon correctly, or buy a bra? At this point, the phrase "I understand what you're going through" is reduced to little more than lip service, and will have very little meaning to a child with a skewed view of gender roles.

This is usually where an astute liberal will try to draw a parallel between children of divorced or deceased parents to children raised by homosexuals. They will usually try to tell you that these children have a way of coping or even thriving under their circumstances. This almost sounds reasonable until you actually give it some thought. Call me crazy, but I don't think people usually *aspire* to die or divorce. These are things that people usually try to avoid...probably for good reason.

Here is a very simple analogy to the gay parenting issue, which results from the gay "marriage" issue. Think of raising a child as being like a child going to school. A homosexual marriage is akin to having two math classes and no English class, as opposed to one of each. Yeah, the kid may turn out to be a math genius, but he may end up with the communication skills of a three year old.

Unfortunately, all the logical arguments in the world (none having to do with hate *or* religion) don't amount to a hill of beans when an activist judge has an agenda to push. You can see evidence of this in the rulings of some State Supreme Court Judges. Some have gone as far as overruling legislation that bans gay marriage, or simply *defines* marriage as being between a man and a woman, basically telling "the people" to stick it where the sun don't shine and giving the green light to gay marriage. This in turn creates a domino effect across the nation. That's because gay marriages in one state will ultimately have to be recognized by all others.

Try as I might, I still have yet to find in the Constitution any line that assigns the United States judiciary the power to conduct social experiments, using us as lab rats. But that seems to be exactly what is happening. Otherwise, *all* Supreme Court justices would realize that there are going to be serious legal, social, and cultural ramifications to allowing anyone to marry everyone, and accept the will of the people, instead of trying to make everyone feel good by essentially throwing the issue at the wall and seeing what sticks without regard for consequence.Granted, some people might feel that they really don't care about the gay marriage fight and I may not be able to convince them otherwise. Consequently, they might not grasp the plight of judicial tyranny either. When it comes to some of our most basic liberties though, even the most socially liberal among us (homosexuals included) should pay closer attention.

Probably our most basic human right is the right to own property. Besides being a matter of common sense, it's also spelled out in pretty plain English in our Bill of Rights. In fact, the right to own property is addressed in two different amendments. I have taken the liberty to include them in this book so you can decide for yourself what you think they say. Consider it a test to see if you are afflicted with liberalism. If you are, you might read the following amendments and see any number of subtleties, nuances, or vague ambiguous concepts; otherwise known as "imagining things." Another symptom of liberalism is a willingness to dismiss the amendments entirely. If you are *not* afflicted with liberalism, you will be able to tell by your ability to read the text of the amendments as written, regardless of what you *wish* they said.

Amendment IV The right of the People to be secure in their persons, houses, papers, and effects, against unreasonable searches and seizures, shall not be violated, and no Warrants shall issue, but upon probable cause, supported by Oath or affirmation, and particularity describing the place to be searched, and the persons or things to be seized.

Amendment V No person shall be held to answer for a capital, or otherwise infamous crime, unless on a presentment or indictment of a Grand Jury, except in cases arising in the land or naval forces, or in the Militia, when in actual service in time of War or public danger; nor shall any person be subject for the same offence to be twice put in jeopardy of life or limb; nor shall be compelled in any criminal case to be a witness against himself, nor be deprived of life, liberty, or property, without due process of law; nor shall private property be taken for public use, without just compensation.

These two amendments have become an issue lately because apparently, some of the Supreme Court Justices that we pay to *apply* them have opted to *ignore* them. Recently, the Supreme Court ruled that is OK for the government to seize the personal property of one private citizen, and give it over to another. In an effort to gain more tax revenue, some local governments have taken it upon themselves to *force* people to sell their land whether they want to or not. The land is sold to real estate or contracting companies who develop it into more lucrative property. This is done under the guise of improving the community. There's just one problem... IT'S

UNCONSTITUTIONAL! The following phrases make that as clear as the nose on your face: "No person shall be deprived of life, liberty, or <u>property</u>, without due process of law; nor shall <u>private</u> property be taken for public use, without just compensation." What about "The right of the people to be secure in their persons, <u>houses</u>, papers, and effects, against unreasonable searches and <u>seizures</u> shall NOT be violated"?

Nowhere does it say that private property can be taken for another's private use so long as the government makes money on the deal. But that's what happens when a Supreme Court Justice starts "imagining things."

The Constitution *does* allow the government to seize property for *public* use such as a highway or schoolhouse (only after due process and just compensation). This policy is known as "eminent domain" and is a necessary evil in order to accommodate the public. But there is a slight difference between a publicly funded interstate highway that everyone can use, and a private beachfront condo used only by those who can afford to stay at a beachfront condo.

As for the concept of using the newly acquired tax revenue to "improve the community," I simply don't buy it as a justification to force someone out of their home. By doing this, you are essentially saying that government has the power to make money at the expense of a citizen's civil rights. You are also saying that it is the *purpose* of government to make money, which it is not. There is nothing in our founding documents that says our government is to be ran like a business and is obligated to turn a profit. That's because our government operates on the *people's* money. I can only assume that it is also because our founding fathers knew that the same kind of power that it would take to run a government as a profitable business would end up usurping our rights as Americans. Basically, we'd end up becoming our own government's business competition. Does the term "conflict of interest" mean anything to anyone? Since the government has the power of enforcement, there would be little difference between a profiteering government and the mafia. Now that the Supreme Court has said that this is just fine and dandy, I can assume that the Justices who ruled in favor of this will start wearing sharkskin suits and pinky-rings.

As basic as it is, our right to own property is only the tip of the judicial tyranny iceberg. The effects that an abusive judiciary can have on our everyday lives are staggering to say the least. It is the Supreme Court that has the power to deem a parent responsible for the health and well being of their children, but is also willing to protect that child's right to an abortion without the consent of a parent. Only the liberal mind could create a system where a sixteen year old needs a signed permission slip to go on a high school field trip to the zoo, but not to have an abortion. Even more ironic is the idea that courts commonly refuse to try sixteen and seventeen year olds as adults. Apparently, if a sixteen year old kills someone *out* of the womb, they are simply too young to fully grasp the consequences of their actions. But if they kill someone *in* the womb, they are exercising their constitutional right as an informed adult. If the same sixteen year old exercises her constitutional right as an informed adult to get into my liquor cabinet, guess who gets to feel the wrath of Child Protective Services.

All in all, I guess judicial tyranny isn't really that big of a deal, unless you want a house, or children...or a job. That's right, even if the whole "family" thing never appealed to you, the whole "employed" thing might have. You see, all levels of the judiciary are constantly upholding brilliant little concepts like "affirmative action." You may recall chapter five of this book where I discussed how racism is actually a *bad* thing. You may also recall my assertion that considering someone's skin color when hiring or accepting them to a college is just another form of racism. Unfortunately, according to the Supreme Court, such a policy gets a green light. So much for equal protection under the law, or the whole "all men are created equal" thing.

It is for these very reasons that I really don't understand why the Supreme Court was ever considered to be such an exalted level of government. We tend to look at it as being literally a *supreme* court. As if they hold some moral high ground that only the intellectually superior could ever hope to reach. Let's not forget that we were well into the twentieth century before blacks and women were first allowed to vote. To this day, issues like affirmative action, abortion, and eminent domain remind us that the Justices who sit on the highest court in the land are nothing more and nothing less than human beings. They go to the bathroom just like everyone else does...their bathroom is just a little nicer than ours. Sure, to hear them speak or to read their opinions, they come across as the pinnacle of legal statesmanship. Keep in mind though that being "well spoken" is a far cry from being on the same page as our founding fathers. All the flowery, legal jargon in the world doesn't have the first thing to do with understanding the Constitution of the United States of America. *Using* flowery, legal jargon doesn't guarantee that you know your ass from a hole in the ground either. Much like a used car salesman, a skilled Supreme Court Justice can use a line of "B.S." to justify selling you a lemon of a law. As citizens, we just need to remember that from time to time.

Maybe you're still not sure that any of this applies to you personally. Maybe you have no interest in a house, family, *or* a job. Maybe you have a "live and let live" policy that suggests you are not directly affected by the rulings of the Supreme Court. Not so fast there, my little hippy friend. You see, the key to a successful "live and let live" philosophy is the whole "live" thing. It just so happens that at this very moment there is an entire population of people all over the globe who believe it is their duty to God to make sure that you are not able to do that very thing. They don't care that you are a pacifist, atheist, environmentalist, Democrat, anti-capitalist, 'live and let live" kinda' guy. All they know is, you're not a Muslim. That's a good enough reason to cut your head off, use their children to blow you up, or fly passenger jets into the building you might happen to be standing in. You can live in the "bluest" town, in the "bluest" county, in the "bluest" state in the union...it doesn't matter; you're not a Muslim. New York City was "blue" long before September 11th. They don't care how many anti-war rallies you attend, or how many pink hats you own...you're not a Muslim.

If you don't see what this has to do with the Supreme Court, consider this. As we speak, there are Justices and Judges at nearly every level of the judiciary who are undermining the war on terrorism on two fronts. First, they are applying the constitutional rights of American citizens to non-American *terrorists* that are captured on the battlefield and sent to Guantanamo Bay. They even go as far as to use the Geneva Convention as a justification for it, even though the Geneva Convention does not apply to terrorists who do not belong to a uniformed, state-controlled army. Second, they are trying to apply a "right to privacy" which is not mentioned in the Constitution, as well as first amendment rights to terrorists that have never even set foot in this country. They are doing this by claiming that our intelligence agencies do not have the right to listen-in on the phone calls of known or suspected terrorists. Apparently, if some Bin Laden wanna-be calls an accomplice here in the U.S. to discuss plans for another attack, the F.B.I. is not supposed to hear that conversation. And after the attack happens and thousands of people are killed, we will all sit back and think of how horrible it would have been if the F.B.I. were allowed to track a terrorist's emails, or tap his phone. On the afternoon of September 11th 2001, a million things were going through my mind, but I don't recall hoping that we hadn't tapped the phones of the hijackers that day. Liberalism is so self-defeating. Ironically, it is the liberal establishment that screams the loudest when we fail to "connect the dots" before a terrorist attack, or an invasion of a Middle Eastern country with a history of using "W.M.D.s." I guess they think we should rely on a "magic eight ball" to gather intelligence. Perhaps they assume that the next terrorist attacker will be kind enough to send a detailed outline of his plan to the proper authorities before he carries it out. This whole mentality makes me wonder what would have happened if we would have had liberal Jurists intervening in World War II. Imagine our own intelligence agencies not being *allowed* to intercept communications between Nazi officers, or Japanese battleships. Imagine them not being *allowed* to counter German espionage methods with those of our own. If today's liberals were somehow "zapped" back to the time of WWII, they would probably be screaming about our attempts to wire tap German officer's phones. After all, if Roosevelt can tap some poor, innocent U-boat commander's phone, then what's to stop him from tapping *my* phone? That <u>GERMAN</u> U-boat commander's constitutional right to attempt to destroy *my* constitutional rights is being violated, and we can't have that. That would be a lot funnier if it wasn't the *exact* judicial philosophy being expressed by the present-day left in this country. Luckily, we have yet to invent the time machine.At this point, you might be wondering why I haven't been naming names or at least been more specific about the who's who of judicial abuse. This is because names and specifics are not relevant to this discussion. The names and faces of the people sitting on the bench will always be in a constant state of flux. One Justice might retire and be replaced by another. Another might get hit by a bus and be replaced by yet another. One could even be impeached or disbarred requiring one more replacement. One way or another, Supreme Court Justices are always going to be coming and going. But no matter how many changes to the bench line-up we get to witness in our lifetime, the things that will remain constant are <u>ideas</u>. Some of the best *ideas* are written down on a piece of parchment that we call the Constitution. Simply put, there have always been and always will be people wearing black robes who just can't seem to understand plain English, but the *idea* of "freedom of speech" is as old as mankind. Equally important are the *ideas* of equal protection under the law, the right to defend yourself and your loved ones, the right to be born, and the right to make our own decisions in life.

Consequently, it is the *idea* that people wearing black robes should have a clear understanding of our constitutional rights that should concern us right now, *and* in the future. As with the rest of the issues discussed in this book, the names and faces will change according to when you happen to be reading it, but hopefully the *ideas* will always apply.

Someone once said, "with great power comes great responsibility." This is never more evident than when you are charged with upholding and applying the Constitution of the United States. After all, very few people have as much "pull" as those who hold the gavel. They have the ability to preserve, extend, or destroy both lives and livelihoods with little more than a decree. To put it in perspective, who other than the Supreme Court has the ability to tell the President or even Congress to "get bent" (metaphorically)? This is not to say that they were ever *meant* to have such power, but for all intents and purposes, they do now.

At the end of the day, we all end up reaping what we sow when it comes to the law. If your second amendment right to protect your family is deemed unconstitutional, whose fault is it? Did you vote in a recent election? Did you know the judicial philosophy of the candidates? If your fourth and fifth amendment right to not be pushed out of your house for the sake of profit is "legislated" out of existence, whose fault is it? Did you pay more attention to pending judicial appointments or the Super Bowl? What name are you most familiar with, Sandra Day O'Connor, or Paris Hilton? Do you know more about filibustering senators, or philandering actors?

Not to beat the topic of education into "dead horse" status, but when you don't take the time to learn about what's going on around you, it is a sure bet that someone will be more than happy to exploit that. The people who are trying to destroy what our founding fathers created are counting on you to care about Brad Pitt's love life, and "A-Rod's" batting averages. They depend on you to play "X-Box" for hours on end, but not take a few minutes to read the Constitution of the United States. You know, the same Constitution that people are fighting and dying to protect as I write this very sentence. The people who are trying to undermine this country are practically begging you to pay even less attention to what your children are or are *not* learning in school. After all, it will be so much easier to pull the wool over the people's eyes if each generation is dumber than the next.

As I watch the news coming out of Iraq and Afghanistan, I realize that each and every one of us have a duty to know more about the rights that so many have sacrificed to protect. I'm not expecting us all to enroll in law schools or become constitutional scholars, but would it kill us to pick up a book once in a while? Don't we owe it to the men and women who have died protecting our freedoms today and throughout history, to pay a little less attention to who's on the bench during the play-offs, and a little more to who's on the bench in the courthouse?

Chapter 15
The Point

There are plenty of reasons for me not to have written this book, not the least of which is my limited amount of free time. As I get older, I find myself in a daily struggle to make time for my family. Earlier in my life, my first priority was making enough money to pay the bills and buy toys for myself. Today, paying the bills is still *a* priority, but not *the* priority. That's because as of today's writing my daughter is nearly two-and-a-half years old. If you've been paying attention, that also gives you some idea of how long it has taken me to write this book. Now that our daughter is old enough to sleep through the night and tell us when she needs something, I can actually stop long enough to see what I would be missing if being home was not my daily goal. As I watch her personality develop, I am more and more jealous of my wife being able to spend the entire day with her. At first, I thought my desire to be home was a result of my deep-seated fear of guilt. Then I assumed it was just a result of simply wanting to do the right thing. I was wrong on both counts. My post-workday mission to find a faster route from my job to my house stems directly from my love for my family.

As it turns out, the whole point of writing this book can be summed up in two simple words: My Family. *They* are the reason, the purpose, the motivation...the point. My family is the only thing of value that I have on this planet. As a father, I believe it is my responsibility to teach my daughter about the many dangers that she might run into as she rolls down the interstate of life. I want her to have a better understanding of things than I did when I was growing up. I also want her to have that understanding a lot *sooner* than I did. I don't want her to have to experience something as traumatic as September 11th in order to develop a curiosity about how the world works. I want her to be able to read between the lines and recognize "BS" when it's being handed to her. Most of all, I want her to be happy and free.

As a husband, I want my wife to have a better understanding of what is bouncing around in my head. I want her to know why I am so passionate about some things, but couldn't care less about others. I want her to understand the things that don't always come out as articulately as I plan them to.

As an American, I wrote this book in hopes of waking some people up around here. I didn't see the point in complaining about the way things are, without at least *trying* to do something about it. Too few of us actually make a conscious effort to exercise our constitutional rights these days. I think that we should remind each other from time to time just what it means to be an American today. Besides, so many people have sacrificed so much to make sure that I even have rights to exercise. It seems almost disrespectful to *not* write a book.

As a conservative, I feel that I have something to offer. Not a handout, or some type of charity, but just a better, more productive way of looking at things. You need to remember, I used to be a liberal. I *understand* that mentality because I used to *have* that mentality. I've been down both roads, and I can tell you from experience that liberalism is a dead end. I can tell you all about *feeling* about every issue rather than *thinking* about them, and being *intention* driven instead of *result* driven. I was there, that was *me*. Did I actually resolve an issue? No, but my *intentions* were noble and that made me *feel* as if I had actually brought something to the table. It was not until I became a conservative that I realized that there are actually some pretty simple ways to deal with just about every problem out there, if you only take the time to think about it, and have the will to accept it. There is no law that says every complex issue must have a complex solution. Some of the most complex issues of our time require only humility and resolve.

I also wrote this book in hopes of dispelling some popular myths about us "right wingers." First, we're not racists. People who are racist are racists, not us. A true conservative pays little-to-no attention whatsoever to something as trivial as skin color. We just don't care what you looked like when you popped out of the ol' baby maker. We do care what you *act* like now that you're a grownup though. *That* has little to do with melanin.

Accompanying this myth is the one that assumes that a "minority" has nothing to gain by being a conservative. Well, in a way that's right. A "minority" will not gain a lifetime of government dependency, or a compulsion to blame others for their personal circumstances by being a conservative. They will also not gain a need for "leadership" to represent them based on something as trivial as skin color. Actually, the only thing a "minority" has to gain by being a conservative is independence, self-reliance, and (dare I say) happiness.

Contrary to another popular belief, there is no law that says a conservative has to be a Christian. In fact, there is no law that says a conservative has to be affiliated with any religion at all. You could just as easily be a conservative Buddhist, Hindu, Atheist, Agnostic, or squirrel worshiper as be a Christian conservative. Sure, the origins of conservatism are up for debate, but the *practice* of conservatism has nothing to do with Christianity or any other religion. Besides, it's not where conservatism came from that keeps me up at night, it's where conservatism is going that concerns me right now. I assure you that even if I had never heard of the Bible, I would still know that tax cuts grow the economy, and killing babies both in and out of the womb is wrong. I don't need a church to explain that to me. You may also have picked-up on the fact that I have not used one Christian reference to argue any conservative point in this book. Not because I can't, but because I don't need to. So basically, the myth of conservatives being a bunch of "Bible thumping extremists" is really just another big pile of "BS" that libs want you to accept...on faith.

Conservatives are commonly labeled as being "intolerant" to new ideas. Not true. We're intolerant of *dumb* ideas. A classic example of this is the idea that there is *never* a need to use violence to solve a problem. Really? OK, let's put a liberal in a room with a captured Islamic terrorist. Give that liberal a pen and a piece of paper, then tell him that he has one hour to guarantee us that the terrorist will never harm another person. At the same time, assign the same task to a *conservative* in a neighboring room with another Islamic terrorist, but instead of a pen and paper, give him/her a .45 semi-automatic pistol with a frame-mounted laser sight, ported barrel, fourteen round clip filled to capacity with hollow-points, and hand-carved walnut hand-grips. Which individual do you suppose will *solve* the problem? Not the lib. He's lying dead on the floor with an ink pen sticking out of his temple, and a wad of paper crammed into his esophagus. Not only did he not solve the problem, but now we have to get a new pen too.

In the other room, we see a dead terrorist and a peacefully napping conservative with feet propped up on a desk, arms comfortably folded, a slightly blood-spattered T-shirt, and a brown Stetson tilted forward over his/her face. The conservative wakes up from his/her nap and goes home to his/her family. As for the lib, well...not so much.

Armed only with years of training in diplomacy, negotiation, and "conflict resolution," the well-meaning lib might as well have shown up drunk and naked. He was totally unprepared to deal with someone whose only goal in life is to kill the "infidels."

Not being shackled by subtle nuance, political correctness, or "grey area mentality," they guy in the *other* room saw the threat for what it was, and dealt with it accordingly. As a result, both he and the terrorist's potential future victims will live to see another sunrise.

Another idea that conservatives are "intolerant" of is the one that claims that money is bad, and pursuing it or having a lot of it is equal to being greedy. This raises a few questions. What do liberals pay their electric bill with? Did they *steal* those hybrid death traps I always see them driving around in? Are they going to *sneak* their children into college?

Bottom line; Money is not bad. *Having* money is not bad. It's how you *acquired* the money that makes the difference. Did you earn your money or steal it? Did you win your money via the lottery, or did you mooch it from the government (taxpayers)? Did you inherit your wealth from someone who thought enough of you to leave it to you, or did you marry someone for money?

In keeping with the theme of "intolerance," it is often assumed that conservatives *hate* homosexuals. I would debate this. Speaking for myself, I don't *hate* anyone. If I were to hate someone, it would probably be for something more substantial than what type of sex they prefer. As for homosexuality, I just don't care. It doesn't apply to me. It's the homosexual agenda of downgrading the institutions of marriage, military service, and adoption that burns me up. As I discussed in an earlier chapter, this has nothing to do with hate, and everything to do with the bulk of the homosexual agenda being nothing more than a series of bad ideas.

Keep in mind that there is no law that demands homosexuality and liberalism be mutually exclusive. It's for that very reason that I have no reason to dislike, let alone *hate* a person who happens to be homosexual. Besides, who says you can't be a gay right-winger? One of my favorite golden oldies of liberal misrepresentation is their constant reference to conservatives being like Adolph Hitler. You can commonly see examples of this in news footage of anti-war protests. Just for the sake of argument, let's compare and contrast.

Hitler invaded other countries without provocation in order to expand his country's borders. No American leader in at least the past hundred years (conservative or otherwise) has done that. This includes the invasion of Iraq, because I have heard of no plans to make Iraq the fifty-first state.

Hitler tried to exterminate an entire population based on ethnicity and religion in order to create what he deemed to be a "pure race." He conducted medical experiments on Jews in an attempt to create the perfect German. As if that weren't enough, he then murdered millions of people for reasons only a madman could understand. Granted, I don't have enough time to watch *every* news channel and read *every* paper, but wouldn't it stand to reason that if someone in this country were attempting something even remotely similar to that, it might make a headline or two? Especially if it were a Republican?

Hitler not only believed in *big* government, but he believed in *total* government. That alone is about as far away from conservatism as you can get without hitching a ride on the space shuttle.

If Hitler disagreed with someone, he usually had them shot. As a conservative, if *I* disagree with you, I'll write a book that explains why. If that doesn't work, I'll probably just make fun of you when you're not around.

Hitler used slave labor and took whatever land he needed to build his country's infrastructure and expand his empire. A conservative government would have *bought* the land, and contracted the work out to the lowest bidding private contractor - saving taxpayers billions.

Hitler believed that it was the duty of the people to work for the expansion of his radical government...and little else. Conservatives believe that it is the government's duty to get out of the people's way so they can pursue their own goals and enjoy the freedoms our forefathers promised us. Asserting that conservatives and Hitler have something in common is pretty ridiculous when you actually stop to think about it. Those of us on the right understand this and usually have a sense of humor about it. But after years of having my core values, and the values of my family and friends slandered in such a way, I've decided that enough is enough. That is why the whole point of this book is to try to set the record straight in as simple a way as possible.

Hopefully, I have sparked your curiosity just enough to look into some of the issues mentioned in this book in further detail. Remember, I'm just a truck driver. Nothing I have written should be taken as "the final word" because I am no authority on the topic of political ideology or anything else (except "Simpson's" trivia). I urge you to *not* take my word for it, but go out and educate yourself. Read a book, pick up a newspaper, watch a political debate, and keep an open mind in the process. Most importantly, before you do any of this...WAKE UP!